S0-BAT-930

RIDING WITH THE BLUE MOTH

Bill Hancock

Foreword by Jim Nantz

www.SportsPublishingLLC.com

ISBN: 1-59670-104-8

www.ridingwiththebluemoth.com

All photos courtesy of Bill and Nicki Hancock, unless otherwise noted.

Publishers: Peter L. Bannon and Joseph J. Bannon
Senior managing editor: Susan M. Moyer
Acquisitions editor: Mike Pearson
Developmental editor: Doug Hoepker
Art director: K. Jeffrey Higgerson
Dust jacket design: K. Jeffrey Higgerson
Book design: Dustin J. Hubbart
Imaging: Dustin J. Hubbart
Photo editor: Erin Linden-Levy
Vice president of sales and marketing: Kevin King
Media and promotions managers: Michael Hagan (regional),
Randy Fouts (national), Maurey Williamson (print)

Printed in the United States of America

Sports Publishing L.L.C.
804 North Neil Street
Champaign, IL 61820

Phone: 1-877-424-2665
Fax: 217-363-2073
www.SportsPublishingLLC.com

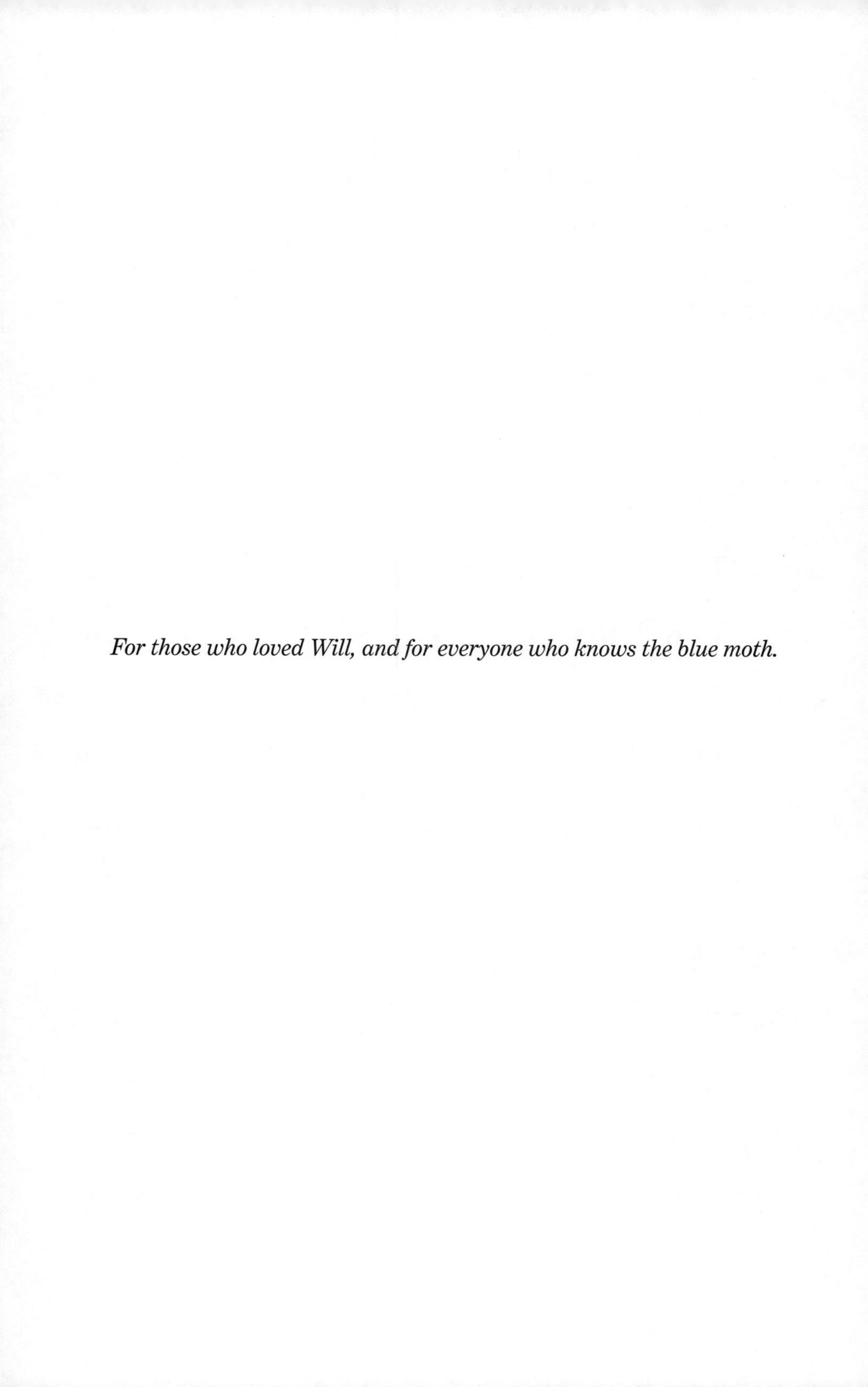

For those who loved Will, and for everyone who knows the blue moth.

CONTENTS

ACKNOWLEDGMENTS

Like SAGs—Support And Guidance—for a bicyclist, many people helped as I wrote this book. Esther Newberg, Jud Laghi, Peter Gethers, and Jim Host got me off to a good start. My friends Bill Althaus, Bill Colby, John Feinstein, Neal Krieger, Steve Richardson, and Doug Vance—authors of their own books—directed me through the process. They know their stuff, which you'll see if you read their works. Retired editor David Frost also provided guidance, and I am indebted to Jim Nantz and Melissa Minker, too.

Former University of Oklahoma basketball student-manager Greg Rubenstein read the manuscript and offered excellent suggestions. So did Tricia Bork, Dale Bye, Jim Perry, Catherine Perry, David Schoeni, and my brother, Joe Hancock. Nicki, my wife and best friend, read the sections that she could, often editing through tears. Nellie Perry, my mother-in-law and novelist in her own right, slogged her way through two drafts.

More thanks go to my editor at Sports Publishing, Doug Hoepker, who simply made the manuscript better, urging me to dig deeper until the book reached the point where it "white lined" (as they say in biker's tongue). Thanks are also extended to the other good folks at Sports Publishing, particularly to Mike Pearson and John Humenik. Two designers also deserve special mention: Dustin Hubbart designed the interior and aided in creating the fine maps of my daily journeys, and K. Jeffrey Higgerson came up with the spectacular cover, using a photo taken by Nicki.

In addition to the people you meet in the book, many others helped during the ride itself. The NCAA's Tom Jernstedt granted the leave of absence that allowed the whole adventure to happen. Greg Shaheen loaned his digital camera to me. Greg and NCAA colleagues Kendyl Baugh, Kelly Kaufman, Jim Marchiony, and Molly Smith covered my back while I was away. Rob Halvaks and Kia Hedlund at the Big West Conference told me about the Santa Ana River Bikeway, and Ray Williams and Don Bowen gave directions from there to the desert. Bob Beane from the Phoenix Metro Bicycle Club helped get me through Arizona. Jim Webber suggested we visit the Owl Café.

Ellen and Richard Johnson, Tim and Tish Allen, Bob Peterson, and Eva Brooks all fed me. Joe and Mary Sine introduced me to Jules Michel.

D. J. and Christy Mackovets suggested Tybee Island as the finishing spot. Dennis Alfton, Anita Cyrier, Dave Fisher, Bob Frederick, Truett Guthrie, Barb Johnson, Belleva Johnson, Jerry Johnson, Khalil Johnson, Bill Lester, Tim Lindgren, Steve Maki, Jeff Schemmel, Bob Shaw, Susan Patterson-Sumwalt, Tommy Sheppard, and Carroll Williams provided encouragement and advice.

Jim Gantert and Jim Shoemaker were excellent as SAGs (Support and Guidance). Cheryl Shoemaker helped, too.

Dave and Bob Clements at Wheeler's bicycle shop in Kansas City sold the Cannondale to me, then encouraged me. Bob even built a special heavy-weight-bearing wheel for the back tire.

Sam Pfenning taught me about boll weevils. Zhongxuan Du taught us about Savannah. Bob Condron taught me about life.

Finally, thanks go to Nicki, Karen, Andie, Nate, Kristin, and William Patrick Hancock—for allowing me to share their lives with the world. Their love is my spiritual SAG.

FOREWORD

By Jim Nantz, CBS Sports

For the past 20 years I have had the greatest job in America.

Forgive me, that is not meant to sound boastful. Actually the statement is made with total humility and gratefulness. I count my blessings.

Imagine having the opportunity to broadcast almost every major sporting event in the world, some of them 20 times over. Traveling to the most fascinating places, documenting the most thrilling games and tournaments, and best of all having the chance to tell the story of the unsung hero. Nothing pleases me more.

I have always considered my friend Bill Hancock to be the unsung hero of the NCAA basketball tournament. His name may not ring a bell, but for the better part of two decades he has worked tirelessly to coordinate every last detail of this true national sports spectacle. Thanks to him, March Madness has never come close to spinning so out of control that it would literally live up to its name. Every year it's a month-long, wholesome, and unifying odyssey—and American tradition—that has operated so smoothly that it seems like the Road to The Final Four is on cruise control. We, as sports fans, have Bill Hancock to thank for that.

Bill's personal life was also like that, always running smoothly and efficiently. He and his beautiful bride Nicki had two wonderful sons, Will and Nate. I remember their joy at the 1995 Macy's Thanksgiving Day Parade when they stopped by our CBS work area. One could only marvel at such a strongly united, loving family.

Years later my snapshot of the happy Hancock family came back to mind. It was the night of January 27, 2001. My CBS Sports colleagues and I were in Tampa preparing for the next day's telecast of Super Bowl XXXV. We were in an edit house making final adjustments and writing scripts for the following day's three-hour pregame show when someone came in with some horrifying news: the Oklahoma State University basketball team's airplane had crashed.

Details were sketchy at first. But soon the information was coming in. Three airplanes left Colorado after the Cowboys' game against the

University of Colorado Buffaloes. Only two of the aircrafts landed safely back in Stillwater, Oklahoma. Someone reminded me of what I already knew, “Bill Hancock’s son, Will, is the basketball publicist at Oklahoma State.”

For the next half-hour it was impossible to work. Suddenly the Super Bowl—the single biggest broadcast in America every year—meant nothing. Phone calls were made, prayers were recited, but soon a colleague tapped me on the shoulder and gave me the news we all had feared: “Jim, Will was on the plane.”

I thought back to the previous year’s NCAA tournament at Syracuse, New York, in March, 2000. OSU had made it all the way to the Elite Eight. For three days I spent quality time with Will talking about his team, his family, his love of golf. I can still see him sitting directly to my left, dressed dapperly in his striped Polo shirt, helping me prepare for the broadcasts by gleaning nuggets of information. He was great at his job and just a classy young man with a tremendous future. He was special. Man, would I love to rewind the tape of life and relive the all-too-brief time I got to spend with him.

After the tragedy, we watched Bill and Nicki put their lives back together with dignity and grace. Just two months after the crash, the Final Four took place in Minneapolis, and of course they were there. It could not have been easy: the constant parade of condolences, the best-intentioned well-wishers who only reminded the family every five seconds of how poorly everyone felt. There was a dinner the night before the championship game, and all the brass from the NCAA and CBS were on hand. We all watched the Hancocks that evening with a heavy heart and a deep admiration for their faith. It was evident to me they were beginning a courageous journey, a transition of stages, from mourning to moving on with their lives.

What they would do next no one would have ever guessed. Well, if you knew them, you knew it would be something inspirational. Bill and Nicki always had a penchant for the outdoors and a love for sports. Together they decided they were going to go coast to coast, with Bill riding a bicycle 80 miles every day for five weeks.

The Road to the Final Four had always given Bill the respect he deserved, but now the Road Across America was going to give him something much more profound. One could only wonder how he and Nicki would muster the strength and concentration to complete a grueling, 2,700-mile endeavor, given the recent tragedy in their lives.

Riding with the Blue Moth is pure inspiration. It is much more than a sports story; it is a glimpse of an enchanting group of people—a snapshot of the American culture. Most significantly, this book offers a poignant, deeply personal and uplifting account of how this family responded to a tragic loss. It will make you want to hug your children and to cherish every moment.

Unsung heroes? You'll see.

1
The Blue Moth Descends

On January 18, 2001, I awoke drenched in sweat and sprawled sideways in a tangle of blankets. I had dreamed vividly that my 31-year-old son, Will, had been killed in an accident. In that netherworld between sleep and consciousness, I was bewildered. Had the accident really happened? I wept with joy when I realized it had only been a horrible nightmare.

Still shaky after a three-mile run and a shower, I telephoned Will at Oklahoma State University where he was the publicist for the Cowboys' basketball team. His calm voice was reassuring. Like George Bailey in the movie *It's a Wonderful Life*, he lived again.

It was always a delight to talk to Will. He was more than a son; he was also my partner, teacher, confidant, and counselor. He enjoyed hearing about my job as director of the National Collegiate Athletic Association's Final Four basketball tournament. I loved talking to him about his work at Oklahoma State.

My wife, Nicki, and I were little more than children ourselves when William Ransom Hancock III was born in 1969. Will's consistent happiness—along with unflinching support from our parents—gave us a fairytale life in a tiny basement apartment across the street from the campus of our beloved University of Oklahoma. We were flower children coming of age just in time to vote for George McGovern. Our second gift, Will's brother Nate, arrived just four years later. With our two long-haired, peaceful sons, we saw unlimited opportunities ahead for our family.

We subsisted on Vienna sausages, Kool-Aid, sports, music, and humor. Our boys loved my silly jokes. Will's favorite was about Mr. Opporknockity, the piano-repair man who only tunes once. We laughed often, cried seldom. Nicki—with Hollywood beauty and Victorian virtue—was the studious, spiritual leader of our cheerful ensemble. I provided the comic relief and taught the boys the nuances of football, basketball, baseball, and Beethoven. Nicki and I were best friends playing house with two little blond roommates.

Time spun quickly. We did everything together and with enthusiasm. Will wanted to arrive early at baseball games to watch the players take infield. Together, we ran the St. Louis marathon in 1986; he sprinted ahead at mile 25, but I caught him and we finished side by side. Along with Nate, we hiked the Grand Canyon, rim to rim and back and climbed 14,000-foot Long's Peak in Colorado. When Nate and I sang in the cockney quartet in a Kansas City production of *My Fair Lady*, Will played trombone in the pit orchestra. Will and I had season tickets to the Kansas City symphony, and he always wanted to arrive early "to watch the players take infield."

Nicki and I liked every friend that Will brought home. We loved the last girl most of all, and he married her. Karen Elaine Horstman became the daughter we'd always wanted. She had been a star soccer player at the University of Tulsa, so she fit comfortably in our sports realm. Later she became head coach of the Oklahoma State University soccer team. Soon, Nate—and the rest of us—fell in love with Kristin Elaine McGuire, a fine athlete herself, and our troupe became a happy sixsome.

Will and I hooted and hollered when Karen became pregnant. Then we wept and hugged when we learned that it was a tubal pregnancy. Then, in April of 2000, he and Karen brought us an ultrasound photograph. "Dad," he said, "this is what a baby looks like when it's growing in the right place!" And so we wept and hugged again in November when Karen gave birth to Andrea Bailey Hancock—Andie for short.

In 2000, Will and I were invited to be media attachés for the USA Olympic team. We sat side by side on the flight to Sydney and talked about life. For a dad, it was the perfect 17 hours. As the airplane neared Australia, Will inserted a CD into his laptop and said, "Dad, this is for you." It was the song "Waltzing Matilda," which I had crooned to him when he was a baby. He and I then sang it together at the Olympics' raucous opening ceremonies. "Once a jolly swag-man camped by a billabong under the shade of a coolabah tree. ...” On our last night in Sydney, we climbed to the top of the fabled Harbor Bridge and shared the highest of highs with millions of stars beaming our way like spotlights from heaven.

On the phone that morning after my nightmare, Will and I talked about how much Andie had grown during her first 62 days of life. “Dad, she’s just great,” he said. “She does something new every day. Yesterday, I think she winked at me. It’s amazing to hold her and talk to her and to know that she is my daughter. I can’t wait to see what is next.”

We discussed less important topics, too, such as Oklahoma State’s chances to qualify for the upcoming NCAA basketball tournament and my dream of riding a bicycle across the country. I did not tell Will about my nightmare. Instead, I ended the conversation, “I love you, William; talk to you later.”

I had no idea what waited for us.

* * *

Occasionally, on a dark, Midwestern January day an afternoon blooms sunny and almost warm—a second childhood for winter. Shadows of bare tree limbs cast over brown lawns resemble roads darting across a highway map. People emerge from their homes to compare cabin-fever remedies. January 27, 2001—a mere ten days after my nightmare—was one of those days.

With the optimism of spring, Nicki and I wore only light jackets as we sought a support vehicle to carry supplies on that dream journey of my lifetime—a bicycle ride across America from the Pacific Ocean to the Atlantic. Although I had worked in athletics for 30 years, I considered myself a non-athlete. I sometimes felt as out of place in the spittin’ and chewin’ world of sports as a pep band member hanging out in the locker room after the game. But I had learned that I could play tortoise to the sports world’s hare. Running 15 marathons had improved my geeky self-image, and the bike ride would add a new dimension to my identity.

On that gorgeous afternoon, sunshine toasted our faces, as if to foreshadow a bright future. I was happy to be home from the Indianapolis apartment where I had camped since 1999, when the NCAA office moved from Kansas City. Nicki, a high school English teacher, was as devoted to her job as I was to mine. So I commuted, flying home to her on weekends as giddy as a kid heading to a slumber party.

We spent the balance of that winter afternoon at the movies, seeing the drama *13 Days*. Then at 6:30 p.m., we shopped for food for our annual two-person Super Bowl party. In the store, Nicki suddenly changed. She looked as if she had been doused with a bucket of gloom. Her plunge was instantaneous, apparently without cause and out of character. One minute she giggled over exotic dips and chips; the next minute she was near tears and unable to function. We returned the groceries to the shelves, held hands and drove home in silence.

A harsh north wind had swept clouds into Kansas City before dark, reminding us that more winter remained. I built a blazing wood fire, which had always cheered Nicki. She climbed into the easy chair with me. "I don't know what's wrong with me," she said. "I'm just really, really sad. The movie wasn't depressing, so it can't have been that. Maybe I'm just tired."

I hugged her, inhaling the sweet aroma of her long brown hair that was now interspersed with a few gray strands. At age 49, she still had the innocent manner that snared me on our first date on January 14, 1967, when she was a high school sophomore and I was a junior. She bore the same delicious scent, the same warm smile. She was still the girl of my dreams. An umbilical cord connected us—when I rejoiced, she was delighted; when she was hungry, so was I; when my team lost, hers did, too. Now, her unexplained sadness passed to me.

We turned on the Weather Channel. The radar showed snow east of Denver. We knew Oklahoma State had played the University of Colorado in Boulder, Colorado, that afternoon. Will traveled with the team, and we enjoyed trying to catch a glimpse of him at the televised games. "Will should be flying home about now," I thought to myself. "I hope the weather won't delay his flight, because he'll be in a hurry to see Karen and Andie."

It was the first time that I had ever thought about the weather when Will traveled.

On television, Duke and Maryland were engaged in a thrilling basketball game. Duke would win by rallying from 10 points behind in the final minute. But basketball could not distract Nicki from her sadness, and so we went to bed. Snow began falling outside and I drew the blankets around us and held her close. The false spring was long gone.

At 10 p.m., we were startled awake by the ringing telephone. In the darkness, we could not find the receiver. The answering machine switched on and we heard Nellie Perry, Nicki's mother, speaking. Nellie's voice had been weakened by Parkinson's disease, but on this night it was particularly strong. And hysterical.

"Will was on the plane," Nellie cried. "Will's plane has crashed in Colorado."

As I fumbled to find the light switch, Nicki collapsed onto the floor shrieking, "Not Will! Not Will! Oh, please God, not Will!"

She tucked her body into a fetal position, as if to create a shell to protect her heart, then reached out and pounded her fists on the carpet.

* * *

Earlier in the evening, while Nicki and I had cuddled in front of the fireplace—aware only in the deepest chasms of our beings that something was terribly wrong—a drama had played out across the state of Oklahoma. Television stations interrupted their regular programming with news bulletins.

Snow in Colorado. ... An airplane crashed at approximately 6:30 p.m. ... Believed to be the Oklahoma State basketball team. ... One of three planes. Two aircrafts landed safely in Stillwater. ... No reports of survivors. ... Two players, one pilot and seven others reportedly were on board. ... Persons who were on the two safe planes somberly gathered in coach Eddie Sutton's office. ... News conference in Stillwater. ... The victims' names:

Kendall Durfey, Bjorn Falstrom, Nate Fleming, Daniel Lawson, Brian Luinstra, Denver Mills, Daniel Noyes, Bill Tietgens, Jared Weiberg.

Will Hancock.

On the surface we had missed it all until the phone call from Nellie. But just below the level of our mortal understanding, we knew.

Hoping the news was a cruel mistake, I telephoned my old pal, Oklahoma State assistant athletic director Steve Buzzard.

"Yes, Bill, it's true," he said. "I am so sorry."

The nightmare had become real. It was an incomprehensible tragedy.

Friends from Asbury United Methodist Church heard the report on the 10 o'clock news in Kansas City and gathered at our home, their hearts broken. Shock mercifully numbed Nicki and me, delaying the pain. But our friends, amateur comfort-givers faced with a test that even the best professionals often fail, had to confront their feelings—and try to soothe ours—immediately. They watched as we pitched clothes into our suitcases to prepare for the 300-mile drive to Stillwater, Oklahoma.

Someone gently whispered, “You’ll want to take your suit for the funeral.”

A funeral? I did not want to believe it.

I placed the most difficult phone call of my life to Nate at his apartment in Hamden, Connecticut. He and Kristin had moved to New England so she could enter Quinnipiac College’s outstanding physician-assistant program. Nate’s employer, the telephone company Sprint, transferred him to New York City, and so each day he rode the Metro North train from New Haven to Grand Central Station. They loved their new lives as Connecticut Yankees.

No one was home. Nate and Kristin were snow-tubing in the pristine New England woods. I left a voice mail: “Nate, it’s your dad, please call me when you get home tonight, no matter what time it is.”

We called Karen. “I love you,” she mumbled. “Come soon.” I paced the floor, waiting for Nate to call back, not knowing how to give him the awful news.

Word spread quickly. The phone rang. It was my old Big Eight colleague Tim Allen, sobbing to the extent that I did not recognize his voice. It rang again; my brother. Again; Nicki’s sister. Again; a dear friend. Again; my emotional boss at the NCAA, Tom Jernstedt.

Again. Finally, it was Nate. The consummate cheerful guy and talker, he launched into a glowing report about his day on the snow tube.

“Nate,” I interrupted. “Is Kristin there?” I wanted to make sure his own best friend was by his side.

“This is the worst news I will ever tell you. One of the Oklahoma State team airplanes crashed when they were flying from Colorado to Stillwater tonight. Will was on the plane. Nate, there were no survivors. I’m so sorry.”

He screamed. “No! Something must be wrong! This can’t be true!”

Something was indeed wrong. All too wrong.

* * *

A blizzard raged at 2 a.m. as Nicki and I loaded our Honda Civic and sputtered gingerly down ice-covered Interstate 35 toward Stillwater. Sparkling white snowflakes flashed across the windshield in surreal contrast to the blackness beyond. There was little other traffic.

I had never felt more alone—it was as if we were on an unknown planet, driving away from our mother ship. Illuminated only by the aqua dashboard lights, Nicki's face resembled an angel's. "What's going to happen to us?" she asked. I didn't know. The road ahead offered only darkness. I thought about beautiful little Andie, 72 days old and now without a daddy.

As day slowly broke to reveal a gray new world, our cell phones came to life. Former NCAA colleague Dave Cawood. My sister. Nicki's brother. Every time we hung up, the phone rang again as others awakened to discover our grief. They called to share, to cry, to comfort. Soon both of our phone batteries failed, and Nicki and I were alone, together, again.

As we arrived at Will and Karen's house in Stillwater at 8:30 a.m., I remembered the last time I saw Will. It was two days after Christmas; he was wearing his goofy blue "Hobart Bearcats" stocking cap and chipping the remnants of an Oklahoma ice storm from his driveway. Now the ice was gone, leaving only the dull gray cement and brown Bermuda grass—each tiny blade holding drops of mist that could have been the tears of the quaint college town that had lost 10 of its sons.

Inside, Karen was curled up in a recliner. Her soft round face was red and swollen. Her cheeks glistened with tears. She and Nicki had both folded their bodies into shells as if to fend off the unthinkable news. "We love you, Karen," I said. "We always will." We kissed beautiful little Andie, who was sleeping peacefully in her crib—unaware that her life had been irrevocably changed.

For the next two hours we talked quietly, still in shock. When had Karen heard the news? When did Karen last talk to Will? I did not know how to comfort Karen, just as she didn't know what to do for Nicki. And so we sat. And talked. Everything moved in slow motion.

Desperate to take some action that might help my shattered family, I drove in the Dickensian drizzle to the Stillwater airport to pick up Will's car. A dozen vehicles sat dripping in the bleak parking lot, each of them like a young wife awaiting a soldier's return from war. Inside Will's car, I found a hamburger restaurant receipt dated January 26 and a laundry ticket. I had not yet cried.

I drove to the OSU athletic offices, found the door unlocked, and went to Will's immaculate cubicle. I sat at his desk and imagined him figuring statistics, writing biographies of basketball players, returning telephone calls from sports writers. There were his books, his notes handwritten in pencil on yellow post-it notes, his calendar, a photo of Andie. His life had been so orderly, so together, so perfect.

Athletic director Terry Don Phillips was alone in his office. A man's man, a former college football player and one of the most powerful people in Oklahoma, Terry was visibly shaken. His hands trembled as he poured a cup of coffee and offered it to me. He faced the biggest challenge ever to confront a sports administrator.

"Bill," he said, "I don't know what to say. I am so sorry."

"What can I do for you?" I asked him. I was attempting to play my role as the helpful NCAA tournament guy. Forget your practice time? Call Bill. Need a bus pass? Ask Bill. Locker room dirty? Find Bill. I was the dad, who could solve any problem. Trumpet valve stuck? Dad can fix it. Girlfriend likes John better than you? Talk to Dad. Algebra problem got you stumped? See Dad. I could always fix things.

But not this. This was beyond anything I had ever experienced—beyond anything I could imagine.

The next few days were a blur, like a videotape on fast forward: *No desire to eat or sleep. ... Order dental records to help the coroner identify the body. ... Visit with the funeral director; can't set a date for the service until we have the remains. ... A phone call from the coroner in Colorado: "Would Will have been wearing a U.S. Olympic team shirt?" ... Consider a 20-hour drive to pick up the cremated remains, to bring Will home ourselves. ... Meet an angel of a pastor, Stan Warfield, at the First United Methodist Church in Stillwater.*

Nicki and I met Nate at Will Rogers Airport in Oklahoma City, the site of many joyous homecomings for our family in the past. At the sight of him walking off the jetway, I burst into tears. Other travelers in the crowded concourse gazed silently as we hugged, both of us sobbing now.

I carried Andie into the public memorial service before 13,000 shocked mourners in OSU's Gallagher-Iba Arena. The many caring speeches were merely background noise. I stared at photos of Will and the nine other men and wondered once again, can this be happening to us?

Hundreds of mourners scribbled messages on massive white walls in the lobby of the storied arena. My note to Will was from a movie that was dear to both of us, *It's a Wonderful Life*: "Teacher says every time a bell rings, an angel gets his wings."

* * *

Bob Condron, an executive on the U. S. Olympic Committee and my foxhole buddy for 30 years, was among the 1,000 people who attended Will's funeral nine days after the crash. He wrote the following about Will's funeral service to members of the Olympic family:

"We filled the First Methodist Church to the rafters and spilled over into the Catholic Church next door. If you arrived after 9:30 a.m. for the 11 a.m. service, you got closed-circuit television.

"We got to see Eddie Sutton and Barry Switzer sitting together. We got to hear the assistant sports information director and the golf coach at OSU laugh and cry about working with Will and the joy he brought each day to the office.

"We heard Will's childhood friend talk about how Will used to organize the softball games and would always put himself last in the batting order. We watched his brother Nate talk about all the mornings that he exploded out of bed because Will's wakeup call was Beethoven at its loudest. How he hated that music, but later learned to love it and majored in classical music. And how we were going to hear 'Ode to Joy' from Beethoven's Ninth Symphony later when we left the church.

"And we heard Bill Hancock talk about his son with tears and laughter as the stillness in that church overwhelmed us. He spoke about Will as a kid, when he decided his name was Georgia Tech Hancock and did mock interviews with anybody within speaking distance. He'd stick a pretend microphone in your face and ask, 'What do you think of President Nixon?' How his exuberance was off the chart and how much he lived life to the fullest. He was smart, scoring higher than 1400 on his SAT—Bill said that would have qualified Will to play football twice at OU.

"And Bill read a letter from Kamon Simpson of the Colorado Springs Gazette, *who wrote, 'Will was what we always knew each of us could be, but only if we tried really, really hard.'*

"I hope you all have a chance to have a Bill Hancock bat cleanup at your funeral. Or have a father like Bill who, in the midst of heart-

break, can walk up to that podium, say 'good mornin' ' and tell you how much he loved his son. And put you at ease and make you laugh—and remember. I also hope that you have a mother like Nicki, who can smile through the anguish and tears and ask how you are doing.

"We in the Olympic family were all involved in a fun part of Will's life. It was recess, a dessert of peach cobbler on vanilla ice cream after a big meal, a rainbow after a summer shower. Being at the Olympics and Pan Am Games wasn't his normal life. It was an important part, though, and it made his real life better. We helped give Will those memories—of a balcony in Bankstown, New South Wales; a night spot in Winnipeg; Opening Ceremonies in Sydney; working late with friends in the Main Press Center in Homebush Bay. Feel good about that gift.

"The whole family stayed several hours after the service to shake everyone's hand and we were just about the last to go through the line. We came across this warm, beautiful lady who said she was Karen—Will's wife. And we realized why he was always smiling. When we said we were Olympic friends of Will, a light came into her eyes, her hand tightened around ours and she lit up like an angel. She said it was important for her to tell us how much the Olympic experiences meant to Will—and to her. Through her tears, Karen made a special effort to thank all of you for those times and those memories and for the joys they brought. I wasn't able to say much, but I smiled for all of us.

"The closing song for Will's service featured a duet with a lone steel-stringed guitar, 'Here Comes the Sun.' You can see it, just in the next meadow, the sun's coming. That warm feeling on your face as the clouds clear and the grass sparkles. When you see it and when you feel it, grab those moments and gather them to your heart—and remember a special friend, a bright shooting star in the night sky, who was with us for too short a time but made our skies light up with a brief, bright, wonderful glow."

Each member of our family cherished Bob's letter; he became our hero. But, I foresaw no wonderful glow ever again in our lives—and certainly no bicycle rides.

* * *

Faith, family and friends carried us through those awful days. Nicki and I busied ourselves with small tasks—cataloging the avalanche of food, flowers, and telephone calls that we received so that we could send thank-you notes later—then invented more chores when we finished those. We slept little and scurried like crazed ants from project to project, carrying six times our body weight. A blanket of pain, fear, and confusion smothered us.

After the numbness of the first several days wore off, the sadness came in waves, like the cold fronts that routinely sweep into the Southern Plains in winter. Because they bring northerly winds and blue skies, the fronts are known as blue northers. When I was a child, my grandmother said in her North Carolina drawl, "blue nawther"; but I thought she was saying, "blue moth." Now, the blue norther of despair—the blue moth—struck often. Just as there is little hope in predicting the 10-day forecast, I could not predict when the blue moth might attack, dousing me with a napalm that destroyed all hope. I despised the agony that came with those waves of sadness. I hated the savage blue moth.

* * *

Oklahoma State University held us with arms made not of brick and mortar but forged of human compassion. As the grassroots nurturer of generations of us proud Okies, it began as a land-grant school, Oklahoma Agricultural & Mechanical College. Now a mighty, world-renowned academic center, the university serves students from 121 countries. Like the kid who succeeds in the big city but cherishes his small-town beginnings, O-State radiates down-home warmth.

People pampered us—friends, colleagues, Oklahoma State alums, grieving Stillwater residents, total strangers. It was as if we had a magic wand that could bring us anything, except the one thing that we wanted more than anything else—for Will to live again. We had to be careful not to take advantage of the wand.

When friends from Kansas City visited Stillwater five days after the crash, they dumped four grocery bags of cards and letters on the floor of Karen and Will's house. It looked like the judge's desk in *Miracle on 34th Street*—the love and concern from others spilled across the floor, covering it wholly. The best medicine was simply knowing that people cared.

The tragedy had caused an epidemic of pain in the sports world. Everyone knew. One man wrote after reading about Will's accident, "If you are the Bill Hancock who worked at the *Oklahoma Daily* student newspaper in 1970, I want you to know I remember you and your baby son fondly. If you are a different Bill Hancock, then please accept my apologies for bothering you at a time like this, and also please accept my sincere condolences."

A week after the crash, eight $10 checks arrived in the mail at Karen's house, then 10 the next day, then 20 and more. Unknown to us, a member of the College Sports Information Directors of America had suggested that people in his field send money to help Karen and Andie. Sports publicists are humble, hard-working, salt-of-the-earth people—and far from wealthy. But they wanted to do something, anything, to convey their sorrow at the loss of a brother. As a percentage of their incomes, the $10 from each of them was golden.

Many people sent books. We had only recently finished reading happy manuals about etiquette for new grandparents, and now we faced a stack of publications about grief. The gesture was heartfelt, but I couldn't concentrate long enough for "Peanuts" in the newspaper, much less a book. The best material for me was a series of easy-to-read paragraphs from Hospice, such as, "When possible, put off making major decisions such as changing residences, jobs, etc., for at least a year until you are thinking clearer."

A friend suggested drugs. Addiction frightened me; we would find another way. But I did wonder if we were taking all the proper steps—would we collapse in 20 years because we hadn't prayed enough, or cried enough, or worked through our problems with countless psychiatrists?

Too many other people had been in our shoes. Steve Owens, who won college football's Heisman Trophy in 1969, had lost his son a few years before we did. "You and I are in a fraternity that we don't want anybody else to join," Steve told me.

The wife of one of Will's high school teachers called Nate on her husband's behalf. "He has tried to call you three or four times," she said, "but he cries every time he picks up the phone. He just can't do it, so he finally asked me to call and tell you that he has been devastated by this."

My heart grieved for people who wanted to help but did not know how. Some people said nothing. Others stepped on our toes in clumsy attempts at kindness. One gentleman gave me a sweet message with spiritual overtones and I began to cry simply because he cared. He panicked and immediately excused himself in order to have a conversation with someone else. It is easier for a man to respond to a tongue-lashing than to tears.

The best words were simple: "I care. I'm hurting for myself and I'm hurting for you. If you ever want to talk to someone, call me."

Each time I encountered an old friend, I cried. Nicki explained why: "It's because you know they care." A reservoir of tears was just below the surface, like oil in our Oklahoma homeland. At each pin prick of emotion, a gusher exploded.

I tried to go for a run but halted on a country road, in tears. Running was too familiar, too hopeful, too ordinary. Simple habits, long-ingrained, became puzzles. I forgot the steps in brushing my teeth. Phone numbers and the names of acquaintances eluded me. Life's customs—from music to work to attending church—became draining emotional distractions. The great hymns made me weep. So Nicki and I moved from our customary spot in the third row to the back of the Asbury Methodist sanctuary. There we had privacy and a quick escape route when the tears came, as they did every Sunday.

Even *It's a Wonderful Life* seemed cruel, because it generated false hope. I was angry with Frank Capra and Jimmy Stewart for creating such a charade. I was embarrassed for having wept every time I had watched the movie, furious at the phoniness of George Bailey receiving a second chance at life. In my head, I screamed, "Clarence the Angel is not reality! Reality is gloom and despair and helplessness! Will Hancock will not say a prayer on an icy bridge and magically live again. No weird angel will save him! Damn! Damn! Damn!"

Nicki and I tried to avoid any emotion, happy or sad. It was as if our bodies were cups filled to the brim with water; add one drop and the cup overflows. Any new feeling forced out other emotions in the form of tears. One particularly thoughtful e-mail from my brother pierced my core so deeply that tears erupted as if I were throwing up. The sob blasted up from my chest, through my throat and out. It didn't seem to have come from me at all, but from some alien who had overtaken my body. I gasped for breath and lurched to the bathroom to finish crying. That's when I noticed how ugly I am when I cry. I vowed to do so away from mirrors—and people—in the future.

I was spiraling out of control, feeling claustrophobic in a lonely room without doors or windows. There was no hope for the future, no reason to live, nowhere to go. My worst moments occurred when I considered how the lives of Nicki, Karen, and Nate had been wrecked; none of them deserved such pain. To keep myself going, I chanted a three-verse mantra over and over: "Put one foot in front of the other. Heaven is real. Will is there." I'm not sure that I really believed any of it, but I chanted hard, pounding the hope into my head like a blacksmith wielding a hammer.

The simple question, “How are you doing?” made a liar out of me. Sometimes when I answered, “Fine,” the questioner would grasp my hand and respond, “No, Bill, really, how are you doing?” Mostly, I did as John Steinbeck suggested in *East of Eden*: “Act out being alive, like a play. After a while, a long while, it will be true."

I did not foresee an end to the awful play. Anything dated before January 27—simple items such as a check written to the electric company, a newspaper article, an e-mail from Will—came from another world, a happy world far away from the sick place we now inhabited.

Before January 27, Nicki often reclined in her easy chair and said, “I am so very, very lucky.” We were a regular family with easy lives—we were the Bobbseys, Cleavers, and Huxtables rolled into one. Now, like out-of-condition athletes attempting to run the Boston Marathon, we were severely undertrained for the obstacle course that we were on. We walked in shoes with bubblegum soles.

Simply wanting to feel better made me feel ashamed, dirty and selfish. How dare I think of myself? From every logical vantage point, I could see no hope for the future. I wished that I had been on that airplane instead of Will. I had walked a charmed path for a half-century. Will had barely begun his journey through life. Why couldn’t it have been me?

“I am just now realizing what my parents went through,” wrote a friend of Nicki’s, whose brother had died in a dormitory fire. “Later, my dad said that his life went on, but that it was like living without one arm.”

It was impossible to relax. I could not sit still for more than 90 seconds; Nicki was worse. She had to stay busy to keep from thinking. If she stopped the frantic activity, the harsh reality set in and she broke into tears. Nicki had always detested crying; it gave her a headache. Now she was reduced to tears several times a day. Nate tried valiantly to minister to her. Karen, bless her heart, was simply paralyzed. I was tremendously worried about all of them.

Strange things happened. Nicki’s mother dreamed she was searching all over her farmhouse for her Oklahoma State University diploma. When she awoke, she found the diploma. Her graduation date was January 27. Meanwhile, I didn’t dream for three weeks. Then, as if a massive dam had burst, a cavalcade of adventures swept through my brain every night. I dreamed that

Will had not been killed, but that the entire right side of his body had been torn away and that he was avoiding Karen, Nate, Nicki, and me because he didn't want us to see him so damaged.

But not all the dreams were so tormenting. Some provided me with a temporary safe haven, a chance meeting with Will. In one, Will sat in a wheelchair and watched an Oklahoma football game with me and ex-Dallas Cowboys coach Jimmy Johnson, a good friend from my Oklahoma days. In the dream Jimmy said, "You are lucky to have such a terrific family." In another dream, Will and I ran a marathon together, only to be frustrated because a group of people from the NCAA kept moving the finish line farther away. In another dream a month after the crash, Will, Nate, and I were playing trivia games with his friends. As always, Will was winning and laughing while trying to make the rest of us comfortable. I was thrilled to see him; he was happy and healthy. But I kept thinking, "This is only a dream and he will go away." Then he started to fade, like some ghost in a movie. "Will," my dream self said as my son dissolved into low-pixel resolution, "please promise that you will keep talking to me. I really need to know you're okay." As his voice faded, he said, "I'll try, Dad. I don't know if I can do it, but I'll sure try. I'm doing fine. Tell Mom not to worry." Then he was gone, and I awoke happy.

Sigmund Freud wrote that dreams are the disguised reflections of our unconscious desires and fears. Dr. Rosalind Cartwright, director of the sleep disorder center at Rush Presbyterian Hospital in Chicago, said people can learn to modify bad dreams. I wanted more of those nightly visits from Will. And I desperately wished to change our family's nightmare—but it wasn't to be. I wanted to ask Dr. Cartwright or some other expert in the study of dreams if it was a coincidence that my recurring nightmare for 40 years had been about my piloting an airplane that was about to crash. Had those dreams—thousands of them over the years—been warnings that I failed to heed? What other messages do we mortals fail to comprehend? What about my dream 10 days before the crash?

I hated waking up in the morning. I felt good for only about 10 seconds—the time between when I heard the alarm clock and thought, "I've had a terrible nightmare" and when I awoke fully enough to remember that it was all too real.

Frightening details of the crash emerged. A Colorado newspaper quoted a National Transportation Safety Board source as saying the airplane was flying upside down when it crashed. That horrific news sent me into a tailspin of depression. I had convinced myself that Will and the others were simply on a routine bumpy ride and then, in an instant, they were in heaven. But no. If the source was correct, they had dangled by their seat belts in terror.

A mother who lived across the road from the crash site said her teenage son ran to the site, hoping to help survivors escape the wreckage. "I followed my son," she said. "He disappeared behind a small hill, and then I heard terrible screams. I knew the screaming could not be coming from my son because those awful sounds were not his. So I became encouraged that the cries must be coming from a person who had survived the crash. And then I ran over the hill and found my son on his knees, vomiting in the snow and screaming in the most unearthly way. No one should have to see what he saw that evening."

Because we decided to have Will's remains cremated, we had no last chance to look at him, to touch him, to say goodbye. I was told that the coroner in Colorado had photos; I cannot imagine ever wanting to see them. One day I put my hand into the oaken box that contains Will's ashes—they are white and coarse, like ground-up seashells—and found the pin that doctors had implanted in an attempt to correct a birth defect that had left his hand two-thirds of the normal size. Touching the pin, which was buried inside Will for 19 years, was like massaging his soul.

* * *

I was lucky in one way—Will and I had no unfinished matters. He loved Karen and Andie and Nicki and Nate and Kristin and me, and he told us often. We all loved him, and we told him often. But even that sense of thankfulness didn't ease the process of coping. It was a difficult business. Death shouted that I had taken him for granted, and the guilt was suffocating. I wished that I had called him more often, sent him more e-mails, stopped my incessant NCAA tournament work, and visited his little family more frequently.

My thoughts sometimes were irrational. I decided that losing Will was punishment for when I lied, when I put too much pressure on others, when I went to the office on too many Sunday evenings instead of staying home with Nicki, Will, and Nate. But, really, I thought, would God punish each of the 10 sets of parents, wives and children all at once, solely for Bill Hancock's sins? No, in rational moments I knew that God didn't make that plane go down; God was crying along with us.

Each of us processed our grief differently. Karen loved photos of Will; the blue moth of gloom descended every time I looked at one. I even had to hide the set of family pictures in my office. Nicki was quiet; I talked. Pounds melted off Nicki; I ate constantly and my weight ballooned. Nate was obsessed with learning why the plane had crashed; I wasn't very interested. Nicki suffered panic attacks in crowds—her pulse shooting to dangerously high levels—and got lost driving on familiar streets; Karen sat alone at home and talked to Will.

The situation was worse for Karen than for anybody else because Will was her constant companion. She kissed him every day, watched television with him every night, and waved goodbye to him when he drove to the Stillwater airport to board that plane for Colorado on January 26. It wasn't unusual for Nicki and me to be apart from Will for a month or more. Now, sometimes it seemed this was one of our little separations and that he would be coming home soon. Karen, on the other hand, had lost her right arm. Thirty-two was much too young to become a widow.

Karen's Oklahoma State soccer players reached out to comfort her. Their coach—their leader, their rock—was in life's most tragic situation and they could have fled in confusion. But they came to Karen's house and helped her in so many ways: baking, cleaning, running errands, and most importantly, talking and smiling. We will never forget them.

And then there was little Andie. Although I knew she would grow up surrounded by love, she would only know her daddy through photographs and the words of all of us who adored him.

* * *

"The game must go on" is deeply rooted in the culture of sports. Athletes, coaches, and fans went back to work—to play—after the Kennedy assassination, the Munich Olympics murders, and the World Series earthquake. Now, I had no taste for games. But because working was part of putting one foot in front of the other, I returned to the NCAA office the day after Will's funeral.

Heavy winds rocked the Southwest Airlines 737 bound from Oklahoma City to Indianapolis; the aircraft bumped, twisted, and lurched. I looked at the ashen faces of the other passengers and thought again about the last few seconds of Will's life. The malicious blue moth slithered through the air, pushed the clouds aside, and dragged me into depression. "Please let this plane crash," I asked God. "Take me to heaven. There's no reason for me to stay here on earth."

God knows to leave some prayers unanswered, just as he knows to when to say, "Sure thing." Take my job, for example. It is a gift from heaven.

My tasks as director of the NCAA Final Four—inspecting locker rooms, arranging refreshments, selecting hotels—help kids realize their dreams during March Madness. Shower heads must be high enough for seven-foot post players, hotel lobbies spacious enough to accommodate 30-piece pep bands, storerooms carpeted for cheerleaders' warmups, concession stands free of alcoholic beverages. Somebody arranges the details; that somebody is me. Surely it is the best job in America.

My job is a position befitting a former player, but I didn't play college sports. I was neither talented nor competitive, but I loved being in the gym, had a fondness for statistics, and reveled in the stories of triumph. And so, sports writing came naturally to me. I had actually planned to study piano or math in college, but found that I lacked the single-mindedness—and talent—for either. So after one semester I shuffled over to the journalism school, mostly because my dad was a newspaper publisher and ink coursed through our family's veins. I worked two years in the print shop of the student newspaper, then stumbled into a job as a student assistant in the University of Oklahoma sports information office.

The sports information staff handles publicity for the athletic department. I was one of four students who helped full-time staff members in a variety of ways—many of which would appear mundane to most. We students kept statistics and wrote press releases for the athletes' hometown newspapers. We hauled typewriters to the football press box on autumn Saturdays, occasionally spilling purple ditto fluid onto our clean clothes. We smudged our hands black making scrapbooks about the Sooner teams and we ran the scoreboard at baseball games on blustery March afternoons. I loved every minute of it. When they paid me each week I felt like a child being rewarded for eating chocolate ice cream.

My career path led from the university to my hometown newspaper—where I covered high school girls' basketball—to publicizing sports in the Big Eight Conference to administering the NCAA's Final Four. As often as possible, Will tagged along to work with me, making basketball a family affair for the Hancocks. His NCAA tournament resume would have been a dream come true for many youngsters. As a boy, he sat under the basket during games and wiped perspiration off the court. Then he graduated to delivering statistics to reporters, carrying soft drinks to television announcers, and cleaning the press room. In college he played in the University of Kansas pep band. Later he sat near the court at the Final Four and kept order among the photographers.

Along the way he saw his dad playing at work, and so he headed down the same road himself when it was time to mull over his choice of careers. He was a brilliant student, and I dreamed of law or medical school for him. But he would hear nothing of it. He wanted to be like his father.

"Dad," he said, "you're the happiest man I know."

No one ever received higher praise.

I loved watching him grow professionally and was proud when he made clever innovations at his job that were unthinkable in my day. It was clear that he had a bright future in college athletics.

But now, just ten days after his death, I was forced to consider my own future. Would I be able to find any solace in a job that I once so thoroughly enjoyed? Could I be away from Nicki and Karen and Andie? It was too much to contemplate, and too soon to make decisions.

I walked into the NCAA headquarters on my first day back not wanting to be anywhere. My colleagues reacted with hugs and tears of their own. The ten members of the NCAA Division I Men's Basketball Committee were assembled in Indianapolis for a workshop to prepare for selecting and seeding the 65 teams for that year's NCAA tournament. They were athletic directors and conference commissioners from across the country, blood brothers and a sister bound together by the immense responsibility of managing an event that commands the entire country's attention. Many of them had traveled great distances to attend Will's funeral.

When I entered their meeting room I saw the faces of ten heartbroken friends and I knew that they had been crying along with us. One member—Big 12 conference commissioner Kevin Weiberg—literally shared our grief. His nephew, Jared, with a future as bright as Will's, was also on the airplane.

I wanted all the committee members to know that I was going to be okay, even though I wasn't sure of it myself. "Okay" meant normal, which meant being at the office offering my guidance to the people in each of the 14 cities who host the tournament games each year. I worked two days the second week after the crash, then three the next week, then four.

My colleague Kendyl Baugh said our co-workers often whispered, "How is Bill?"

"Go in there and ask him yourself," she told them. "He's still the same person."

No one cared more than Kendyl. She and I are different in almost every way. She was an NCAA champion track and field athlete at the University of Texas, and is a city girl, young and impulsive. Yet she reached out as if I were her brother. One day, she told me, "You have no idea how much support you have out there. For the first week, everyone who called asked me about you. Every single person. It has been incredible." I was shocked to discover that huge reserve of caring people, like a geologist stumbling onto a previously unknown oil field.

When I returned to NCAA tournament business, it was a signal to others—an inaccurate signal, I realized later—that I was prepared to move forward. The majority of my co-workers were more patient than I was; many were willing to give me a decade, if that's what it took, to find my way out of the quagmire. But I wanted results immediately and couldn't convince myself that wounds heal by degrees.

Dragging my grief to work was awkward—even inappropriate. It was also desperately draining for me and everyone in the basketball circle. One person later complained that I was dysfunctional. Indeed, "functional" had taken on a new meaning; getting out of bed and remembering what day it was were high functions for me.

For everyone else, the routine business of life went on—as I knew it must—even though I was hardly prepared. A constituent phoned: "So sorry for you and your family. Oh, and by the way, we sure could use 20 more hotel rooms in Minneapolis and we don't have enough double-doubles at the Marquette and we need two more parking passes." A basketball fan, unaware of my personal involvement with the crash, sent this e-mail to me: "Please assign Oklahoma State to a site in the NCAA tournament near Stillwater, so they can take a bus to the game. I cannot bear for them to fly again."

I bounced back and forth among Stillwater, Kansas City, and Indianapolis, dealing with tournament business and personal business and absorbing dozens of attacks from the blue moth each day. After two weeks, Nicki decided that she, too, was ready to return to work. She was still quite shaky, but felt it was time to put one foot in front of the other. I drove her to school and cried when I watched her walk bravely toward the building. It reminded me of the first day that we dropped Will Hancock off at kindergarten some 25 years earlier.

When I picked her up that afternoon, she collapsed into the car and said, "Those are the most wonderful people in the world." Her colleagues and students had reacted in a way that had become so welcome to us—with an outpouring of love.

For me, selection Sunday—that day in March when the committee announces the tournament pairings—was drawing near and I was forced to cope with an exhaustion unlike any I had ever experienced. It was a painful kind of fatigue, much worse than I had endured after any marathon. My weary body simply couldn't support the weight of the last five weeks. I was omitting words from correspondence, misplacing documents, and forgetting my thoughts in mid-sentence. I knew I must get some rest. I had always feared becoming addicted to medicine, but something had to be done. So I broke down and took two aspirin. After going to bed at nine, I awoke ready to begin a new day. Trouble was, it was 1:15 a.m.

* * *

A week before selection Sunday, a reporter gently asked how the committee would evaluate Oklahoma State's team in light of the games the team lost shortly after the crash. I said the committee members would consider the effect of the crash, just as they do the myriad of other influences that all teams face: injuries, travel difficulties, and special occasions that give extra incentive for particular games. I hoped Oklahoma State would be either a solid "yes" or a solid "no" for the tournament field. Instead, the Cowboys appeared to be a definite "maybe." The team had lost three of its five games immediately after the tragedy, but had drawn courage from coach Eddie Sutton to finish the regular season with a 20-9 record.

On the first day of the selection meeting, my mind drifted as it had so often in the preceding weeks. I remembered six-year-old Will Hancock begging to join me on the golf course, then collecting broken golf tees in an old coffee can. He was thrilled. "Dad, I have enough to last the rest of my life!" he said. The can—still full—remained on a shelf in our basement. As my eyes filled with tears, my colleague, Jim Marchiony, nudged me back to reality. "Bill, are you okay?"

That's how it went during selection weekend—I was up, down; in focus, out; lucid, loopy. Still, the game must go on. Thanks to the dedication of the staff and the committee members, the teams were selected and the pairings were announced. Oklahoma State did make the field. I hoped it had not been a sympathy vote. The Cowboys would go on to lose in the first round.

It was time for March Madness and my annual trek to the first-round, second-round, and regional tournament games. For me, the tournament had always been like a big happy reunion of coaches, staff members, arena managers, sports writers, and broadcasters. They were my second family. I went on the road with trepidation because I would be away from Nicki for ten days, and because I did not know what to expect from all those people.

My fears were quickly dispelled upon arrival in San Diego, the first site. Everyone in the tournament family knew about the crash, and the response was overwhelming. Many of these sports giants hugged me; some cried. A hundred or more remembered Will and said kind things about him. On the other hand, a few fled in the other direction when they saw me coming. I did not blame them; they simply did not know what to say. There is little training for confronting a friend in grief.

Part of me wanted to make myself invisible or isolate myself in my hotel room like a disfigured hermit to avoid disturbing people to whom my presence bespoke "unclean!" The attention was embarrassing and awkward. Mostly, though, compassion was exactly what I needed, and my parched body absorbed it like an Oklahoma cotton field during an all-day August drizzle.

A strange thing happened. On the first day of the tournament, my first thought upon awakening was not, "Is this a nightmare, or is it real?" Instead, I returned to my mantra: "Put one foot in front of the other. Heaven is real. Will is there. Believe it." Such progress came slowly. Sometimes I struggled to move two inches forward only to fall three back in the same day. Like a rose blooming in the desert, the few good moments were brighter because of the sadness that surrounded them.

On the airplane en route to games in Kansas City, I studied the topography below and thought about my now-abandoned plan to ride across the country on a bicycle. I concluded that the frivolous part of my life was over. I could barely function. The old dream seemed insane.

Then the plane moved over the very pasture east of Denver where the ground had caught Will. I pressed my nose against the window, not certain what I was looking for. Blackened earth, maybe? A makeshift road in a field? Investigators in white overalls sifting the dirt for clues? Or perhaps Will waving his arms and saying, "Dad, I'm down here! Come get me!"

Instead, I saw only brown roads dissecting barren gray earth. From 35,000 feet, the terrain revealed no sign of the airplane crash. I realized my seatmates had no idea why I was peering out the window so intently. Emotionally, the others on board were flying 35,000 feet above me. From that perspective, my face gave no hint of heartbreak. All too often, I realized, I had observed people from that same cold distance, expecting them to behave normally when their own horrid fires of depression raged inside.

I thought I saw Will sitting four rows in front of me on the airplane. Same close-cropped brown hair, same perfectly shaped head, same broad shoulders. Of course, I knew it wasn't really him. But I wanted it to be, so I didn't leave my seat to investigate. I thought, "How nice that Will and I are on the same airplane together," and was happy in a fantasy—if only for a few moments.

* * *

Nicki and Karen comforted each other during my absence, each more worried about the other than about herself. A bond was growing between them—they were almost like sisters. Karen also had developed a special connection with Will's grandmother, Nellie. The 32-year-old widow and the 71-year-old widow had much in common. Too much.

We all talked to each other on the telephone for hours. It was as if none of us—Karen, Nicki, Nate, Kristin, Nellie, and me—could stand spending more than a few minutes apart. One night I told Karen that the accident had positively affected the lives of many in the basketball tournament family because it had opened their eyes to all that they had taken for granted. "That's nice, and I'm happy for them," she said. "But the price we paid was too high."

* * *

Will and I had been like brokers—all too often the persuaders whose role was to convince reluctant sports stars to speak to journalists in the wake of emotional defeats. Now I was a news item myself at the NCAA tournament, dealing with a calamity that made even the most disappointing sports contest seem laughable.

"Reporters are just doing their jobs," Will had told Karen—the soccer coach—when a writer phoned at an inopportune moment to discuss her team. Now we tried to follow Will's example, although the public attention was discomforting. We thought often about the hundreds of other families in the United States who lose children each day; it wasn't fair that our stories were in the newspaper and theirs weren't.

Almost every interview began with an embarrassed disclaimer. "My editor wants me to write a story about your family. I am very sorry to trouble you, and I will understand if you say no, but would you possibly have five minutes to spare?" I sensed that television reporters wanted me to be emotional, like people are after tornadoes and floods and forest fires. I was determined not to cry on TV. When I knew that tears were coming, I said, "Can we please stop the interview?" and asked for a Kleenex and a cookie, and then we would start over. The reporters and photographers always understood.

Journalists are trained to be indifferent, but they failed in our case and poured their hearts out to us. Sam Farmer from the *Los Angeles Times* wept as he interviewed me in the Metrodome before the Final Four in Minneapolis. It was clear that many writers were imagining what it would be like to be in our place.

Some did not have to imagine. An Atlanta reporter eavesdropped during an interview in San Diego, then sat next to me later.

"I don't know you, but I heard your story," he said to me. "I want to tell you I lost my 17-year-old son in a car wreck several years ago, so I do know what you're going through. No one else does. At first, my wife and I had good seconds every day. And then good moments. And then good hours. It took three years until we could function as normal. But, believe me, it will happen."

At age 50, I didn't have three years to waste. In fact, I didn't want time to pass at all, because every day marked more hours since Will had last been alive.

To honor the Oklahoma State victims, other schools' coaches and players wore orange ribbons imprinted with the number ten. Tom Kensler from the *Denver Post* looked at the one on my lapel and smiled.

"I hope you won't take this wrong," he said, "but Bill Tietgens (the OSU radio announcer who was on the plane with Will) never did like those memorial ribbons. He said, 'They have a ribbon for AIDS, a ribbon for a cheerleader with a strained hamstring, a ribbon for someone's lost dog.' And now people are wearing ribbons at the Final Four to remember him. How ironic."

Four-month-old Andie Hancock wore an orange ribbon as well to her first Final Four. She was good medicine. So was Bill Lester, who manages the Metrodome. Bill christened the stadium's media work room the "Will Hancock Press Room" during Final Four weekend. Will's colleagues took things a step further, leaving one chair empty under the north basket, among the photographers, where Will used to sit. The heartfelt outpouring of kindness made us realize that we were not alone.

I spoke to Duke coach Mike Krzyzewski as the Blue Devils warmed up on the court before their semifinal game against Maryland.

"Bill, I don't know what to say," he told me. Standing on the court in front of his team's bench, Mike shook my hand and would not let go.

"Thank you, Mike," I replied. "I just wanted to say hello and wish you good luck. I know you need to spend time with your team now."

"My team can wait," he said, still grasping my hand. "This is more important. I want you to remember that all of us are thinking about you and your family. We care. Don't ever forget that."

The Blue Devils went on to defeat Maryland and then Arizona to win the tournament. While Mike's team celebrated after the championship game, Nate and I stood arm in arm on the Metrodome basketball court and watched the traditional playing of the song "One Shining Moment" on the stadium's big video board. Nate looked at me with tears in his eyes and said, "Dad, what do we do now?" I knew we had to find shining moments. Somewhere.

* * *

After the tournament I returned to work in Indianapolis, and away from Nicki and the supportive embrace of hundreds of friends, the blue moth invaded again—with a vengeance. Things were no better for Nicki. She had joined me at the Final Four and had found the same consolation from friends, but now her confusion returned and I was not home to help her. I hit bottom on the roller coaster of emotion. After even the most devastating loss, coaches know that there will be other games in the future—other opportunities for happiness. For Nicki and me, there was no hope, no tomorrow. It seemed that the season of our lives was over.

I was driven deep into the abyss of depression. Late one night, alone in my small downtown apartment, unthinkably, suicide seemed a plausible solution. But I quickly realized that my choosing the coward's way out would only multiply the pain for Nicki, Nate, Kristin, Karen, and Andie. It was nearly 1 a.m. I stumbled outdoors onto the deserted street and screamed at the moon.

In the days that followed, I attempted several maneuvers to escape the shadow of misery. I went to a baseball game, but it was a disaster. Never before had I noticed how many fathers and sons enjoy baseball together. Their smiling faces brought back too many memories. I tried reading but couldn't concentrate; I tried playing piano but always erupted into tears.

One thing did help: eating. I gorged myself with food. Exercise had once given me the confidence to survive as a musician in an athlete's world, and in those days I had thought nothing of rising at 3 a.m. to run 12 miles before work. But now I could not summon the self-discipline to ride the bike around the block.

The progress that I had made during the tournament was lost. There seemed to be no permanent passport out of the ugly land of death—only a temporary visa good for a precious few moments.

2
Rebirth of the Bike Ride

In the early 1970s, I was a skinny Beethoven aficionado geeky enough to know the value of *pi* by heart. Journalism had eased me into the world of Sooner sports, but I remained a trespasser among the jocks until basketball coach John MacLeod sensed my discomfort and threw me a lifeline. "You can become an athlete yourself," he promised. "Come running with the other coaches and me. You'll enjoy it."

Specialized running shoes hadn't been invented yet—or at least they hadn't made their way to Oklahoma. So, MacLeod and I and a dozen others jogged barefoot around the luxuriant Bermuda-grass football practice field in the shadow of the university's storied Memorial Stadium. It was not fun at first. Covering 100 yards left me breathless and I lost my lunch nearly every day. But slowly I gained muscle and confidence.

Running was my ticket for the long, lonely bus ride from Nerd to Cool. Later I would wear out a hundred or more pairs of running shoes while completing 15 marathons, including Boston and New York. My mathematician's running diary—faithfully maintained for 25 years and more than 22,000 miles—tells of distance, weather, health, people, and places.

In 1973, I tore the cartilage in my right knee while playing touch football. It was a Norman Rockwell autumn Sunday after the Sooners had whacked Colorado, 34-7, and the student newspaper reporters had challenged the sports information staff to a game. Barry Switzer, in his first year as head football coach, stopped to watch us run a few pass patterns. "Don't give up any day jobs you're offered," he said. We laughed and enjoyed the attention of the gregarious coach, even though my knee hurt like crazy.

I continued running through the years until the bones in my knee ground each other into painful splinters. Before I knew it, I was nearly 50 years old. The rest of me would wear out soon. So I sought out less-battering outdoor adventures—I climbed Mt. Rainier, hiked the Grand Canyon, and took up bicycling.

The bike and I did not get along well at first. Riding unsteadily on the very first day, I smashed into a bridge railing over I-435 in Kansas City and bent the handlebars like a pretzel. A week later, waiting at a stop light, I lost my balance, fell over and slammed my head on the door of an idling automobile. Thank goodness for my helmet.

Eventually I stopped crashing into things and grew to love riding. I pedaled across Kansas with a group, then spent five days alone, riding the 500 miles from Kansas City to my hometown of Hobart in Southwest Oklahoma. Like astronaut Alan Shepard's up-and-back fling into space, the experimental solo bicycle trip proved that bigger adventures were possible. With the awe that is reserved for the unattainable, I had pledged to give myself a 50th birthday present by riding coast to coast. Biking across America would be a fitting gateway to my last half-century—and as challenging as Neil Armstrong's trip to the moon. Running had changed my early life; I hoped that biking would enrich my middle one.

But I gave up those dreams after Will's death—or so I thought.

* * *

It had been a tradition for Will and his close circle of friends—a band of brothers who grew up to become doctors, financial planners, lawyers, and dentists—to call in sick at their jobs, meet for a tailgate party and attend the Kansas City Royals' season opener. As baseball season began anew on April 6, 2001, the party went on without Will, in part as a memorial to him. The guys invited Karen, Nate, and me to join them.

Losing their friend Will was life's first great calamity for most of the young men. The looks on their faces said, "What do we do?"

What would I have said if one of them had been on that plane instead of my son and Will had asked that same question? "Live," I thought. I would have told Will to remember his friend forever, and to honor his memory by living every minute as if the whole world were watching and learning from him.

A light went on in my head while I was eating a bratwurst in the stadium parking lot on that chilly afternoon. I decided the future *was* something to explore. I knew that little Andie needed our love, but she also needed Nicki and me to be strong, happy role models. I went home and said to Nicki, "How would you like to be tour director for a bicycle ride?" Her answer? "I was hoping you would ask."

Not once did we discuss the journey as a balm for our souls. "The best thing you can do with death is ride off from it," said Augustus McCrae in Larry McMurtry's *Lonesome Dove*. That was not our intent. We were going on an adventure. Nothing more.

* * *

According to *Adventure Cyclist* magazine, some 2,000 people ride bicycles across the United States each year. Many others begin such trips but ultimately give up. Like the man who falls in love with a dimple and then makes the mistake of marrying the whole girl, these bicyclists learn that there is more to American geography than meadows and shady lanes.

Most cross-country cyclists travel in groups, often with guides. I chose to join the handful who set out on their own, finding their way from scratch. I didn't want "If it's Tuesday, this must be Prescott."

Temperate northern routes, basically from Seattle to Boston, are the most popular. But the southern distance is shorter because the country narrows at the hips. I wanted to ride through my Oklahoma home; so with Soonerland as the fulcrum, Nicki and I picked Southern California as the departure point. We would be John Steinbeck's Joads—in reverse.

After considering more eastern-seaboard harbors than that wandering Philadelphia garbage barge, we decided to finish at Tybee Island, 18 miles east of Savannah, Georgia. There was little science in the decision; it was simply the shortest route that we could find. Plus, in the same way Nicki picks horses at the track, we liked the name. In our awful world, we savored every ray of sunshine. Merely enunciating the words "Tybee Island" made us smile.

Next, we selected the most practical spots to enter and leave each of the nine states that we would cross. Then we pored over American Automobile Association highway maps, which gave our lives the first modicum of purpose in months. We connected the dots, choosing back roads and booking overnight camping accommodations in towns roughly 90 miles apart. We wanted to avoid the homogenized interstate highways, where each McDonald's, Waffle House, and moccasin shop is duplicated at every exit. We preferred the back roads, hoping to find, in Betty's E-Z Stop and the Blue Goose Station, folks like us.

For a place to sleep, we purchased a Coleman pop-up tent-trailer with a stove, refrigerator, cable-television outlet, and, most importantly, an air-conditioner that would chill Arizona in August.

Our home on wheels needed a name, other than "The Trailer." I suggested the "Good Ship Lollipop." That seemed too juvenile. "The Enterprise?" Too futuristic. "Pequod?" Nicki shied her slippers at me.

Then I submitted "Rocinante," after Don Quixote's mule. The name also worked for another American who traversed the nation in the hopes of reconnecting with his countrymen and rediscovering the passion of his earlier work. Steinbeck, at the age of 58, did just that when he and the family dog traveled the country in "Rocinante," his RV. Steinbeck's journey became the basis for his next book, a travelogue titled *Travels with Charley*. Nicki, a non-plagiarist, approved of the name as well, but shortened it to "Roci," pronounced ROE-see. Our trailer was officially christened.

The game plan was for me to depart early each morning before Nicki, the neighboring campers, and the sun arose. Nicki would "un-pop" Roci, drive to the next destination, set up camp, and wait for me. When she caught me along the route, we would stop for a roadside picnic. If I couldn't complete that day's prescribed distance, she would return to pick me up and we would mark the quitting spot as the place to begin the next morning. We e-mailed an itinerary to family and friends. Announcing our intention to see the task through was the first of many points of no return.

We forwarded our mail to Nicki's mother's house in Hobart, halted delivery of the *Kansas City Star,* and asked neighbors Rita Mouber and George Brzon to watch over our house. Finally it was time to test the plan.

* * *

Feeling like Granny and Jed Clampett in their trek from the backwoods hills to Beverly Hills, Nicki and I pulled Roci from Kansas City over the Rocky Mountains and across the desert to Los Angeles. We could cover ninety miles in the car in less than an hour and a half; on the bicycle, it would take ten hours. I decided not to think about it.

With the awe of naïve Midwesterners, we negotiated the Los Angeles freeways and arrived at Huntington-by-the-Sea RV Park in the community of Huntington Beach, across Highway 1 from the blue Pacific.

We walked along an asphalt path that bordered the surprisingly cool and breezy beach, among bikini-clad power-walkers, roller-skaters, hand-holding lovers, and little families that reminded me of ours back when Will and Nate were young. One ponytailed man on roller blades said to Nicki, “This beach is awesome, man; but—bummer—I gotta go to work tomorrow.” “Not me!” I thought. Tomorrow I would be on my bike, living a dream.

But with that dream came nervousness; I was experiencing reasonable doubt. Could a regular guy actually ride across the country?

“Your chances are 50-50,” said an NCAA colleague. “Fifty you'll quit because of boredom and fifty you'll quit because a truck runs over you.”

Generally, my health was good. But because I had salved my grief with gluttony, I looked like a third-rate sumo wrestler. My training was brief and inadequate: I tackled one 30-mile practice ride, which hardly put a dent in my 15 pounds of newfound weight.

The biggest reward from marathon running is the training. The fruits of the 12-week buildup exceed the race itself, which is almost anticlimactic. So to attempt a bike ride of this length with no training was like being born rich. Yes, it sounds fabulous—until you consider what you missed. I hoped to rely on what remained of my marathoner's heart and leg strength. Could I ride myself into cross-country condition?

As Nicki and I ate our last (pre-ride) supper, Roci's tent sides quivered in the ocean breeze like aspen leaves. So did I.

Day Zero felt like the night before a heart transplant. I was anxious, to say the least. How did John Glenn feel? Or Christopher

Columbus? Christa McAuliffe? Meriwether Lewis? I thought I understood.

I scanned the first-day instructions that a California bicyclist had sent in response to my e-mail plea for advice and directions: "Get through Corona and connect to Victoria (our most scenic route in the area, lined with orange trees and a wide bike path). Victoria leads into Alessandro/Central which takes you out to Moreno Valley, where you can take a left on Redlands Boulevard, then a right on San Timoteo Canyon Road into Beaumont. Any way you do it, you've got a climb into Beaumont, but this route is less work than going out on the boring (and smelly) Ramona Expressway, then climbing up the nasty 79."

I gazed at lovely Nicki asleep on Roci's queen-sized bed—her soft brow furrowed as if she were studying that ambitious route in her dreams. What had I gotten us into?

3
Into the Sea of Sand

DAY 1

Too Much to Chew

Date: Monday, July 9.

Distance traveled: 77 miles in California, from Huntington Beach to 10 miles west of Beaumont.

Starting temperature and time: 62 degrees at 6:30 a.m.

Finishing temperature and time: 91 degrees at 4 p.m.

Food: breakfast—Raisin Bran and toast; lunch—two tacos; dinner—spaghetti.

Additional fuel: 19 Fritos, two gallons of water, one root beer.

Overnight: Stagecoach Campground in Banning.

The alarm buzzed at 5 a.m. and we parted Roci's curtains to reveal an overcast, sad world outside. Many days on California's benign coast begin this way; then the sun melts away the gloom. The only optimism at this early hour came from the birds. Gulls squawked as if to say, "Go for it!"

I followed bicycling tradition by dipping the bike's rear tire into the salt water of the Pacific near the Huntington Beach Pier. If all went as planned, I would walk my Cannondale bicycle across a similar sandy beach and slip the front wheel into the Atlantic in a month. I filled an empty hotel-shampoo bottle with ocean water and packed it away in my bike bag.

My mind raced. I was overtaken by complete fright. My body shuddered as if clamped into a hardware-store paint shaker. The cold morning air raised goose bumps on my arms.

"Riding across the country, are you?" said a female jogger in a bright blue warm-up suit. "What's your cause?"

"Cause?" I wondered aloud, connecting the chin strap on my bike helmet.

"Yessir, what are you riding for? I assume you are collecting money for a deserving charity."

My cause was to fulfill a dream and to keep myself moving. Nothing more. I walked toward a beach-side shower to rinse the ocean salt off my bike. She followed, waddling like Charlie Chaplin.

"Well, you ought to have a cause," she said. Her shrill voice sounded like the sea gulls that were circling around us. "Many people in this country are poor, sick, and desperate. Healthy people with time on their hands, like you, must help them. Do you hear me? Help somebody!"

"Uh, okay," I responded. "I'll think about a cause." I had nearly 3,000 miles to ponder her point. She departed, apparently satisfied. I kissed Nicki goodbye and headed east toward the Atlantic.

The Santa Ana River Bikeway is the autobahn of bike paths, as wide as a road, with a dotted yellow line down the center and a smoother surface than most highways. The bikeway passes beneath streets, freeways, and railroad tracks. A biker can ride 32 miles across the teeming City of Angels without encountering a stoplight. The bikeway winds like a serpentine peninsula into a sea of chaos, piercing poor neighborhoods and rich ones, parks and business districts. The back yards and loading docks are like movie-lot facades—the real world is hidden behind false fronts.

The path also skirts two golf courses, and I stopped to watch four albino-legged men launch eight-iron shots across a ravine toward a large green. One dumped his ball into the gunk and asked his partners for a mulligan. I wished for a mulligan myself—a second chance at life with Will Hancock.

"Where you bound for?" asked a golfer, munching on a soggy cigar.

"Oh, Banning," I said, not willing to admit to a stranger—nor perhaps even to myself—that I was attempting to ride to the Atlantic Ocean.

"Man, ain't no way I could ride a bike all the way to Banning," he replied. "I don't even like driving a car that far."

I rode off, inhaling the blended fragrances of the golfer's full-bodied Rigoletto cigar and the surrounding, sweet eucalyptus. The Los Angeles basin was my humidor.

There was nothing sweet about the aroma of the homeless people who lived like modern-day trolls under many of the path's overpasses. I couldn't even discern whether one person—who reclined next to a shopping cart that was loaded with clothes, bottles, shoes, and a baseball bat—was a man or a woman. What drove the person to the street? Perhaps the loss of a loved one? Life is wretched for many; Nicki and I were not alone. But I realized I had very little in common with the street people. For one thing, by handing over the money that I planned to spend on this leisurely bike ride, I could start them on new lives.

An angular old woman with a little dog in her bike basket pedaled past in a frenzy like the Wicked Witch absconding with Toto, which reminded me of Will and our Kansas home. The blue moth of sadness perched like an albatross on my shoulder.

The path—probably unnoticed by most sports fans—meandered past Anaheim Stadium and Arrowhead Pond Arena. After 32 miles, as the foggy dawn melted into a glorious sunny morning, the bikeway dead-ended without warning at a 10-foot chain-link fence. I looked up and slammed on the brakes just in time to avoid tattooing myself. I backtracked and found the proper route, which put me on city streets for the first time, where I was forced to stop at traffic lights and inhale the exhaust of vehicles. After the serenity of the bike path, I was surprised by the sheer agitation of the real world. I did enjoy a $1.79 pork soft taco at a *mama y papa* restaurant in the blue-collar town of Corona. The clerk looked at my sweaty body and long-sleeved shirt and said something in Spanish. Probably, "This guy is nuts."

Resting at the Corona city park, I shared a pavilion with three short Hispanics fiddling with ropes and a man who danced with such enthusiasm that his long gray pony tail flopped around on his backside like … a pony's tail. He had no radio, no CD player, and no headphones. But he was moving his feet, hips, and arms in rhythm elegantly, as if the Glen Miller Orchestra were performing "Moonlight Serenade" beside the swing set. Clearly someone—or some *thing*—was playing in his head.

"Hey, man, that bicycle is cool," the dancer said in a sing-song voice that took me back to the early 1970s when people looked at Will's shoulder-length blond curls and called him a "hippie baby." The dancer was also a talker. "I had a bike once, a long time ago," he said. "Sold it for money to buy a guitar. I thought I was gonna become a star. Are you a star?"

"Nope, I'm just a regular guy," I responded.

Perhaps would-be stars worked down the road at Angel's Sports Bar. In the back of the building was a sister establishment, "Angel's Other Place, Topless Dancing." As I watched, a well-proportioned employee stepped from the sunny afternoon into the dark life at Angel's Other Place. I knew something about plunging from daylight into darkness; unfortunately, my form of darkness didn't pay the rent.

Victoria Avenue in Riverside was lined with oleander bushes and eucalyptus, palm, pine, and oak trees. Feeling like a 10-year-old, I stole an orange from a tree.

The 12 miles on Alessandro Boulevard carried me up and over the gorgeous coastal range of mountains—percentage-wise, today's ride offered the most significant altitude gain of the entire trip, from sea level to 2,500 feet. Alessandro offered a variety of lifestyles, too, symbolizing what I expected to encounter across America. Initially the street climbed past immaculate seven-figure homes and top-dollar shops, but then it sliced through a forest of fast-food restaurants and finally became a two-lane road dissecting wide fields of grain.

I laid the bike on its side and strolled into the dusty wheat stubble, figuring few people had the opportunity to walk in ocean fog, orange groves, and wheat fields in the same day. I had better take advantage of it. In a mere 50-mile ride, I traveled the agricultural equivalent of 1,000 miles. In that way, California is a microcosm of America: ocean to orchards to Oklahoma wheat. At this rate, I would be in Georgia by tomorrow.

In reality, though, I ran out of gas and couldn't meet the day's goal. I had estimated the distance from the ocean to Banning to be

80 miles, but it turned out to be 94. As the sun reached high noon, my legs turned into boiled cabbage. I wallowed in a sea of nausea. A football coach would have said that I had out-kicked my coverage—bitten off more than an unprepared cross-country cyclist could chew. I was so tired that I forgot to be sad.

Nicki, who had backtracked on the route in a frantic search, found me at the bottom of a hill on Redlands Road. “Dr. Livingstone, I presume?” she mused. She loaded the bike and me into our minivan.

“How are you?” she asked, doing a lousy job of pretending to be calm.

“Just fine, you?” I answered, faux cheerfully. Both of us were rotten liars.

I vowed to be more diligent about measuring distance from this day forward. Laying my right index finger on the map nine times as I had done today (“let’s see, one knuckle equals 10 miles”) wasn’t going to work.

Happily, Nicki had set up Roci in paradise. The Stagecoach Campground, sandwiched among granite mountains and shaded by leafy oaks, could have been a western movie set. I expected Silver to gallop past any minute, with the Lone Ranger aboard. Roci’s air conditioner was unnecessary because of a stiff breeze and the abundant shade.

The granite hills surrounding the campground reminded me of hiking with four-year-old Will in the ancient Wichita Mountains of Southwest Oklahoma. Just a tyke, he struggled over the boulders in order to keep up with his dad. Luckily, the beauty of our current surroundings tempered the pain of that memory.

Swimming in the campground’s cool pool chased away the blue moth and restored my legs. I was only slightly embarrassed when dirt, salt, and leftover sunscreen formed an oil slick around my body, making me look like the Exxon *Valdez*. I made a mental note to shower next time before swimming.

My queasy stomach limited my enjoyment of the scrumptious spaghetti dinner that Nicki had prepared on Roci’s outdoor propane stove. As I dawdled with the food, I looked across the table at my best friend. Nicki is every man’s dream—smart, warm, loyal, trusting, clever, and owner of a natural grace that radiates like a sunrise. She was a sophomore in high school and I was a junior when she accepted my invitation to a movie. Her saying yes is still viewed by my friends as one of the all-time upsets in Oklahoma history—it was beauty and the geek.

The date was January 14, 1967, a frigid night in Oklahoma, but Nicki's smile melted me into August. She was the smartest girl in school and I was the scrawny clarinet player. The movie was *Nashville Cats* and I don't remember a thing about it; in the small town of Hobart it didn't matter what was playing—you went. Nicki wore a burnt orange wool skirt with matching jacket and her perfume, called *Ambush*, made my knees tingle. I was too scared to touch her, too nervous to eat popcorn, and too tense to talk. Words were important to her even then; so, she must have wondered why she hadn't stayed home to read *Our Town* or Shakespearean sonnets instead of going out with a mute date.

We had another date the next weekend, then another. On that magic third date, the kid-rock radio station KOMA played a new tune called "Georgy Girl," and it instantly became our song. Later that night, she and I were devastated when KOMA reported that astronauts Gus Grissom, Ed White, and Roger Chaffee had died in a fire aboard an Apollo 1 capsule. Like most children of the '60s, I was absorbed in the space program, and the news broke my heart. It was January 27, 1967—of course, we had no idea of the ultimate heartbreak that awaited us 34 years later.

Pretty soon Nicki and I were "an item" in our cozy small town. In addition to her looks and my lack thereof, we were different in many ways: she was a Baptist, I was a Methodist; she was an Oklahoma State University fan, I was a Sooner; her dad was a lawyer, mine the publisher. But, as the saying goes, the opposites clicked. One night I reached across the front seat of my dad's Buick Electra 225 and touched her hand. Never—not in any of my 15 marathons nor in any of my Final Fours—has my heart raced as fast as it did in that instant.

Nicki is even more stunning at 50 than she was at 15. I hope Andie will wait a little longer to begin dating her husband. But if she chooses to start early, I hope she'll be as lucky as her granddad.

Thoughts of tomorrow's ride put my daydreams on pause. Ahead lay America's most remote desert. I had allocated three days to cross it. Those three days would go a long way toward determining whether I could ride all the way to Georgia or not.

After dinner, I contemplated the woman's demand that I ride for a cause, pondered the lessons that I had learned on my first day as a cross-country biker, and wished for a way to convey them to Andie. I decided this bike ride could be a journey of discovery; the lessons could benefit Andie—and perhaps me, too.

DAY 2
THE BATHTUB

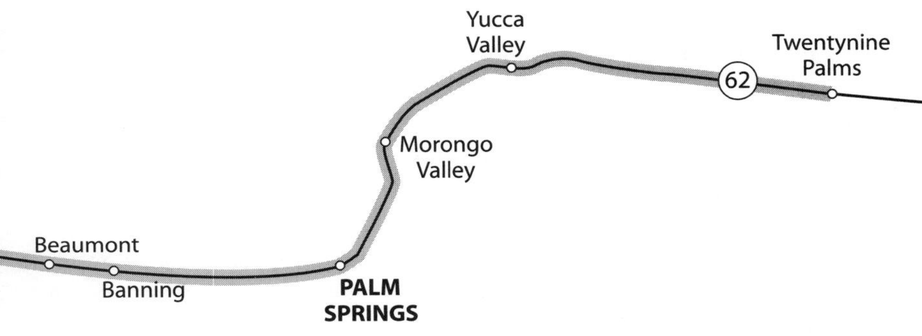

Date: Tuesday, July 10.
Distance: 83 miles in California, from 10 miles west of Beaumont to Twentynine Palms.
Total miles completed: 160.
Miles to go: around 2,500.
Starting temperature and time: 56 degrees at 5 a.m.
Finishing temperature and time: 101 degrees at 5 p.m.
Food: breakfast—Raisin Bran, banana, toast; lunch—four bites of a peanut butter sandwich; dinner—cheese sandwich, carrots.
Additional fuel: six cheese crackers, two gallons of water, half-gallon of Gatorade, one root beer.
Song stuck in my head: "Play That Funky Music" (by Wild Cherry, 1976).
Overnight: Twentynine Palms RV Resort.

I knew that today would be difficult, like riding into and out of a bathtub—down from Beaumont (elevation 2,582 feet) to Palm Springs (400 feet) and back up to Yucca Valley (3,256 feet) and Twentynine Palms. I had planned a short journey of only 67 miles, but "short" went out the window because I had to make up those 16 extra miles that I had failed to complete from yesterday.

I wanted to begin the ride each day at precisely the spot where it had ended the day before. This was my chance to pedal across the country, and I wanted to be sure to ride the entire way. We found the stop sign where I had wilted the afternoon before, and I started from there.

I was several miles up San Timoteo Canyon road before good-morning calls from roosters began to pierce the cold pre-dawn darkness. Rabbits hopped across the road, which ran parallel to railroad tracks. For an hour, the only people I saw were train engineers.

At 7 a.m. a woman wearing a micro-skirt and fishnet hose climbed out of a sleek red sports car at a stoplight in Beaumont. A curtain of unnatural blond hair partially hid her heavily painted eyes. The car sped away and she stumbled toward me.

"Which way to Los Angeles?" she said. It was a classic case of the lost seeking directions from the lost. "Uh, west," I muttered.

The light changed and I rode away. I glanced over my left shoulder to see if Ms. Fishnet was still standing along the road and nearly ran head-on into a young boy on a bicycle. I looked up just in time to see his startled face, grateful that he swerved north and I veered south. I realized that, for the next month, misfortune would be only an instant away. This was the first lesson for my granddaughter: *Andie, for crying out loud, pay attention.*

At the village of Cabazon, I missed a chance to purchase moccasins because the tourist shop on Interstate 10 was closed. Are moccasins sold anywhere other than at stores along interstate highways? Perhaps I would find out on my trip.

Nicki and I had spent hours studying maps in search of a safe way to travel from the I-10 frontage road near Cabazon to California Highway 111—the road to Palm Springs. But we failed; the only choice was to ride a quarter-mile on the mad interstate. I dreaded trucks whizzing past my left ear at 75 miles per hour, but there was no alternative. I reluctantly rode up to the entrance ramp, only to see a sign reading "No Pedestrians or Bicycles

Permitted on Interstate." Now a new element—breaking the law—entered the picture. Two highway patrolmen sat in their vehicles near the ramp as if shielding the freeway from bikers. I scanned the desert for a footpath through the sage, so I could walk the bike to 111.

"Do you know how I can get to 111 from here?" I asked one of the officers, playing innocent.

He nodded to the east. "Hey, man," he said in a 1960s-hippie voice that was in stark contrast with his buttoned-down shirt and military-style haircut, "the 111 is right over there." He didn't mention the no-bicycles sign, and I adopted a "don't-ask, don't-tell" policy. He even pulled his car onto the entrance ramp, lights on, to alert freeway-bound drivers to my presence. So I dashed down onto the shooting gallery.

I had stewed and sweated about this brief segment for weeks, but the two minutes on the interstate turned out to be uneventful. Three dozen vehicles passed, but I guided my bike safely on the edge of the shoulder like a tightrope walker balancing on a wire. Without incident, I exited onto 111.

Between the 10,000-foot San Jacinto and San Bernardino mountains, wind whistles through the San Gorgonio Pass as if Los Angeles were blowing on a giant soda straw toward the desert. The gale shot me down into the Sonora Desert and glitzy Palm Springs like a pinball out of its chute. No passenger in a chauffeur-driven limo ever had an easier time. I sailed eight miles without pedaling and wished that all of life could be so simple.

Palm Springs is a checkerboard of landscapes. Spectacular green-grass squares abut barren desert. A gray-haired gentleman in a service station explained it to me thusly: in the 1800s, the government gave half of this land to the Agua Caliente Indians and the other half to the Southern Pacific Railroad. Over the years, the railroad people sold their land to developers. The Indians decided to lease, rather than sell. Preferring ownership, early-day developers avoided much of the Indian property. Of course, those Indians now own most of downtown Palm Springs.

While traveling through town, I began to daydream. Those disparate patches of ground caused me to envision two incongruent worlds. On the lush, green side of a weathered split-rail fence were mothers, fathers, and children who had not been affected by death. Their lives were simple and happy. They spent their days reclining under willow trees and listening to "Oh, What a Beautiful

Mornin'" from the musical *Oklahoma!*. On the desert side, my mind's eye saw people—our family and others who had faced tragedy—wandering in circles and staring blankly ahead as the strains of Mozart's *Requiem* wafted across the desolate acreage. Occasionally, the gray, hooded figures glanced sadly at the fence as another weeping family crossed a rickety wooden stile into the world of gloom and despair.

My bike drifted into the traffic lane.

"Get your head outta your butt," yelled a young driver in a green Chevrolet, jarring me back to reality. I hadn't retained that "pay attention" lesson any longer than a fourth-grader who memorized the 20th-century American presidents just before recess.

Recess was over. I had enjoyed coasting down into the bathtub; now it was time to climb back out. After two miles of struggling uphill, I spotted a store with a sign proclaiming "Ice Cream ... Date Shakes ... Open." But when I pulled the door handle, it wouldn't budge. I peered into the window. What I saw was dark and dusty. Obviously, the place hadn't had a date in many months.

Longing for a rest after three more miles of climbing, I soon spotted a white plastic patio chair—was it a mirage?—in the ditch next to the highway and dismounted to have a seat. Unfortunately the chair had only three legs; the blue moth fluttered down upon my wrist. Not even the furniture was open for business in "the bathtub." But to my relief, no one could close a grove of tamarisk trees in the median of Highway 62, where I stopped and fell asleep in the shade, using my bike helmet for a pillow.

I awoke to a cool breeze and a breathtaking view down to Palm Springs and the mountains beyond. The blue moth was gone. Could Nicki and I ever wake up and see beauty like this in our lives?

Beauty was one thing; obsession was another. Since the crash, I had been unable to listen to music. Even the national anthem at NCAA tournament games made me cry. And now, without warning "Play that Funky Music" began to play in my brain. It continued for hours, as if an obnoxious neighbor was hosting a rave in her backyard. Later, a friend said that bikers frequently get tunes stuck in their heads and can't get them out. Perhaps the hypnotic rhythm of the pedal strokes is the cause. In any case, I could now relate to that dancing hippie in the Corona city park.

With the music blaring like a bad dream, I fled the Sonora Desert and pedaled the bike upward to a new one. The Mojave is higher and supposedly cooler. Cooler? Well, the high temperature would be 107 in the Mojave today. Palm Springs hit 110.

As I struggled uphill amid heavy traffic on four-lane U.S. Highway 62, the bike speedometer showed four miles per hour. That's barely fast enough to keep a two-wheeler erect. Just one week later I would be in better shape, and hills such as these wouldn't be difficult. But now I was riding in quicksand. I rested every quarter mile.

I recognized that I could not complete a ride through desert—or anyplace—without Nicki's help. She was my "SAG," which is bike rider lingo for Support And Guidance—or perhaps it's SAG because bikers sometimes, well, sag. In group rides with support vehicles, bikers who give up and ride an automobile to the finish are said to be taking the "SAG Wagon." SAG can be a noun ("Nicki is an efficient SAG.") or a verb ("Do you want me to SAG you?") It's one of the most versatile non-four-letter words in our language. We all need SAGs in real life.

Along this horrid but starkly beautiful stretch, Nicki met me frequently with water, granola, and a smile. The smile helped, but the water and granola made me gag. Nausea set in. I became disoriented. My eyes wouldn't focus. A bank thermometer showed 103, but I saw 110033. As a marathon runner, I'd learned how to hydrate, and today I had consumed enough water to float a small aircraft carrier. But this was different; for one thing, I was out in the sun for 10 hours every day on the bike. My body craved more potency. I was woefully undertrained for such a climate and incredibly naïve.

DAY 2

I had always believed bananas and water were as beneficial as those highly advertised electrolyte drinks, but this was a crisis. So I decided to experiment with Gatorade and sipped the orange tonic while sitting on a stack of Sprite boxes and listening to a pair of convenience-store clerks complain about their boyfriends' poor money management. Something—perhaps the Gatorade, the cool air, or the conversation—diminished the nausea somewhat.

Nicki drove past on the highway while I was lollygagging in the store. I dashed out of the store yelling at her, but she couldn't hear me. I tried her cellular phone but got a "looking for service" message. There was nothing to do but ride on. A few miles up the road, a highway patrolman pulled his cruiser across the lane of traffic and skidded to a stop on the shoulder facing me. My front wheel bumped his hood like a kiss.

"You're in trouble," said the burly officer, twirling his silver moustache as fine white dust settled around us like snow. Then he smiled, but his humor couldn't hide the concern in his eyes.

"Your wife is worried and is looking for you. You keep going, and I'll find her and tell her where you are." He made a U-turn and soon our minivan came down the hill toward me. Nicki rolled down the window; her face was beet red and she gripped the steering wheel like a child riding a roller coaster. She was crying. We had both become experts at that.

"Oh, Bill, I thought I had lost you, that you had been mugged and dragged off into the desert. I can't bear to lose anything else, ever again," she said, sobbing.

Ever the humorist, I asked why any self-respecting mugger would be out here in the desert in mid-day. It was inappropriate—what she needed was a hug and I proffered only a sophomoric joke. Fact was, we hadn't come on the bicycle ride to be sad. To improve our communication and to protect her own sanity, Nicki bought a two-by-five-inch EXIT sign to put in the highway when I left the road. It was much too small to be effective, but I was grateful for anything that made her feel better.

As the temperature topped 105 near the town of Yucca Valley, a forest of enchanting Joshua trees formed a greeting committee. The trees offered no shade but added mystique to the afternoon. According to legend, the cactus-like plants got their names from 1880s Mormon pilgrims who thought that each one resembled the prophet Joshua, his limbs outstretched, guiding the travelers westward.

The trees pointed me to the day's finishing spot, a taco restaurant in Twentynine Palms. As I relaxed in the air-conditioned dining room, munching a *grande* burrito to celebrate having made up the 16 miles that I lost yesterday, a Marine from the nearby Air Ground Combat Center approached me.

"I know who you are," he said. "I read about you in the newspaper. You're one of those two rich guys from Detroit who ride their bikes all over the country every summer." I wished it were true. For months I had wanted to be anybody but me.

Outside the restaurant, I discovered that I had rolled the bike's back wheel onto a thorn and the tire was flat. It was a rookie mistake. Removing the chain and sprocket were difficult, and so I employed profanity as an aide, which is an essential tool for changing a rear tire. A group of curious German tourists gave me instructions that I could only partially understand. Under their scrutiny, I surgically removed the thorn with Nicki's eyebrow tweezers and inserted a new tube.

Tomorrow I would test the tube and myself in an attempt to ride 110 miles alone, across the merciless Mojave desert.

Andie, learning is a slow process. Your grandmother and I had never attempted a bike ride like this before. We were like two school kids working with our multiplication tables for the first time—making mistakes, erasing our papers, and starting over. In the same way, we were attempting to rebuild our lives without your dad. We would keep trying.

The Bicycle

Thomas Stevens was the first person to ride a bicycle across North America. He piloted a "highwheeler"—also known as the Ordinary—from Oakland to Boston in 1884, with no SAG and no Gatorade. There were few maps, fewer paved roads, and even fewer bridges over wild rivers. The bike probably rode him part of the way. I can only imagine how the astonished citizens greeted the high-hatted adventurer during the 104-day trip.

His bicycle was a Model A compared to my exotic Cannondale. But his was a modern marvel itself, when matched with what probably was the world's first self-propelled vehicle—a four-wheeler that was powered by a long rope connected to wheels by gears, built by Italian Giovanni Fontana in 1418. About 1817, Baron Karl von Drais of Germany created the Swiftwalker, an improved wooden model with iron wheels and no pedals. Riders moved themselves forward by pushing off the ground with their feet. According to legend, Scottish blacksmith Kirkpatrick Macmillan added foot pedals to the Swiftwalker in 1839.

Pedals of early bicycles were attached to the front wheel. Riding those vehicles any significant distance was exhausting because each pedal stroke rotated the front wheel only one time. To achieve more results from all that work, inventors in the 1870s enlarged the front wheel—the largest were nearly five feet tall—so the bike would cover a greater distance with each pedal rotation. Thus was born the comical Ordinary that has become a cultural symbol of the gay 1890s.

Common people seldom rode the Ordinary because it was uncommonly dangerous. Riders frequently flipped head-first over the handlebars or flopped over on their sides. That changed in

1887, however, when the Victor bicycle was invented; its two wheels were the same size, and it had a chain drive similar to today's bikes.

A bicycle revolution began in 1888 when John Dunlop's cushiony air-filled tires replaced leather and solid rubber wheels. For the first time, people were able to transport themselves comfortably without relying upon animals or other humans to pull or push them. A bicycling craze swept America and the world like nothing ever seen before. As Eugene Sloane noted in *The Complete Book of Bicycling*, "by 1896 the watch and jewelry business had fallen almost to zero, piano sales had been cut in half, and book sales had dropped disastrously. Apparently, no one stayed home and played the piano or read, and instead of buying jewelry, people bought bicycles."

DAY 3

ALONE IN THE DESERT

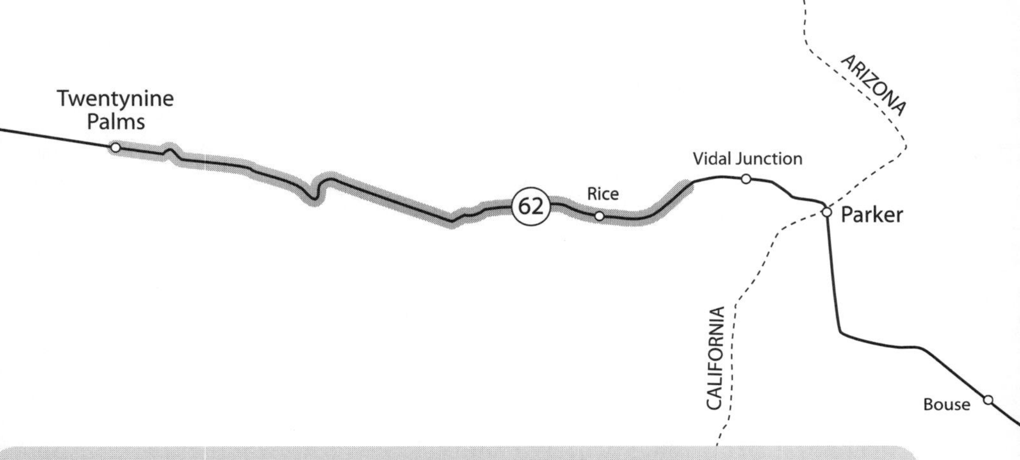

Date: Wednesday, July 11.

Distance traveled: 85 miles in California, from Twentynine Palms to near Vidal Junction.

Total miles completed: 245.

Starting temperature and time: 74 degrees at 4:30 a.m.

Finishing temperature and time: 104 degrees at 2 p.m.

Food: breakfast—toast; lunch—Vienna sausage and 17 Fritos; dinner—chalupa, taco, Fritos, and jar of cheese dip.

Additional fuel: three gallons of water, four quarts of Gatorade, one root beer.

Health: queasy stomach, double vision, and minor tingling in my right hand.

Song stuck in my head: "Like a thorn in the desert, like a sleepy blue ocean..." ("Annie's Song" by John Denver, 1974). I know the correct lyric is "storm," not "thorn," but yesterday's flat tire played tricks on my mind.

Overnight: Fox's Pierpoint RV Resort, located north of Parker, Arizona, on the Colorado River.

"Next Services 100 Miles."

That sign on the outskirts of Twentynine Palms was ominous. And true. A handful of houses within five miles of town clung to the ground like gray spiders. Most were surrounded by tall chain-link fences. A Confederate flag flew in front of one. Two bad dogs bolted from another house to chase me. I'd own a bad dog, too, if I lived in the heart of a desert. Certainly these people were independent folks. I wanted a taste of independence as well, so I asked Nicki to meet me at noon instead of mid-morning. I wanted to tackle the Mojave alone.

The desert wrapped me in a blanket of silence just before sunup, when I sipped water and built a miniature sand castle near a creosote bush. The only sound was my breathing. The colors of the sky changed as if someone were testing theatrical lighting gels. Carbon black at first, with millions of flashing stars. Then lilac-purple. Then pink like a strawberry milkshake. Then steel gray. And, finally, azure blue. Unfortunately, I couldn't linger and enjoy the transformation because the sun marched aggressively over the horizon. And the sun was my enemy.

Highway 62 traverses places with hardy names: Iron Mountains, Granite Range, Sheephole Mountains, and Coxcomb Mountains. Beyond Danby Dry Lake, I struggled up long hills, then coasted down the other sides, hanging on for dear life. It was rugged territory—the Tommy Lee Jones of deserts. For years it had been flyover country for me. Cycling through it was different, like sitting courtside instead of watching a basketball game from the budget seats up high near the rafters.

By 10 a.m. the temperature was already 97 degrees and I was down to my last half-bottle of water. Cooked by the sun, the water was as hot as English tea. Drinking it made me want to vomit. I rested under a speed-limit sign that afforded shade the size of a rolled-up newspaper. It was hardly adequate, but even a sliver of relief from the obstinate sun was better than none. There was no traffic and little apparent life except a red ant, which I killed when it began to explore the pale landscape of my left thigh. I felt guilty for doing so. I pledged not to kill anything else on purpose—except mosquitoes—and apologized to gentle Will Hancock, the animal lover. As a young boy, Will watched a tourist feed popcorn to a squirrel in Rocky Mountain National Park and said, "Dad, that's totally uncool; what will the squirrel eat when the people are gone?"

That ant had lived among the world's toughest plants. The desert is a vast greenhouse full of sage, creosote, and desert lavender. To survive here takes tenacity, much like what is needed to pedal a bike across the country. As I rode eastward through the heat waves, I pondered those plants. They survived by changing to fit climates and cultures that threatened to overwhelm them. Over the millennia, they adapted as continents shifted, oceans inundated valleys, and mighty wind storms scattered boulders. After the airplane crash, my family similarly adapted to a new world, except our evolutionary pace was draconian, not Darwinian.

The frightening double vision and nausea of yesterday returned. I drank all of the hot water, ate a cracker, rested every 15 minutes—but nothing helped. As the blue moth circled overhead, I spotted civilization up the road. At the bottom of a long hill were two road-graders and a pickup truck, although it looked to me like four graders and two pickups. As I approached, a man stepped from the pickup. "Here, you take some of our water," he said. "We don't want you to die out here."

Spectacled and trim, he carried himself more like an MBA candidate than a construction worker. I filled each of my three bottles with Siberia-cold water, which he had hauled fifty miles from his home in Lake Havasu City, Arizona. "A good place to live," he said. "We even have a Wal-Mart—and London Bridge, of course."

Indeed, in 1962 experts discovered that the English icon, which opened in 1831, was sinking into the Thames River under the weight of modern-day traffic. The city of London put the bridge up for sale; Arizonan Robert McCulloch bought it for $2,460,000, and had it dismantled and shipped to Lake Havasu City. London Bridge belonged in Arizona about as much as I belonged in the kingdom of the malevolent blue moth. But we were both here, immobile and misplaced.

Buoyed by the cold water and the stranger's warm compassion, I set sail into the blistering afternoon as giddy as a fifth-grader escaping piano lessons. I saw only two other people in the first 50 miles of the trek—tourists from Connecticut who sternly prepared peanut butter sandwiches on the sizzling hood of their blazing red Cadillac at Clark Pass in the Sheephole Mountains. I stopped and said hello, but the taciturn Yanks wanted no conversation.

After I had ridden 62 miles, Nicki arrived. SAG to the rescue! While we ate lunch in the air-conditioned van—it wasn't the pleasant picnic we envisioned before the ride, but practical given the hot weather—a co-worker back in the NCAA office called on my cell phone, and we chatted about telephone service for the tournament. Later, I scolded myself for worrying about the NCAA eight months before the next Final Four. I loved my job, but now I wanted to throw the phone far into the vast desert. It was time to play, not to serve the NCAA. I realized that I had developed Baby Boomer Syndrome. Work had become play for me and play was work; writing specifications for courtside media seating was more fun than attending games.

Before the tragedy, the most enjoyable part of my life—besides hanging out with my family, of course—was work. There was never a day when I dreaded going to the NCAA office. Helping to manage the tournament was a dream come true, part of a storybook life that included a beautiful, brilliant wife and two happy sons. Sometimes I felt that I didn't deserve such an existence; I hoped in my secret heart that I'd never be exposed as an imposter swiping all the good stuff that belonged to somebody else.

Success in sports requires hard work and long hours. Media folks, coaches, athletic directors, ticket managers, sports information directors, trainers, conference commissioners, and the people who work with them are all in a big boat together, rowing like crazy toward triumph. All that time in the boat leaves little opportunity for outside interests, but most of us squeeze in a few moments for ourselves.

Bob Dekas, the brilliant Northwestern graduate who is the coordinating producer for NCAA basketball on CBS Sports, wistfully says that everyone should be bored for at least a half hour a day. Few people in our sports world actually follow his advice because the work provides such joy and an adrenaline rush of excitement.

Still, this bike ride had to be a holiday from work for me. As difficult as it would be, I vowed to put basketball on the back burner and concentrate on the bike-riding moment in this grand desert. Those moments were easy to enjoy along a bizarre 17-mile stretch of Highway 62. Passersby had created messages by placing stones and pieces of glass on a railroad embankment. It was art, vandalism, and graffiti all in one package: "ABW," "Class of '63," "Suzy Loves Jose." People make their marks in many ways, I thought, and the vile blue moth descended when I remembered that Will had been given only 31 years to make his.

A few miles along, I spotted a salt cedar tree that was draped with hundreds of shoes—like a clever cobbler's Christmas tree. It gave me a good laugh, and the moth flew away. Sandals, hiking boots, cowboy boots, running shoes, and almost every other kind of footwear were tied to the branches of the spirit-lifting shoe tree. It was the first living thing more than six feet tall that I'd seen in 60 miles.

Highway 62 passes the site of Camp Rice, one of 10 desert-warfare training bases operated by the U.S. Army during World War II. Nothing remains of the camp, although Rice was listed on our map.

Just after noon, the construction crew rumbled alongside, headed home. "Glad to see you're still alive," my pal from Lake Havasu City said with a grin. Truth is, I was nowhere near death and was actually having fun in the 101-degree sun. He filled my water bottles again; then he and his mates drove away. I continued east, now with the sun on my neck instead of my nose, treasuring my time in the desert despite the blistering heat, poor eyesight and nausea. I realized that I would view this magic place differently from the airplane the next time I flew overhead. The desolate tract was even more engaging close up. That made me feel guilty again; in the same way I had not fully grasped the beauty of the desert before diving into it, I had also not understood the grief experienced by the many others who had suffered losses like ours.

Nicki made me stop every five miles to rest; she asked how I was doing and then tried to read the real answer in my bloodshot eyes. I knew how she was doing—she was worried.

A miracle occurred on one of those rest stops. When Nicki fed me one Vienna sausage and two Fritos, the nausea and blurred vision vanished. Later I learned that I probably had been suffering from hyponatremia, a potentially serious medical condition caused by a deficiency of salt. The Fritos and lowly Vienna sausage, which are scorned by the healthy elite, injected salt into my veins. They became the staple of my bike-ride diet. The fat might clog my arteries, but by golly, I wouldn't die with an upset stomach. I washed down the salt with Gatorade mixed half-and-half with water; a full dose was too strong.

Despite the new-found nutrition, my legs, arms, and brain ran out of steam, and I stopped 28 miles short of the planned distance. I was disappointed and angry. I'd been riding three days and had wimped out on two of them. At this rate, I would arrive in Savannah in time for Groundhog Day, 2023. But when I adopted a pragmatism like that of the peanut-butter Connecticut Yankees, I realized that 110 miles in the desert had been an unrealistic goal.

Frankly, I knew precious little about what it took to ride a bicycle cross-country. I hoped to learn on the fly.

Nicki drove us to our resting point, a campground north of Parker, Arizona, where we swam in the cool Colorado River. My body seemed to sizzle like a cheeseburger frying on a grill as I settled into the clear water. Twenty million people get their drinking water from the Colorado, and on this day it replenished my soul. I can't speak to whether my little swim improved the quality of anyone's glass of water, though.

"You've picked a great place to visit," said a 50-ish gentleman named Charlie, as Nicki and I toweled off. We followed as he ambled toward an open-air bar on the river. "I moved here from Michigan myself, 20 years ago. I work construction. There's as much work as I want. Don't want too much, not in this sun."

A ruddy-headed man who was busy adding layers to his beer belly nodded at our new pal and said, "Ole Charlie has a poet's insight into life, but you only know it when he's really drunk."

In fact, all the men and women on the riverside bar were silly from alcohol, or headed there. Mist floating down from overhead water pipes kept the patrons cool—along with postage-stamp-sized bathing suits, that is. Nicki led me away to Roci before I could get harebrained along with them.

Our camping spot in the desert beside the mighty river was paradise until the sun went down. Then a swarm of small moths invaded. Unfortunately, these were the literal kind. They filtered into the trailer and crawled into our shirts. The real moths opened the door for the goggle-eyed blue moth to enter and sit with its hairy elbows propped on Roci's dining table.

A mother, father, and three children occupied the trailer next door. The dad, a California police officer, went into Parker to get groceries and pizza for the family. He returned with Ajax for us, which veteran RVers spread around the wheels and the hitch to keep the ants away. It didn't help with the real moths, of course. But his kindness drove away the blue one.

Andie, that construction worker knew that it was not wise to bike across the desert alone. And the father knew that we would be overwhelmed by ants without the Ajax. I was a total stranger, yet they were worried about me. The best thing we can do is care for others. No man—or little girl—is an island.

DAY 4

A SUBSTITUTE FAMILY

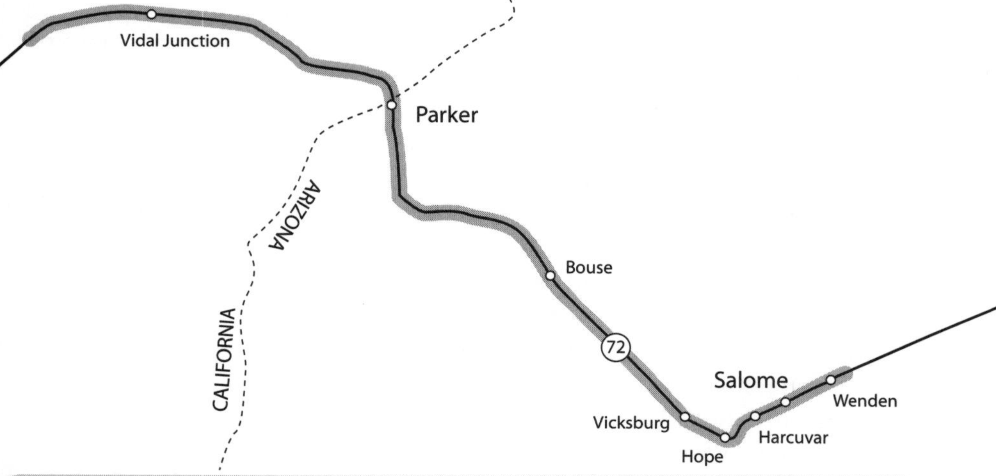

Date: Thursday, July 12.

Distance traveled: 91 miles, from 8 miles west of Vidal Junction, California, to just east of Wenden, Arizona.

Total miles completed: 336.

Starting temperature and time: 71 degrees at 4:30 a.m.

Finishing temperature and time: 102 degrees at 3:30 p.m.

Food: breakfast—Cheerios, banana, toast; lunch—Vienna sausages; dinner—Rice-a-Roni, bread and butter.

Additional fuel: peanut butter crackers, a handful of Cheez-Its, three gallons of water, four quarts of Gatorade, one root beer.

Health: I took two potassium pills to combat nausea; then, via e-mail, a friend suggested magnesium. Maybe I should just eat the Periodic Table. My fingers began to tingle, and I could not bend them. My journal entry read: "twping vety sloely and not at all accurgtely."

Song stuck in my head: "Do you know where Hell is? Hell is in hello. Heaven is goodbye forever, it's time for me to go. I was born under a wanderin' star." ("Wanderin' Star" from the Broadway musical Paint Your Wagon, Lerner and Loewe, 1951.)

Overnight: Morenga Palms RV Park, Wenden.

After Nicki dropped me off in darkness at the railroad crossing that was our "memory marker" from the day before, I flew downhill to the Colorado River, officially ending my stay in California. One state down, eight to go. I arrived in Arizona just in time to see three shirtless caramel-skinned men leap from a slow-moving freight train and sprint toward downtown Parker, Arizona. Creating stories about their intent occupied my mind for a dozen miles. Were they buying apples for comrade warriors in a secret desert shantytown? Seeking medical treatment for snakebite? Applying for jobs as greeters at Wal-Mart?

The sun was already broiling the sandy landscape at 8:30 a.m. when I rested in a dry creek bed east of Parker. In the shade of a palo verde tree, with a fresh breeze and the silver remnant of the morning moon in the blue western sky, my rocky enclave felt like a tropical island. The chalky banks created a protective shell. Out of sight to travelers on the highway, I scratched tic-tac-toe games into the sand and decided the blue moth would never find me in this secret nest. Then the words to "Waltzing Matilda" came back to me: "Once a jolly swag-man camped by a billabong, under the shade of a coolabah tree." The song crept into my soul as if to remind me that I couldn't stay put; I had to place one foot in front of the other. So I moved on, deeper into the desert.

Each year, an estimated one million RV owners flock to the western Arizona town of Quartzsite to escape the northern winter. Their presence shapes—and grays—the culture of the town. Many flee that Quartzsite throng, creating desert sprawl in nearby villages. To serve them, camping spots have sprouted; many of them are merely gravel parking lots, which now—in the summer heat—sat forlorn, like baseball fields in December.

I loved the soothing solitude. Although Nicki and I had relied upon others during those first weeks after the crash, being alone now was sound therapy. There was time to think, to daydream, to remember Will's life.

Twenty-seven miles from Parker, I stopped to examine a monument to Camp Bouse, another of those World War II training bases that had once housed 9,000 soldiers. It was now little more than a ghost town. A tall, distinguished-looking 70-year-old gentleman was there, too, and he wanted to hear all about my bike ride. He had an athlete's body and a journalist's mind full of questions. "I wish I'd started running marathons when I was in my 60s," he finally said. "I think I could have been good at it. You're lucky to have so much life ahead of you, young fellow."

Southeast of Bouse, I crossed the Central Arizona Project (CAP) canal that carries water from Lake Havasu through 336 miles of aqueducts, tunnels and pipelines to near Tucson, Arizona. Boosters say the CAP helps Arizona's metropolitan areas conserve a dwindling ground water supply by importing surface water from the Colorado River. The bad news is that the water that once flowed south now is siphoned to the east. The lower flow of the Colorado has hindered agriculture near Yuma and leached life from former wetlands further downstream at the mouth of the river in Mexico.

The hot, dry air had once again begun to drain away my common sense, and so I pondered swimming in the canal's seductive water. But the steep concrete sides and the *Peligrosa* (danger) sign caused me to reconsider—those and the 10-foot-high chain-link fence running as far as I could see on both sides of the canal. So I pedaled on.

To keep from being intimidated by the distance I was traveling across the country, I had decided to take one day at a time. My thoughts were only on the town of Wenden, today's goal; dreaming of tomorrow could wait. Then I subdivided each day into 10-mile segments. It was easier to break the endeavor down into small, achievable tasks. The journey would be a series of short trips placed end to end until I reached the Atlantic. Nicki and I were trying to deal with grief similarly, concentrating only on the next few hours—not the rest of our lives.

On this particular day, I was forced to concentrate on my current health. I stopped every 10 miles to sip Gatorade and eat salty crackers. I hoped the regular vaccination of potassium and salt would medicate my stomach.

The town of Hope, Arizona, consisted of a few houses, two large RV parking lots, and a new convenience store. Sweating like one of Bear Bryant's football players at his famed Junction training camp, I staggered into the spectacularly air-conditioned store. Following my personal rule of courtesy—buy something every time you enter a store—I paid two dollars for a bag of Cheez-Its and sat down in a corner on the shiny gray tile, like a sodden Cinderella.

"Don't sit on the floor," said the elderly cashier, as if I'd tried to drink all his Welch's Grape Soda without paying.

"Sure, no problem," I said. "If you have a mop, I'll clean up the wet spot."

"It ain't that," he said in a growly voice that was more bear than human. "Sittin' on the floor ain't classy. You can sit on the icebox, if you want to. Or here, take my chair." He passed a white plastic chair over the counter to me. I sat on it for 30 minutes. He stared at me for a while as if something were on his mind. He said nothing more to me but chatted politely with three other customers.

"Suppose that young feller is gonna try to ride that bike up Yarnell Hill?" a patron stage-whispered to him. I thought nothing of it; one day, I would learn to listen to such warnings.

Riding on these desert roads, and trudging through the sands of grief, a person sometimes moves higher gradually, sometimes suddenly. Just beyond Hope—pun intended—I popped up a nice hill to a plain where the rocky desert was interspersed with honest-to-gosh dirt, apple orchards, and wheat fields. On the plain was the Morenga Palms RV Park, where Nicki had turned down Roci's air-conditioner to something well below glacial. Inside, I shivered with delight.

Bruce and Dorothy O'Hara, the kindly RV park owners, basically adopted Nicki and me for the night. We were their only customers, so they treated us like the king and queen of Wenden.

"A biker stayed with us last year, too," said Dorothy. "He said he was writing a book and would mention our names. We never did see the book. If you write one, put us in it."

I explained that I had no intention of writing, because authoring was for professionals and I was just a regular guy out for a simple adventure. But then I played reporter.

"Do you get lonely in the desert?" I asked.

"Not at all," said Dorothy, who was a journalist's dream because one question opened her floodgates to a torrent of information. Roll her together with the stoic store clerk in Hope and the result would be one average person. She gestured at the deserted gravel RV lot; its utility-connection poles reminded me of Civil War tombstones.

"The park is full from November through May," she continued. "Most of the people stay the entire time. They come from all over, but primarily the upper Midwest. They are our family; they help Bruce and me take care of the place. We could never keep it up ourselves. And, goodness, do we have fun. We have pot-luck dinners. We play cards. We sit around a bonfire in the evenings. It's just one big family. In fact, it's better than our real family."

I wondered: how can anything in the world be better than a real family? Nothing could surpass the joy of our own clan at the

Thanksgiving table. I thought back to the last dinner before the tragedy, when Will insisted that Nate not be served pumpkin pie until he finished his broccoli/rice casserole, and Karen and Kristin giggled at the antics of their brother-husbands. The blue moth cut figure eights overhead like a buzzard ready to feast on carrion as I realized that such happiness was gone forever. Words from Bruce grabbed my attention and distracted the moth.

"Are you riding to Prescott tomorrow?" he asked. "Do you know about Yarnell Hill? It's difficult to *drive* up Yarnell Hill. I can't imagine riding a bicycle up it."

Yarnell Hill was beginning to get my attention. The name sounded more like a football player than an icon of geography. No reference to the hill appeared on the map, but the locals treated it almost as an idol. Their awe frightened me, forcing me realize how little I really knew about what lay ahead on the road across the continent. Yarnell Hill obviously was as prodigious as an NFL all-star, and I would try to tackle it as a third-string pretender.

Despite all its amenities, the Morenga Palms RV Park had no pool, so the next best thing for my legs would be a cold shower. Alas, in the summer heat, there was no cold water. Of all the millions of people who used campground showers, I was probably the only one who would complain about not having enough *cold* water.

But there was cause for celebration, because for the first time on the trip, I didn't need to throw up after supper. It was a turning point in my health; the steady, day-long consumption of salty snacks and Gatorade, plus the late-afternoon mini-meal of Fritos and Vienna sausages had returned my stomach to normal. In my new, morbid world, anything close to normal provided great comfort.

Nicki and I held hands and walked under stars across the soundless desert.

Andie, the 70-year-old who dreamed of running marathons knew that it's never too late. He thought 60 years old was just the beginning of prime time and that I was a lucky youngster at age 50. On the other hand, he regretted having missed his opportunity. Remember, "Carpe Diem." As my friend Bob Condron said, "That's Latin for 'seize the carp.' Tomorrow is promised to no one, and you always must come into the day, enjoy the sunrise, and grab whatever fish float into range." Make full use of every day, Andie. That's the way your dad lived, and that's what he wanted for you, too.

4
Over the Hump

DAY 5
YARNELL HILL

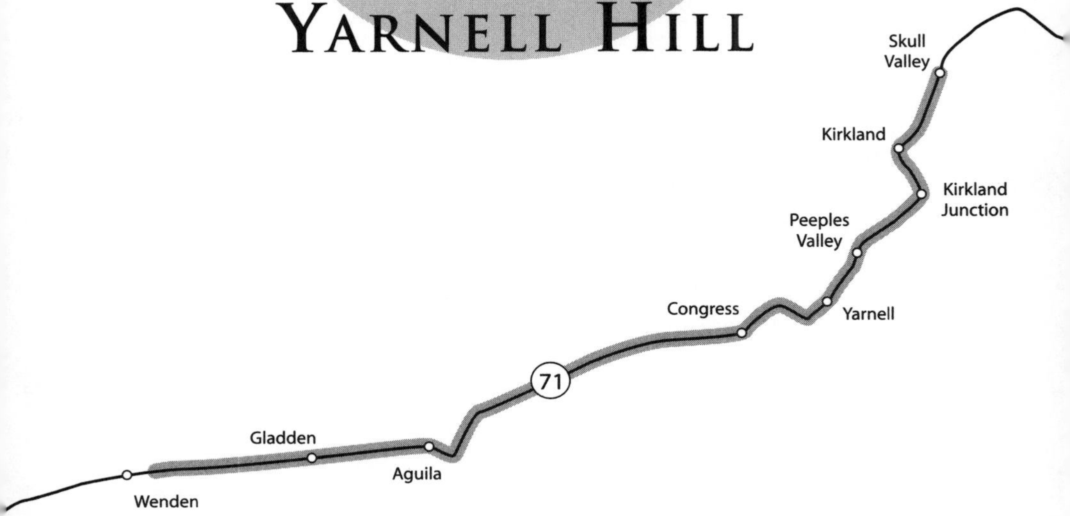

Skull Valley
Kirkland
Kirkland Junction
Peeples Valley
Yarnell
Congress
71
Gladden
Aguila
Wenden

Date: Friday, July 13.
Distance traveled: 78 miles in Arizona, from just east of Wenden to Skull Valley.
Total miles completed: 414.
Starting temperature and time: 80 degrees at 4:30 a.m.
Finishing temperature and time: 85 at 3:40 p.m.
Food: breakfast—shredded wheat, banana, toast; lunch—Vienna sausages; dinner—ranch-style beans, summer sausage, peaches, Fritos, cheese dip, bread and butter.
Additional fuel: cheese crackers, apple, two gallons of water, four quarts of Gatorade, one root beer, one Big Red soda.
Health: Stomach problems almost gone. Potassium did it, plus Gatorade-and-water mix and Fritos and Vienna sausages at end of day. Hands still stiff and painful.
Song stuck in my head: "I got to Kansas City on a Friday; by Saturday I'd learned a thing or two." ("Kansas City," from Oklahoma!, Rodgers and Hammerstein, 1943.)
Overnight: Willow Creek RV Park near Prescott.

I had fallen in love with the desert and did not want to leave. I realize that people define "desert" in different ways; remember that the "Great American Desert" turned out to be the verdant Great Plains? I knew I would visit more remote territory later, but this was the end of the Mojave Desert. And I would miss its seclusion and rugged scenery.

I nearly remained in the desert a while longer. Just before dawn on otherwise-deserted U.S. Highway 60 east of Aguila, a car slowly passed me from behind. I squeezed the bike as near to the shoulder as possible. Normally if there was no oncoming traffic, a vehicle would move to the left lane to give it—and me—some space. But this rusty Ford remained in my lane and dangerously close to me. Only three of its wheels had tires; the other was only a rim, which spat sparks and smoke.

A projectile shot out the back window and bounced off my rear wheel. It was a half-full can of beer. Clearly, the six occupants were busy producing empties. A man in the passenger seat glared at me in an evil way, like Hannibal Lecter eyeing his next victim. My heart pounded and I prepared to turn around and ride as fast as I could back to the safety of Wenden. But then the car veered off down a dirt road and rambled into the desert. I released my tension by dreaming up identities for the passengers: bank robbers, car thieves, a weird family limping home from vacation.

The morning was 80-degrees warm when I left Wenden. But eight miles east of town, a blanket of clouds rolled in, and it was as if I had ridden into a refrigerator. The temperature dropped at least 10 degrees.

Over the next few miles my pulse returned to normal and the orchards yielded to a veritable forest of saguaro, mesquite, and prickly pear. A coyote crossed the road ahead, and its graceful gait was in sharp contrast to the screech of the rubberless rim on the beer wagon. I may have even glimpsed the rare jackalope, a species derived from the accidental breeding of an antelope and a jack rabbit. Some claim the jackalope is mythical, like Smokey the Bear or Wolfman Jack; others think it is merely extinct.

As I sat under a mesquite tree in a dry creek bed—an activity that I highly recommend to anyone seeking peace—three military jets roared overhead, bursting the comfortable bubble of silence. Of course, the pilots had no way to know that I was down here meditating. On the bike, I influenced life in perhaps a 15-foot radius. A passing automobile affected a wider circle, the rumble of its engine traveling a half-mile. But the jets influenced life for miles and miles. I preferred being merely a regular guy with a small circle.

A few miles ahead two archaeologists in wide-brimmed hats were examining rocks by the side of the road. They smiled sweetly and chatted amiably, but their voices reminded me of the desert gravel that surrounded us. "You're dern lucky it's cloudy this morning," one said. "Yarnell Hill is up ahead. It's a real bear. Are you ready?"

I couldn't honestly answer the question. But I pondered it until I topped a small hill covered with saguaros and labored into the village of Congress, where I was surprised to find road construction and a new housing addition. The buzz of civilization filled the air.

While I sipped a Big Red soda in a wood-floored store, a woman purchased 30 bags of ice.

"She's havin' another party," said the burly proprietor, who sat behind the counter watching his wife take care of customers. "Everyone here is havin' a party these days. Our population has doubled in the past two years; 2,000 people live here now. We're gettin' a new post office, new school, and maybe a new grocery store. The snowbirds are movin' here and buildin' houses. Our lives have changed, and they're fixin' to change more. I look for some of the more independent folks to move out. I told 'em, nothing ever stays the same, so get used to it. But they don't have much use for anything new."

Outside, on the store's dusty cement front porch, I watched the parade of life. It was easy to tell the old-timers from the newcomers. The long-time residents drove pickups and wore beat-up running shoes. Their faces bore deep lines and fissures; looking at the textures of their countenances was like seeing the Grand Canyon from the air. The newbies had round, smooth, pink faces, piloted SUVs, and sported new cowboy boots. Their grimaces indicated that their feet hurt.

As I hooked up my helmet and prepared to depart, I saw for the first time a gigantic mass looming in the path of the road just north of town. It was as if someone had built a brick wall across a bowling lane. Yep, confirmed a man in baggy blue jeans, it was the dreaded Yarnell Hill.

Riding closer to the base of the beast, I could see diagonal lines on its stone face. They were—frighteningly—the ascending curves of the road. I took a deep breath, switched the Canondale into "granny gear" and started my climb. To take my mind off the task, I returned to my roots and pondered a little math.

Today's lycra-clad cyclists have the same desire as the 1890s riders in their morning jackets and pantaloons: to go forward with the least effort possible. Our bikes are more efficient because of modern gearing, which works by moving the chain among the three disks next to the pedals and the nine smaller cog wheels on the rear axle. Thanks to the options offered by the 27 gears, I could move as little as 92 inches with every pedal stroke or as far as 287 inches. Resistance is greatest at the high end of that scale. Riding in the 92-inch end of the gear spectrum requires very little work. The low gear—when the chain is on the smallest of three front chain rings—is called granny gear because the pedals rotate so easily that your frail grandmother could ease the bicycle forward. Granny gear is for climbing. The far end of the spectrum, let's call it the testosterone gear, is for high-speed downhill runs.

Yarnell Hill was brutal. I rested every quarter-mile and was indeed grateful for the clouds. On a sunny day, this southern exposure would have been hotter than Julia Roberts in *Pretty Woman.*

I became a gnat magnet. A cloud of the little black creatures descended like Nantucket fog. Four dozen were stuck to my sweaty face after 15 minutes.

I was not equipped, mentally or physically, for Yarnell Hill. Cooler mountain air awaited at the top, I hoped, but getting there would take some doing. When my speed dipped to 3.5 miles per hour, I decided to walk. But then the bike speedometer dropped only to 3.0. I figured, what the heck, might as well ride. Nicki, bless her heart, photographed the colossal climb and offered Gatorade and sympathy. And—most importantly—she didn't lie about how far it was to the top.

"I don't know," she said. "You're not there yet."

Two motorists saw Nicki parked on the shoulder and asked if she needed help.

"No, I'm just waiting for the biker."

"Oh. He's a half-mile back and he looks real bad."

The road ascended in an s-curve, so I could not see the top of the hill. At every switchback, I thought, "Okay, the summit will be just around the next corner." Finally, after nearly two hours in granny gear, I paused to look back at Congress. The town now resembled an ant village far below. While I rested, down the hill came a gentleman on a three-speed Schwinn bicycle, like the one I rode to deliver newspapers in 1962. He sat on that old bike with an uncommon grace, like a king on his grand carriage.

The elderly man stopped to wipe his white brow, and I could tell from his trembling hand that he was going downhill in more ways than one. Yet he was an inspiration—I hoped that he was metaphorically coasting now, enjoying the fruits of a life's labor. Besides, if he could ride on this hill, surely I could, too.

Was I at the top of Yarnell Hill? Like the Ghost of Christmas-Yet-to-Come, the old man didn't say a word, but pointed a bony finger toward the peak. So I struggled up one more rise, then glided into the town of Yarnell as a conquering hero, although no one stood among the pinion pine trees and junipers to toss rose petals or ticker-tape. I rejoiced with a watered-down Gatorade and two cheese crackers, which were as rich for this celebration as champagne and caviar.

Fifteen minutes later, I set off through Peeples Valley, its broad green pastures and white fences reminiscent of Kentucky horse country. A choice presented itself at Kirkland Junction: I could ride to Prescott on a county road in a great 30-mile circle, or I could take the 22-mile direct route on busier Highway 89. As Nicki and I sat by the fork in the road and pondered our options, a pencil-thin, steely-eyed man with rumpled gray hair rattled his dusty truck to a stop, ambled on bow legs over to us, and squatted on his haunches in the gravel. In a Bob Dylan-like voice, he asked if we needed help.

"I'm a bicycler myself," he said, squinting and puffing on a cigarette. "Rode from San Diego to Jacksonville, Florida, one time. All on the interstate. We ran out of money 'cause we broke down and we needed beer. I put a sign on the back of the bike that said 'NEED MONEY.' People gave it to us, too."

Actually, a frosty beer—"root" or regular—sounded tasty.

"If I were you," he continued, "I'd take the long way up to Prescott. It's more gradual and also less dangerous. On 89, the guard rail is right next to the road in some places. And you go up and down, up and down. It's your decision, but that's what I'd do. Ain't no sense gettin' killed trying to save a few miles."

He got up, stretched, slid into the truck and drove away. Nicki and I looked at each other, and she paraphrased Robert Frost: "two roads diverged in the yellow Arizona country; let's take the one recommended by an aging hippie."

Andie, along this journey I often found myself thinking, "Should I have taken a different route?" Although we knew it was a waste of time, your grandmother and I were guilty of thinking about what might have been. Don't worry about the roads you don't take. Concentrate on the ones you do.

DAY 6

CATCHING UP

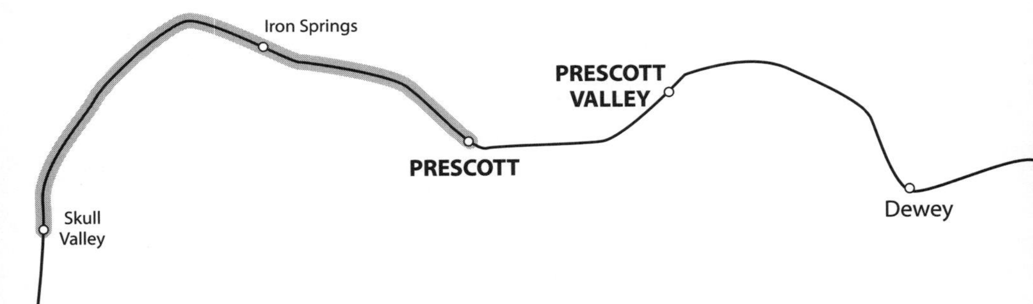

Date: Saturday, July 14.

Distance traveled: 21 miles in Arizona, from Skull Valley to Prescott.

Total miles completed: 435.

Starting temperature and time: 59 degrees at 6:30 a.m.

Finishing temperature and time: 75 degrees at 10 a.m.

Food: breakfast—toast; lunch—omelet, pancakes, hamburger, French fries; dinner—pizza.

Additional fuel: 24 Fritos, one blueberry scone.

Health: Fine, thanks.

Song stuck in my head: none, which caught me by surprise. Admittedly, the ride was short, but couldn't I at least have heard the Minute Waltz?

Overnight: Willow Creek RV Park in Prescott.

Today was the first of four catch-up days written into the itinerary. If I'd been on schedule, we'd have relaxed at the pool. But I was behind, so I rode.

The country was different—higher and rolling. On the climb to Prescott I spotted a hand-crafted roadside memorial, the kind that dot Southwestern roads at places where fatal auto crashes have occurred. In keeping with the Hispanic heritage of the area, the memorials are called "descanos"—from the Spanish word *descanar*—which means "to rest."

A calmness came over me as I dismounted from my bike and stepped off the pavement, as if I were entering a chapel. I removed my bike helmet and knelt beside the two white crosses that were planted in a circle of glistening white rocks and entwined with artificial green ivy. Two names—a boy's and a girl's—were written on the crosses. Inside the rock circle were a locket, a class ring, a book, and a football. Two empty wine bottles also rested in the circle; I read the labels—it was the good stuff. I hoped the family and friends had sipped the wine while remembering happier times.

Before our family's tragedy, I had considered such markers morbid and unnecessary. Now I understood the need to preserve the memory of loved ones. I knew the pain that these mourning families endured; this memorial was no different in essence from the one at the site where Will's plane crashed. A shiver of recognition raced down my spine. I was alone at the memorial, but I could feel the presence of people who were on the same, grieving side of the fence as me. The brief encounter with unknown kindred souls was enriching. Together, either spiritually or physically, perhaps we could keep the blue moth at bay.

I pedaled away with a lighter load, enjoying the brisk atmosphere that reminded me of an autumn football morning. Those September days had always signaled a new beginning for me, and I wondered if such hope was now possible in my life.

I had chosen to enter Prescott through the city's back door, so there was no traffic. Although nothing like the monumental ride up Yarnell Hill, the climb was strenuous. But I was in no hurry, and soon I inhaled the pine-scented air at the summit. Then I effortlessly scooted downhill into a bustling city such as I had not seen since Los Angeles.

Prescott is an alpine retreat where Phoenix residents flee the downstate summer heat. Nicki and I visited an Internet café to download e-mail. The establishment had it all: live music, soft sofas, free phone lines, sandals-clad customers, crunchy scones, and blue-haired high school girls sitting next to blue-haired old women. It was good to be back in civilization and away from the turmoil of the highway outside. Apart from a shady arroyo, it was the most pleasant place I could imagine for unwinding. And unwind we did.

Every day I looked forward to my evening alone with Nicki when we would relax in Roci, exhausted from our labors. Her days were as taxing as mine—it was quite difficult to hitch the trailer, negotiate tight turns in parking lots, use maps to find her way in strange territory, then push and pull our pop-up home back into position by herself. I knew the activity was good for her; perhaps I saw signs of life returning to her deep brown eyes.

Later at the campground, Nicki and I held hands and watched electric-blue lightning illuminate giant cauliflower clouds as thunderheads above the Mogollon Rim reached maybe to heaven. My own time on the rim awaited tomorrow.

Andie, I pray that you live out the rich, full life that your dad dreamed for you, and that you leave something behind. Perhaps you will write a novel, paint a masterpiece, score more goals than any soccer player in Oklahoma State University history, or simply be a wonderful friend to many.

An E-Mail Support Crew

I could take but one member of our family along on my bicycle tour on the nation's highways. But those left behind still participated via the information highway. I had e-mailed a brief journal of my trip to a dozen people after the second day. Several shared it with others, and I began to receive e-mail questions from strangers who were interested in my quest. In Prescott, responding took a half-hour, as inquisitive minds wanted to know:

What technical gadgets are you carrying to keep in touch with everyone? Only my laptop computer which Nicki carries in the car, and the cell phone, which seems to have been manufactured by "looking for service."

How do you remember what happens during the day? I write notes on folded-up legal paper. Yesterday, when I couldn't find the paper, I scribbled the following on the back of my hand: "damn gnats."

What do you carry on the bike? In a small bag under my seat are bike-repair tools, a poncho, $40 in cash, $100 in travelers' checks, a Visa card, my NCAA business card (is it possible to need "connections" in the middle of the desert?), a compass, the EXIT sign at Nicki's request, a spare tire tube, and a tube-repair kit.

A black bag sits on my rear fender. Inside are a water bottle, road map, camera, reflective vest that I wear each day before sunrise, cheese crackers, and a granola bar. Oh, and the little bottle of Pacific Ocean water. In my fanny pack are the cell phone, sunscreen, note paper, a pen, lip balm, and pepper spray (for bad dogs).

We carry five extra tubes in the car, plus one extra tire, one extra rear wheel, two bike-repair manuals, and enough Gatorade to quench the thirst of an entire Boy Scout troop.

What kind of bike are you riding? The bike is a 27-speed Cannondale R600 model with aluminum frame, Shimano 105 components, CODA Slice Echelon fork, and Shimano RSX hubs. I don't know what all that means, but the bike almost goes by itself, which it ought to do, since it cost twice as much as our first car. It also has an odometer and speedometer. I move my hands to one of the five positions on the handlebars every mile or so.

What do you wear? A blue Giro helmet, long-sleeved cotton t-shirt, padded biking gloves, padded biking shorts with nylon running shorts underneath, cotton socks, and running shoes. I tie a bandana around my neck and wear another on my head; it hangs like a curtain from the sides and back of the helmet to cover my ears and neck. Yesterday an elderly man called me the blue sheik.

Are you nuts? Who counts Fritos? That's a two-part question. Yes, perhaps. And I do count Fritos. It's the math thing; I can't help it.

Are you riding for a good cause? I really don't think so.

DAY 7
FREEWAY SAMARITAN

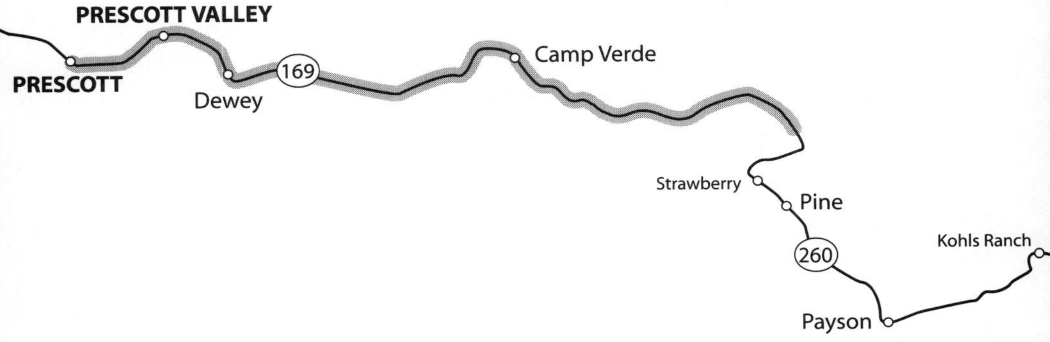

Date: Sunday, July 15.
Distance traveled: 74 miles in Arizona, from Prescott to 25 miles west of Payson.
Total miles completed: 509.
Starting temperature and time: 59 degrees at 4:15 a.m.
Finishing temperature and time: 85 at 3:30 p.m.
Food: breakfast—toast; lunch—Vienna sausages; dinner—apple sauce, Fritos and cheese dip, cheese sandwich.
Additional fuel: 18 Cheez-Its, two gallons of water, five quarts of Gatorade, one root beer.
Health: Hands still numb. Nicki's sister Catherine advised that her secretary cured carpel tunnel by swimming. So I began to do swimming strokes—windmills—with my arms while riding.
Song stuck in my head: "By the time I make Albuquerque, she'll be risin'. She'll find the note I left hangin' on the door." ("By the Time I Get to Phoenix," as performed by Glen Campbell, 1968.)
Overnight: Ox Bow RV Park near Payson.

Nicki and I calculated that I could save 10 miles by riding on Interstate 17 downhill to Camp Verde instead of tackling the narrow road through the mining town of Jerome. So I decided to risk it and coasted down the on-ramp to the wide four-lane highway. The interstate was a frenetic artery, starkly different from the quiet lanes that I had been traveling. The wake from each truck buffeted my bike like an aircraft carrier passing a dinghy. The wide shoulder was an obstacle course of tire treads, broken glass, metal and stones.

While I zipped downhill at 30 miles per hour, a hunk of garbage punctured the back tire—flat number two. I sat in the gravel between the freeway lanes and pried the tube from the tire. A car pulled off the freeway and stopped a few feet from me. Out stepped a fuzzy-haired 30-ish woman and an imposing German Shepherd dog. The woman wore granny glasses and a flowing skirt from the '60s. The dog wore a snarl.

"You okay?" the woman asked. "I was headed south and saw you. I've been in trouble on the freeway before, so I know what it's like. I went to the next exit and doubled back to see if you needed anything. I'll stay with you until you finish fixing your flat."

Stay she did. And her big dog, too. I made friends with the animal by allowing him to lick my salty face. I made friends with the woman by listening to her as she spoke 100 miles per hour. I learned that she was a special education teacher who lived in Phoenix, had a cat but gave it away, loved her mother, and wanted to buy a canary. Sometimes I have a curmudgeon's impatience with rambling raconteurs, but this woman was a blessing—like the familiar company of a radio station on a solo all-night drive. I was prepared to tell her about Will, who, of course, was never more than a few seconds from my mind. But I couldn't get a word in.

"You should be more careful about stopping to help strangers on the interstate," I finally said as I used my 10-inch hand pump to inflate the replacement tube. "I could have been weird."

She looked at the dog, studied my spindly pale forearms, looked back at the dog and said, "He knows 'weird' when he sees it. He takes care of any problems before they happen."

Then a highway patrol car turned off the northbound lane and crunched to a stop in the gravel next to her car. Suddenly we were hosting a convention in the noisy median. "Good grief," I thought as the officer stepped out. "It must be illegal to ride a bike on an interstate; he's going to arrest me, put the bike in his car, and drive me to jail in Camp Verde."

"You okay, sir?" he said, removing his perfectly blocked trooper hat to reveal a bald head that was dappled with perspiration.

"Yes, I'm fine, and I'm just about finished changing this flat tire. Beautiful day, isn't it? This is—er, what's your name, miss?—and her dog. They stopped to help."

"Well," he said, "both of you be careful when you get back on the interstate." He wheeled his shiny black cruiser back onto the highway, leaving me alone with the dog and the woman. Saying goodbye took her a long time; I wished the patrolman had stayed to help listen. Finally I bade farewell to my long-winded Samaritan, dodged a passing Budweiser truck, and returned to the interstate shoulder.

The rest of the ride downhill on the interstate was without incident. At Exit No. 287, I signaled with my right arm and coasted down the ramp. I visited the obligatory moccasin shop in Camp Verde, and watched grandmothers rifle through Indian moccasins and turquoise jewelry. Their grandkids—unimpressed with the shopping and antsy from long hours of captivity in seat belts—begged to cross the street to McDonald's.

I visited historic Fort Verde, crossed the Verde River, then finally headed up Arizona Highway 260 toward the Mogollon Rim (pronounced two ways: MUGGY-own or MUGGY-on). The wall of the rim, which extends southeast from near Flagstaff almost 200 miles toward New Mexico, looked like a series of castles built side by side. Geologists say it is an escarpment marking the southern edge of the Colorado Plateau. Bikers say it's a killer.

The riverside fields of Camp Verde quickly yielded to broad treeless foothills covered with tall brown grass. I paused to take in the view back down to the green valley below and the mountain ridges beyond. Then, I rode upward, along what is basically the route where General George Cook constructed a road in the 1870s to connect Fort Verde with Fort Apache, nearly 200 miles to the east. Cook's troops were stationed out here to protect settlers from Indians; perhaps, I reasoned, vice-versa would have been better in the long run. During the great silent stretch devoid of towns, I had plenty of time to compare the reality of those days with the imagined culture of today's moccasin shops.

The average elevation of the Mogollon Rim is 7,000 feet—quite a contrast from Camp Verde at 3,160 feet—and I was sneaking up the rim on a ramp from the west. The climb was not as abrupt as Yarnell Hill, but plenty taxing. At one point I spotted two other bikers ahead and tried without success to catch them. Later, a man told me that Olympic cyclists train up here on these quiet roads through the Prescott, Coconino, and Apache National Forests.

Three trucks lurched downhill toward me, accompanied by the acid smell of hot brakes. The truckers' brake-tapping caution was another warning—I had plenty more climbing to do before reaching the Mogollon Rim. I cried "Uncle!" more often than a first-grader being force-fed asparagus, pausing to rest every two miles while reminding myself that this climb was just like dealing with grief. I had to put one foot in front of other—again and again and again.

I left the grassy foothills and entered a land of pinion, juniper, and oak. There, in a particularly winding stretch of road, I spotted a nasty message spray-painted on the highway's narrow shoulder: "Bikers Suck. Stay off Rode." I didn't want to meet that person, nor the English teacher responsible for such poor spelling.

The ground became more rocky, and the climb seemed to be endless. I grew irate. Old marathon runners actually relish anger because it provides a shot of adrenaline that revs up the muscles. But now I was *really* steamed. My frustration was focused on the American Automobile Association because my map seemed to be incorrect. After miscalculating the distance that first day in California, each night I had carefully evaluated the next day's mileage and terrain. Squiggly lines were bad; they indicated hills. Straight lines near towns weren't good, either; traffic would be heavy. Mostly, the AAA maps were outstanding, but this one was the exception. I interpreted the map to show 32 miles from Camp Verde to the town of Strawberry. Actually, the distance was more than 50 miles. Eighteen miles isn't much in an automobile. On a bike, it can be like several light years.

Thankfully, when I reached the rim, my heart and mind were resuscitated by mountain air so clear and crisp that I thought I could break it with my hand, karate-style. Through a gap in the majestic Ponderosa pines, I glimpsed smoke from a forest fire wafting over a distant ridge, but it was in another life removed from mine. I rode through burned-out areas where tiny new pines were emerging from the slate gray earth. New life from ashes—I appreciated the concept.

Andie, that woman on the interstate highway took a chance by stopping to help me. But she felt safe because she knew her dog would protect her. People will protect you, too: your mom, your grandparents, others who aren't even a part of your life yet. But you might also want to get yourself a big dog.

A White Afro

As a three-year-old, Will—the hippie baby—had a white Afro hairstyle that glistened like Angel hair from a Christmas tree. When we visited Mexico, friends said, "Hang onto that boy; someone will try to steal him."

His appeal went way beyond the curls. His bubbly personality drew people to him. He was happy and genuine and honest almost to a fault. Like another Okie named Will, our son never met a man he didn't like. But he had more depth than a simple quotation could reveal.

Will absolutely loved sports. He and I began playing tackle football in the yard when he was two years old. At age four, he kept score at Sooners baseball games. He wrote his first sports story in third grade—a sign of what was to come.

After my daily long runs, six-year-old Will would meet me at the front door. "Can we please go for a walk, Daddy?" he would eagerly ask. And we would hold hands and go, with me sweating and him singing, to the tune of "Rock Around the Clock," "Walk, walk, walk, around the block...."

Will was on the cross-country and track teams in high school. He took good care of his body. Unlike me on the bike ride, he was a healthy eater, often choosing health food over fast food. He was also so cautious that we teased him for driving his car like a 93-year-old librarian on Ritalin. Will was the least likely member of our family to put himself in harm's way.

Thankfully, he looked like his mom, but Will's interests were much the same as mine. His love for music was always evident. He learned to sing the National Anthem ("what so proud we-lee-hailed") when he was three. He memorized the trombone countermelody to the University of Oklahoma fight song, "Boomer Sooner," in seventh grade and played it incessantly, annoying his Kansas Jayhawk-rooting friends. Later, he and I played trombone-and-piano duets together. Will was as comfortable reading a Bach score as he was examining a box score—just like his dad.

But as much as he learned from me, I too learned from him. I taught him to treasure Beethoven's majestic *Ninth Symphony* and the tradition of college fight songs; he led me to Mahler. He was patient with my passion for Chopin waltzes and etudes; I appreciated his love of the rock band U2. I explained the infield fly rule to him; he introduced me to Slate.com on the Internet.

Oh, we didn't always think alike: I failed to convince him to read Stephen Ambrose; he couldn't persuade me to try Stephen King. He loved Monet; I preferred Norman Rockwell. He never really grasped the joy of personal finance; I was lousy at PlayStation 2 games.

But I truly treasured time spent with Will. During his 31 years on this planet, I was blessed because he was always willing—even excited—to do things with his dad. We were bound together by more than genetics. More even than our twin careers. Along with Nate, we formed a trio connected by a love of music, literature, sports, and off-beat humor. The three of us even developed our own private language from movie catch-phrases which we employed with abandon, often to the bewilderment of others:

"Teacher says every time a bell rings, an angel gets his wings." *(It's a Wonderful Life)*

"I am pitching to Shoeless Joe Jackson!" *(Field of Dreams)*

"No more rhymes now, I mean it." "Anybody want a peanut?" *(Princess Bride)*

"Do you think I could make one of those bats?" *(The Natural)*

"When the Lord closes a door, he opens a window." *(The Sound of Music)*

A massive door slammed shut when Will died. Nicki and I were seeking the window.

DAY 8

Boost from a Son

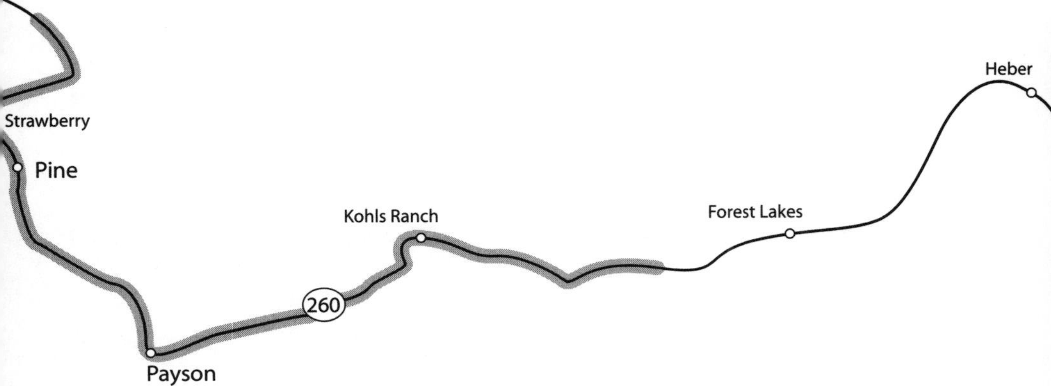

Date: Monday, July 16.
Distance traveled: 56 miles in Arizona, from 25 miles west of Payson to near Forest Lakes.
Total miles completed: 565.
Starting time and temperature: 49 degrees at 6 a.m.
Finishing temperature and time: 85 at 2 p.m.
Food: breakfast—toast, banana; second breakfast—McDonald's breakfast burrito; lunch—Vienna sausages, peanut butter crackers; dinner—Pringles, squash, cream-style corn, Fritos and cheese dip, hot chocolate.
Additional fuel: one gallon of water, three quarts of Gatorade, one root beer.
Health: Much better. Nausea is long gone. Hands are improving. I will continue to swim on the bike.
Song stuck in my head: none.
Overnight: Sinkhole Campground in Apache-Sitgreaves National Forest.

Coasting is possible because the bicycle's back wheel is a freewheel, which means it spins freely in one direction and locks in the other. Pedals on a tricycle turn constantly because it doesn't have a freewheel—children riding three-wheelers must pedal all the time; adults have learned to coast. But, I could not enjoy coasting downhill on the bike, because an uphill climb always followed. It was like dealing with the rollercoaster of emotions that I had endured since the crash—each moment of peace was only temporary. The persistent blue moth always waited in the valley ahead.

At dawn I sailed down through the picturesque mountain hamlets of Pine and Strawberry, whose gingerbread houses rested under a canopy of massive pines. "These are Mormon towns," a man in coveralls told me. "I can't imagine anyone, anywhere, has a better life. I drive 90 miles down to work in Phoenix every day, but that's a small price to pay to be able to live in such peace."

Peace was impossible to find east of Payson, as the traffic became frightening on narrow Arizona Highway 260. To my distress, the road had plunged down off the Mogollon Rim to Payson's 5,000-foot elevation. Then, the highway carried me and a passel of cool-weather seekers on a long climb through the pine-studded neck of the Rockies back up to the Ponderosa-pine country. A Winnebago passed inches from my left heel, sending my heart rate soaring. The timid driver of the next car saw that big RV nearly hit me and refused to pass, and so a string of 15 vehicles slowed to a six-miles-per-hour crawl behind me. I wanted to pull off the road to let them by, but "off the road" was a 10-foot plummet to boulders below. I was a trapped Pied Piper and so were the poor rats in vehicles crawling impatiently up the hill behind me.

I couldn't see the top of the climb, so I employed a trick that I had used to avoid disappointment on Yarnell Hill: I convinced myself that there was no summit—that I would be riding uphill forever.

A sudden gust of warm wind hit from behind. I had the eerie sensation that I was not alone.

"Will, is that you?" I said out loud.

I was sure he was behind my right shoulder. Certainly, I could *feel* him, pushing my bicycle up the hill just the way I pushed his when we first removed its training wheels. It was not ghostly or illogical or even spiritual; Will was simply there, helping me ride up the hill. Despite the steep climb, I pedaled almost effortlessly. And while I pedaled, I talked to him.

"How you doing? Your mom and I really miss you; we know you miss us, too. Andie is beautiful, and she is quite happy. But I guess you know that."

He didn't respond, but that didn't stop me from talking to him.

"Thirty people stood with us at Andie's christening. Thirty or 300 or even 3,000 couldn't take your place, but we're trying. We're trying hard.

"But I'm worried about your mom. Remember that she used to read a book every night? Well, she can't read at all nowadays. And sometimes the sunshine makes her cry. Doggone, that breaks my heart.

"Nate and Karen are struggling, too. Of course, you also know that, don't you? Sometimes they call me when they're sad, and for some crazy reason that makes me happier. Am I losing it?"

The wind—or Will—continued to propel me upward. Soon, almost to my disappointment, the road flattened, and I was back up on the Mogollon Rim. That climb had been an awesome moment of grace that left me serenely happy. The blue moth had been shooed away.

A minute later, the happy moment vanished when a snarling bare-chested man strode out of the woods and onto the road in front of me. He put his hands on his hips and glared at me with bloodshot eyes.

"You there, stop! Come over here," he said, gruffly, pointing to his scruffy pickup truck. A chill shot through me. A mugger! I wanted to flee, but I knew the Cannondale could not outrun his vehicle. So, with fear and trembling, I followed him.

"We watched you fight your way up that hill," he said as we walked to his rusted white pickup. "After that long climb you might need one of these." He reached into an ice chest and pulled out a glistening can of Budweiser.

I had been contemplating a mugging, and the unkempt man delivered manna. As far as I was concerned, he was the king of cheers. The moment froze in my mind like a favorite vacation snapshot. On the fireplace mantle of my heart, that photo would sit beside the frame of Nicki in fetal agony on our bedroom floor—everlasting symbols of the wonderful and the horrible in life. I popped the top and took a small sip of cold beer.

"We come up here to fish," he said, now smiling like a court jester and hitching up his cutoff gray sweat pants. "We watched you ride up that hill; it didn't look like fun. We thought you were nuts, because you were smiling. I told my pal that we were damn lucky to be in our pickup.

"When we got to the top, we hatched a little plot to help you out. We've got plenty of beer—take all you want."

I'm not sure how he figured I could carry an armful of beer on my bike, but the offer was generous nonetheless.

"We live down in Mesa," he continued. "We work in the winters, fixing snowbirds' cars. They drive crazy—going the wrong way on one-way streets and going so slow that people plow into their backsides. We love 'em.

"In the summer, we fish and drink beer. It's a good life."

After more small talk he hopped up into his truck, slapped five with his partner, waved out the window, and drove away. I was only one mile from the campground, so I rode on with the can of beer in my right hand. It was B.W.I.—biking while intoxicated by the kindness of a stranger in cutoffs.

Nicki had parked Roci deep in the woods. Sedated by the beer, I took a power nap and awoke to the spicy scent of warm pines in the afternoon sun. Later, other campers roasted chocolate-and-marshmallow s'mores over crackling wood fires in the cold darkness. Enjoying our first night away from electricity, Nicki and I slept in long pants and socks and used towels as extra blankets. We cuddled like newlyweds, savoring the stars and the silent night.

DAY 8

Andie, my brother—your uncle Joe, who is not a preacher or a philosopher but just a regular guy like me—wrote this to me after the airplane crash:

"I feel so inadequate. I don't know how to help you. Anything I try to say can be responded to by the phrase, 'He doesn't know—he hasn't been there.'

"This is what I believe: Will is not gone. He's here right now. He's everywhere. He's with you every minute and with Nicki and Nate and Karen and Andie, too. He's just like Mother and Daddy. They're not gone. I feel their presence every day. The Bible says something about 'we'll all be together again.' How does God manage that with millions of people? I think it's really simple. We all have souls. We are souls. We can't see them, can't touch them, but we all have souls just the same. When death comes, as it will to all of us, the soul remains just as it always has been. It's a wonderful thing, too.

"I believe Mother's and Daddy's souls are still with us. Nothing changes really, does it? Will's here watching and enjoying everything

we do and say. That's why I believe we should say and do only the things that will make them happy and proud of us. Someday, our souls will be reunited with our loved ones. But until that time comes, God expects us to live our lives to the fullest. We must continue as the persons God intended us to be. Our every action must reflect favorably on those departed souls that are magically still with us."

DAY 9
THE FOREST

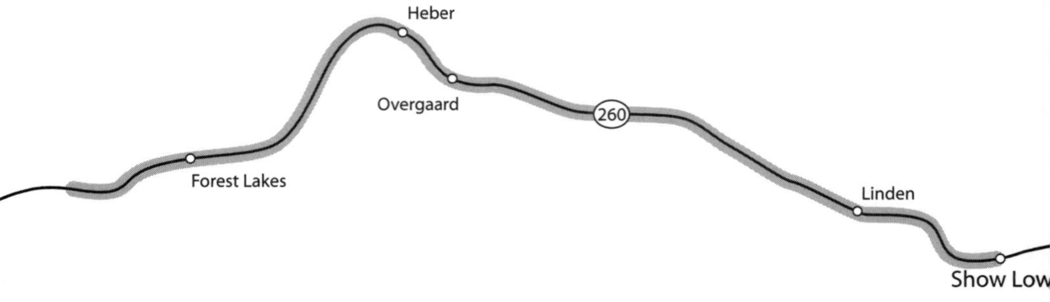

Date: Tuesday, July 17.

Distance traveled: 58 miles in Arizona, from 22 miles west of Heber to Show Low.

Total miles completed: 623.

Starting temperature and time: 49 degrees at 5 a.m.

Finishing temperature and time: 75 at 1 p.m.

Food: breakfast—toast, banana; lunch—cheese crackers, baloney and cheese sandwich; dinner—KFC all-you-can-eat buffet: chicken, salad, chicken, corn, mashed potatoes, chicken, biscuits, gravy, chicken, pudding.

Additional fuel: 12 Fritos, two gallons of water, three quarts of Gatorade, one root beer.

Health: Just fine, except for still slightly numb hands.

Song stuck in my head: "Lots of curves, you bet. Even more when you get to the Junction. Petticoat Junction." ("Petticoat Junction," as performed by Flatt & Scruggs, 1966.)

Overnight: "Bates RV Park" (not its real name), Show Low.

My hands tingled from the cold as I rode fast through a construction zone at 6 a.m., before the highway crew arrived. Later in the day, Nicki waited here for nearly two hours because the workers had closed one lane. But I zig-zagged around the heavy equipment and rolled easily over the newly laid asphalt, which was as black as a new bruise. The windless air was refreshing. Mysterious, long, black shadows hung onto my surroundings; my own shadow chased me down the road.

The world awoke as I passed. A rooster's cock-a-doodle-doo brought a smile to my face. A pair of elk fled into the woods. A two-inch beetle zipped across the road like a miniature brown Indy race car. A grasshopper ricocheted off my upper lip. Then, as I was meditating and spinning in the silence, I was slapped back to reality when something came crashing through the forest. Was it a bobcat? A bear? Big Foot? Vanished hijacker D. B. Cooper?

It turned out to be merely an old tree limb that had dropped from its lofty perch, crashing with a great flourish. The limb was doomed to rot away in the loam of the forest floor. The blue moth swooped down when I concluded that Will could be forgotten like that tree branch, his existence slowly fading as his friends and colleagues found substitutes to take his place.

It was difficult to shake that irrational thought. But thankfully, riding hard through the quiet pines chased the moth away. Perhaps I was growing mentally tougher? I was certainly physically stronger; my marshmallow-soft flab was hardening. After yesterday's climb to the Rim, the riding today was so easy that it felt like cheating.

Traffic increased as the morning progressed. Once the world woke up, vehicles of all kinds were my constant companions. Cars, trucks and motorcycles sped past my creeping Cannondale. I had come to know three distinctive horn honks. One was delivered by friendly drivers: "Hey, I'm back here, so please be careful." The second was the male equivalent of a cheery, "You go, girl." The third was nasty: "Get the hell out of my way, you granola-eatin', tree-huggin', Democrat-votin', bike-ridin' liberal, because I'd just as soon run over you as look at you." The two happy honks were by far the most common, thankfully.

In the magnificent Arizona high country, there were plenty of people around to honk.

A mother in Heber told me, "We moved up here from Phoenix six years ago. This place is booming. There were 34 kids in the average high school graduating class five years ago; the class of 2002 will be 54. I don't like it. They should have closed the door right after we got in."

As I eavesdropped, a convenience store clerk said to a customer: "You shoulda seen the police reports in the newspaper last week. In St. John's, they broke up a fight between two turkeys and a dog. Up here, they kicked a kid out of school for throwing a pop tart. What's the world comin' to?"

As a high school English teacher, Nicki didn't enjoy the pop tart story. Nicki is the kind of teacher we all had—or wished we had. She grinds away at exposing her classes of college-bound seniors to Shakespeare and logic and clear writing. It's difficult for some of them. But in the autumn, her former students troop back from college to thank her for having been so firm and to boast about how they are far ahead of their freshman English colleagues. She loves them all.

I felt terribly sorry for Nicki's high school students in the days after the airplane crash. Those youngsters were a part of the vast circle whose lives were changed. I'm told they huddled together at school the Monday after the accident, comparing notes about how they heard the awful news and how to react when Mrs. Hancock returned to the classroom.

Nicki and I also compared notes—and continued doing it at the end of each day during the bike ride. From the bicycle, I saw things that she didn't, such as two empty Taco Bell sauce packets on the side of the road 50 miles from the nearest fast-food emporium. Nicki saw things that I missed, too; today, she encountered a young man moving down U. S. Highway 60 on roller blades. She learned the man was skating from Boston to Los Angeles, raising money for cancer treatment. His cause was clear; mine, still murky. A couple of days ago, she watched a dust devil—a mini-tornado created by wind swirling over newly plowed ground. Together, we enjoyed wild flowers, pillow-soft hillsides, golden sunrises, and mellow sunsets.

In Show Low—which indeed was named because of a poker game—I dubbed our campground the "Bates RV Park" because of a domineering mother and a quiet, obedient, Hitchcockian 50-year-old, who I assumed was her son. The mother peeked through window curtains as we drove to our parking spot, then stepped out to give orders as we backed Roci into our parking space.

Later, I lay on my back on the sidewalk with my eyes closed, doing my evening routine of hamstring stretching. Suddenly I heard a shrill voice.

"Young man, what are you doing?"

I opened my eyes and was shocked to see the mother's face inches from mine, as if she were looking for a lost contact lens. I screamed in terror. She squealed in response. Her son came running to see what caused the commotion. I wanted to laugh about the entire affair, but the mother's icy glare was too spooky. The next morning, the restroom light fixture fell on Nicki, then I burned my toast and melted the alarm clock on top of the toaster. We were happy to flee the mysterious RV park.

Andie, remember that your grandmother spotted different things at 60 miles per hour than I did at 15 miles per hour. When you were a crawling baby, even though we were all in the same room, you observed a whole other world on the floor. That's okay; each person has a different viewpoint. Don't expect others to see life as you do.

DAY 10

The Purple Anvil

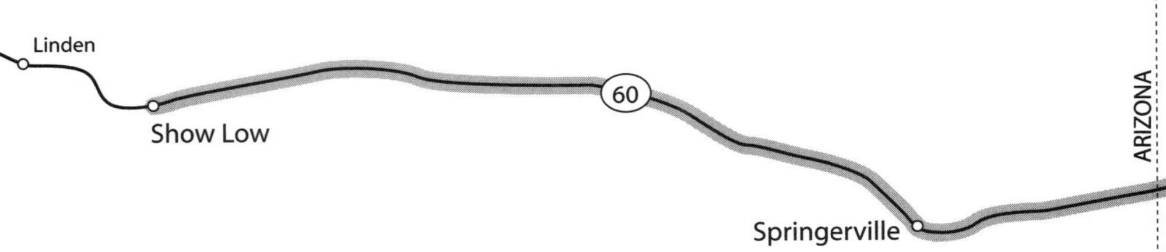

Date: Wednesday, July 18.

Distance traveled: 64 miles, from Show Low, Arizona, to two miles east of the New Mexico state line.

Total miles completed: 687.

Starting temperature and time: 59 degrees at 5 a.m.

Finishing temperature and time: 75 at 1 p.m.

Food: breakfast—toast, banana; lunch—two cookies, cheese crackers, baloney and cheese sandwich; dinner—two hot dogs, apple.

Additional fuel: two cookies, six Twizzlers, 17 Fritos, one gallon of water, one quart of Gatorade, one root beer.

Health: Darn fine. Hands back to normal thanks to the swimming exercise. If you ever see a windmill on a bicycle, c'est moi.

Song stuck in my head: "I wonder what the king is doing tonight? What merriment is the king pursuing tonight?" ("I Wonder What the King is Doing Tonight?" from Camelot by Lerner and Loewe, 1960.)

Overnight: Casa Malpais RV Park, Springerville.

Pedaling through the deserted streets of Show Low long before dawn, I felt like the only human running from the end of the world and remembered the old pun, "Armageddon outta here." I didn't want to get out of Northeast Arizona, a wide-open land as emerald as Oz.

After nearly three days among the pines, the highway dropped off the Mogollon Rim through forests of pinion, juniper, and aromatic cedar into high ranch country with air so fresh and clean that it made me want to weep. And so I did, right in the middle of the road, wishing Will were here to enjoy the mud and green grass and wildflowers as white as wedding dresses. I'd had no inkling that *this* Arizona existed. What other surprises awaited on the road ahead?

A sign read, "Rough Road Next 16 Miles." The sign-makers weren't kidding; there were cracks and ripples and ruts that slowed the pace more effectively than any set of speed bumps on the Kansas Turnpike. I believe the Oregon Trail was smoother. But the blue sky was so big and the aroma so tangy that, if the road had been smoother, I might have circled back and ridden it again.

Cruising a velvet sea of grass west of Springerville, I spotted two forest service workers sitting in a parked pickup truck, its bed shaded by a huge multicolored umbrella that bobbed in the breeze like a jib sail. One of them was orderly and trim like a Junior Leaguer preparing for the next charity ball; the other, frumpy and warm like a day-care director. An antelope bounded past their little oasis. I pulled over for a visit. They smiled and laughed at my southern accent and offered two homemade cookies and a Twizzler, then filled my bottles with well-water smoother than any that ever came from a two-dollar bottle. I never did learn why they were parked in the middle of that glorious rangeland.

"We live in Springerville. St. John's is 25 miles north," said the Junior Leaguer. "They got the county seat, we got the grocery store."

In sunny Springerville, I could smell rain. It's always raining somewhere; someone is always crossing to our sad side of the fence. But I was oblivious to sadness in the splendid high country. It was 11 a.m. and I was well ahead of schedule, so I explored the town. A man reported that Springerville boasts the country's only domed stadium for high school football, with 3,500 permanent seats and 1,500 removable ones.

Frisky after the spin through the town, I rode into New Mexico, 15 miles farther than planned. Just after noon, the jubilant white clouds gathered together, and the western horizon turned the color of pencil lead. Wisps of rain hung from the sky like gray bridal veils. Lightning flashed from a blacksmith's purple anvil high above. Sitting tall in the bike's saddle, I rode on a ridge, taking in the celestial show of light and sound. The air around me was as still as the inside of a chapel—the hairs on my arms stood on end.

Later that evening, as Nicki and I savored hotdogs and chili while snug inside Roci, a rainstorm whipped through the campground. The rain smelled so sweet that I wanted to have it for dessert. Tomorrow I would sample something better: Pie Town.

Andie, that indoor high school football stadium reminded me that people are mighty good at sheltering themselves from the world. And maybe that's a shame, because rain and snow give us an appreciation for the warm, dry times.

DAY 11
PIE TOWN

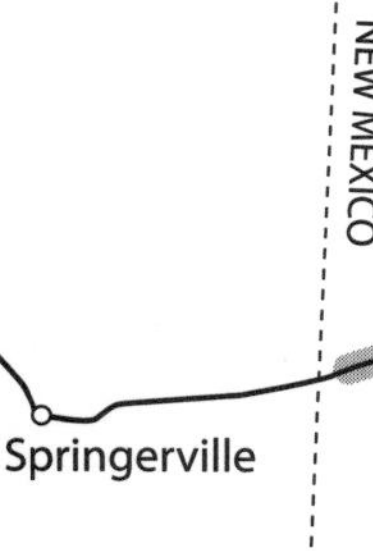
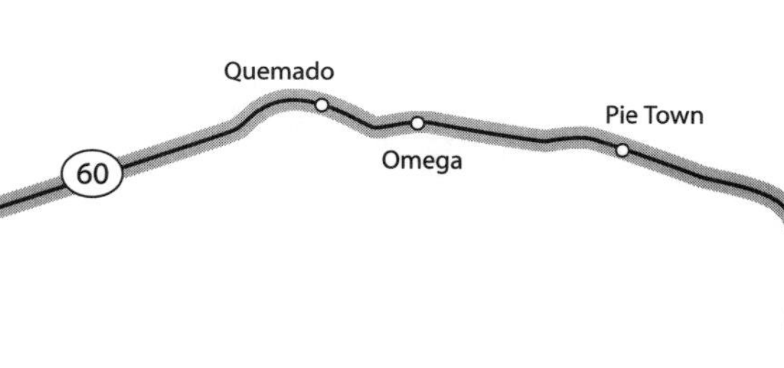

Date: Thursday, July 19.

Distance traveled: 83 miles, from near the Arizona–New Mexico state line to a few miles east of Datil, New Mexico.

Total miles completed: 770.

Starting temperature and time: 51 degrees at 5:30 a.m. Mountain time.

Finishing temperature and time: 75 at 2:30 p.m.

Food: breakfast—toast, banana; lunch—cheese crackers; dinner—spaghetti, cookie.

Additional fuel: 22 Cheez-Its, a slice of cherry pie, one gallon of water, two quarts of Gatorade, one root beer.

Song stuck in my head: "Georgia on My Mind" (Hoagy Carmichael, 1930). But I wanted to focus on the journey, not the destination. It was way too early to think about the Georgia coastline. So, I forced it out. Into my brain popped this one: "Away out here, they got a name for rain and wind and fire. The Rain is Tess, the Fire's Joe and they call the wind Mariah." ("They Call the Wind Mariah," from Paint Your Wagon by Lerner and Loewe, 1951.)

Overnight: Datil Well Campground, operated by the Bureau of Land Management.

When Nicki and I had studied the maps before our trip, Pie Town had been the most intriguing site, simply because of its name. I looked forward to savoring a slice of cherry pie once I arrived there. Yet Pie Town provided much more.

As I headed out, the moon was still a silver sliver in the cold, black, morning sky. Nicki left me alone in the silence. Then, a coyote howled, sending a tingle down my spine.

Riding east on the dark road, my bicycle headlight flickered and then quit entirely. I fumbled in the darkness for spare batteries, but found none. Angered by my carelessness, I rode through pitch-blackness for the next half-hour. Yes, to be safe I should have stopped and waited for the dawn to arrive. But it became an exciting game: only blind faith told me there would be no Sousaphone in the road, no pirates waiting in the ditch. As my eyes adjusted, the tiny moon and the plethora of stars provided a surprising degree of illumination. I was actually disappointed when the purple dawn broke.

In full daylight an hour later, I again set a personal bicycle-land-speed record—42 miles per hour on a downhill in the rugged pinion-pine country west of the village of Quemado. Skiing down the Matterhorn could not have been more exhilarating. Even when rocketing down steep hills, a bike rider can't just sit back and relax. I had to hold on, stay alert, and, because of bugs, keep my mouth shut.

Near a low-slung motel in the small town of Quemado, I encountered a couple riding a bicycle built for two. They were the first long-distance riders that I had met, and I lapped up the conversation like a parched desert hiker gulping water at an oasis. The man was in his mid-fifties; his very blonde female companion was a lot younger. Together the Californians were exploring a 250-mile loop south and east from Holbrook, Arizona. They pulled a small trailer that contained their food and a tent. The man offered advice: "Before you buy a tandem bike, make sure you have a very strong relationship with the other rider." His perky partner placed her hands on her tidy hips, rolled her eyes, then smiled. We shared water and candy and they took off.

East of town, my bike developed a squeak that sounded like Chewbacca in childbirth. Cross-country cyclists are like paranoid parents: we constantly listen for signs of trouble with our bikes and sometimes invent them. We never let the two-wheelers out of our sight and seldom allow others to touch them.

Nicki and I had tried not to be that way when we were raising Will and Nate; we hoped to give them wings. Like everything else he did, Will studied parenting until he knew every detail. When Andie was born and hadn't learned how to breathe quite right, Will was anxious in a way that I never had been. I never worried about Will and Nate; perhaps I should have.

Goodness, now I was worrying about not having worried more. The blue moth of guilt and grief fluttered onto my left shoulder. I wished to put it to work fixing the annoying squeak, but it wouldn't budge.

I stopped fretting about the squeak—and about the moth—when I arrived in Pie Town. Yes, the town, population 55, got its name in the 1920s because restaurateur Clyde Norman served pies hearty enough to stop traffic. The eatery, the Pie-O-Neer, was still going strong. Nearby was another cafe that appeared to be trying to take advantage of the legend. Sort of like Pepsi.

"The restaurant gives me someplace to go and chat," Pie Town resident Pat Hutton told a newspaper reporter in 2001. "I've been in there with people from Japan, Germany, Switzerland, and other places. I ask them, 'Where'd you hear about this place?' They'll say, 'In Germany.'"

A round-faced young woman welcomed me into the Pie-O-Neer with a smile and a scrumptious slice of cherry pie. When I asked who baked the pies, she pointed to a corner booth. "My mom and that lady over there," she said proudly. Two pretty, middle-aged women blushed, smiled, and waved.

Two gentlemen sat with me at the Pie-O-Neer's dark brown wood counter. I learned that one-eyed "Pop" was 81 years old and his lanky, bearded partner was 70. The waitress wouldn't let Beard pay for his coffee.

"Come back later, we might have some scraps for you," she whispered.

"Much obliged," he said softly, sipping his coffee and hardly glancing up at her. Then he turned to me. His faced was deeply etched by time and—I thought—no small amount of pain.

"Ain't much to do in this country 'cept live and die," he related. "My daddy died at home over yonder last year. He was 91."

I wanted to tell him about my own father, who died when I was 23 years old. Instead, I said, "You had him for a long time."

He studied his coffee cup in silence and then changed the subject. "You say you're ridin' that bike to Georgie?" he asked me. I nodded.

"It's hot down there in Georgie, you know," he warned. "You orter stay right here with us."

While the thought percolated in my mind, my SAG arrived as a reminder that there was more work to be done. Nicki lost herself in a piece of apple pie, which allowed more time for Pie Town's serum to inoculate me. Then, as we sat together on the Pie-O-Neer's shady veranda, massaged by a refreshing southerly breeze, my mind raced: *I could help manage the Final Four from right here. My assistant could forward the mail. I could correspond by e-mail with the staff at the Georgia Dome. I could drive to Albuquerque and fly to Indianapolis for selection weekend.*

That dream ended when one-eyed Pop walked onto the porch. He said, "I'm the man who drove that team of mules around the country for 41 years." I could think only of the 20-mule team on the old Ronald Reagan television show, *Death Valley Days*. My face must have looked blank because his shoulders slumped and he seemed disappointed that I hadn't heard of him.

Then, seeming to read my impatience, Pop said, "This ole stuff of gettin' in a hurry just ain't no good." Without saying another word, he ambled to his pickup and drove away.

Did he know that Nicki and I had been dashing from project to project as if we were on some maniacal Easter egg hunt ever since the crash? Or, could he sense that I was drowning in obsession with my NCAA work? We desperately needed to slow down. I watched his old truck rattle away in the dust and hoped that I would remember the lesson.

I took Pop's advice for a few moments, relaxing as long as I dared on that heavenly veranda. But the schedule was set. There were more miles to ride before I could rest tonight. So I bade farewell to Pie Town. Five miles east, I paused at the 7,797-foot Continental Divide. This was the spine of the nation. I spat onto the pavement to test folklore. Myth says that half the spittle will end up in the Pacific Ocean and half in the Atlantic. Mine simply sat in the road like a spent wad of Juicy Fruit.

I had conquered the desert and Yarnell Hill and the Mogollon Rim. I had experienced heat and cold, bugs and trucks, traffic and solitude. I had reached the dividing crease of America, but I had to keep going—putting one foot in front of the other. It seemed that I had already forgotten Pop's words of wisdom. I raced downhill to the evening's destination and, for the second day in a row, decided to proceed a few miles farther. Being ahead of schedule was like extra money in the bank. It made me think that perhaps I could actually ride all the way to Tybee Island.

A sign above the cash register in a wood-floored grocery store in the tiny town of Datil stated: "Impeach Bill—Jail Hillary." Another sign read: "Due to the shortage of paper and wood products, please wipe your ass with a spotted owl." Knowing that bike-riders are supposed to be nonpartisan, I decided that it would be inappropriate to ask for a copy of *Harper's Magazine,* a stem glass of Merlot, and the coordinates for the local National Public Radio station.

I pedaled around a small mountain east of Datil and down onto the 40-by-15-mile Plain of San Agustin. Geologists say it is an ancient lake bed; it seemed to me that a giant had steam-ironed the mountains. The immensity and silence took my breath away. The Plain was the inspiration for Conrad Richter's novel, *Sea of Grass,* but there was no discernable grass on this July afternoon—from the speeding bike I saw only a dry tan carpet dotted with sage. In the middle of the plain was a spectacular collection of basketball-court-sized satellite dishes called—no kidding—the Very Large Array (VLA). The VLA is part of the National Radio Astronomy Observatory. It consists of 27 dish-shaped antennas spread over an area the size of Washington, D.C. The Very Large dishes are hooked together to form a single Very Large radio telescope. "Very Large Array" was the working name when the facility was planned, and it stuck. Scenes in the movie *Contact* were filmed here.

VLA scientists wait at computer terminals to "hear" radio waves created by violent explosions that occurred billions of years ago in incomprehensively distant galaxies and are only now reaching earth. From all that racket, the experts learn about the history of celestial objects. As I left the VLA, a military jet created a sonic boom among the clouds like a million cars backfiring simultaneously. Perhaps a scientist on some distant planet would someday hear that boom and wonder what on Earth we were doing over here.

The day's ride ended at the informative VLA visitors center. Then we packed the bike into the minivan and drove back to the Datil Well Campground, which was refreshingly simple. There was no electricity. No noise. Few people. While Nicki hiked alone in the pinion woods, I listened to familiar music in my head ("Once a jolly swag-man camped by a billabong under the shade of a Coolabah tree.") until a rain shower drove me inside Roci. I fell asleep to the soothing rhythm of the rain and the sweet smell of the pines. The blue moth was in a galaxy far, far away.

Andie, like those scientists listening to other worlds at the VLA, people are always watching you. People will listen to you, too. Many will admire you, and wish to learn what they can. So be aware of the signals that you send.

The Last Cattle Trail

From near Springerville, Arizona, to Magdalena, New Mexico, I rode along the Magdalena Livestock Driveway, the last cattle trail regularly used in the United States. Cattle first moved down the trail in 1885, prompted by the 1884 opening of a railroad spur in Magdalena. To ranchers at that time, that railroad must have seemed as convenient as an interstate highway appears today. Cowboys drove herds from those Eastern Arizona ranches—the ones I passed yesterday—120 miles along the trail to Magdalena, where they were loaded onto trains and shipped to markets in the East. There were few places where the cattle could get water, but the Civilian Conservation Corps partially solved the problem in the 1930s by fencing the trail and drilling wells every 10 miles.

The state paved the road between Datil and Magdalena in the early 1950s. The trail crossed the road several times and sometimes the pasture-raised cattle, especially the bulls, refused to cross the white line in the middle. Cowboys ultimately obscured the line with sand, and then the cattle stepped across. I wished that mere sand could mask our sadness in the same way.

The Great Plains cattle trails ceased existing by the early 1890s, victims of barbed-wire fences, railroads and a Kansas cattle quarantine. But when the rest of the world had advanced to Captain Kangaroo, electric football games, and Etch-a-Sketch in the mid-1950s, why was the Magdalena Driveway still in use? I learned that the ranchers experimented with shipping the cattle to Magdalena on trucks in the 1920s. The effort failed because the trucked cattle couldn't graze along the way and arrived at the railhead in much worse condition than the cattle that had walked the trail.

Using one's own power to move across a great expanse of land is healthier than riding in a motorized vehicle. The cattle-drive lesson made perfect sense to this bike rider.

DAY 12
THE OWL

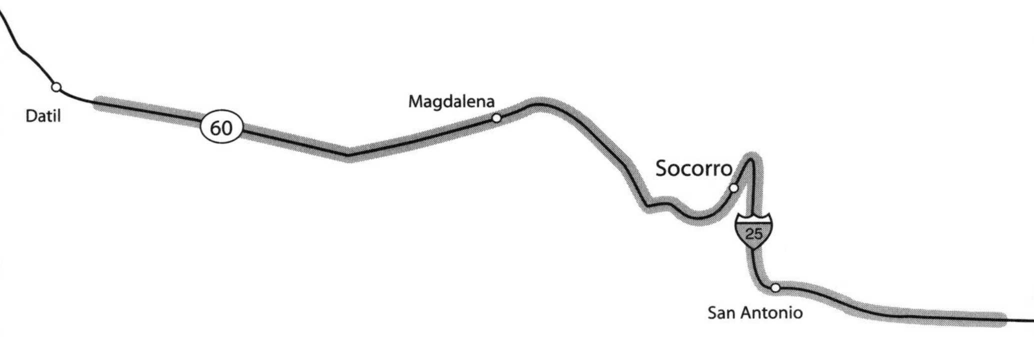

Date: Friday, July 20.

Distance traveled: 86 miles in New Mexico, from six miles east of Datil to 22 miles east of San Antonio.

Total miles completed: 856.

Miles to go: don't really want to think about it.

Starting temperature and time: 50 degrees at 5:30 a.m.

Finishing temperature and time: 87 at 2 p.m.

Food: breakfast—toast, cheese crackers; lunch—green chile cheeseburger, green chile cheese fries; dinner—beans, carrots, bread and butter.

Additional fuel: cookie-dough ice cream, carrots, six quarts of water, three quarts of Gatorade, one quart of cherry cider.

Song stuck in my head: "Slow down, you move too fast. Got to make the morning last, just lookin' for fun and feelin' groovy." ("59th Street Bridge Song" by Simon and Garfunkel, 1967.)

Overnight: Casey's RV Park, Socorro.

Dissention divided Team Hancock this morning when I attempted to repeat my stunt of riding in the dark. Team Captain Nicki protested, and I was frustrated. I had enjoyed yesterday's adventure, plus there were many miles to go, and I wanted to beat the heat.

"But your bike light is broken," she pleaded. "Please don't take any chances with your life. Please."

That was enough. I realized my recklessness was arrogant at best, dangerously stupid at worst. So Nicki followed behind in the car at 18 miles per hour, with me in the headlights, until another deep violet dawn crept slowly across the horizon in front of us. Then Nicki turned the minivan back toward Datil Well Campground to fold up Roci. I watched her taillights fade away and remembered driving away from her farm house after our first date in 1967. She was 15 years old, and neither of us had ever dated anyone else. No lucky frog ever found a better princess than I did in Nicki.

In Magdalena, the town's historic hotel had been converted into low-income housing. Much in the West "used to be" something or other. Later, I poked around the derelict Water Canyon Resort, 10 miles east of Magdalena on Highway 60. Birds were the only guests in the tiny, crumbling old motel rooms. The restaurant's windows were broken and it—like an abandoned urban housing project—marked the failure of someone's dream. That made me think about my own dream—this dream, the bike ride. What if I failed? Would I be able to handle the humiliation?

The doubts sang a cantata in my mind as I stopped at a laundromat, looking for water. A kind-faced man—his cheeks shining like two moons—said, "My wife and I have dreamed of riding our bikes across the country, but now I'm too fat. Do you think I could do it?"

"You can do it," I heard myself responding. "Just put one foot in front of the other." I chuckled at the irony. Here I was, a pitiful character who had abandoned hope himself, acting as the teacher, the saver of souls, a SAG to a stranger without giving it a second thought.

The man continued, "You be careful. Folks drive fast around here, and they're not used to seeing gentlemen on bicycles."

His words reminded me that those of us in the high-travel world of sports often part company with others by wishing them a safe journey. Before the plane crash, I said, "Safe travels" absentmindedly. No more.

All along the route so far, people had told me to be careful. In fact, others were more concerned about my safety than I was. From the outside, biking along busy highways appears impossibly dangerous. I hardly noticed as a large truck passed while I talked to a man by the road today, but he leaped fearfully into the ditch. Since the crash, I was no longer afraid of much, and certainly not of death.

Karen—who, along with Nate, was in my thoughts constantly—said it best when she explained that it would not be long until she was with her husband again. "I don't mean suicide," she said. "I mean the time I have left on earth, whether it's 40 or 60 years, is like a few seconds compared to all eternity."

* * *

In just one hour, I covered 27 miles to Socorro, a city of 8,700 nestled in the fertile Rio Grande River valley. Socorro also straddles Interstate 25 and is replete with fast food restaurants and moccasin shops. One store even displays a "human skull hit by a blunt instrument." The highway sustains the people as the river nourishes the land.

A city-dweller would have found Socorro soft, remote, and gentle, but from my perspective it was a ferocious place where traffic and confusion contrasted sharply with the peaceful certainty of the countryside. I could relax when riding through pastures and forests, but the tumult of a freeway town was a shock. It was as if I were stepping into a foreign country, not unlike the world after Will died where I felt like a visitor from outer space who had come home to the wrong planet.

At a bustling service station, a well-coifed father lectured a tow-headed youngster who stood no taller than the man's belt buckle. "Listen to me, Michael," yelled the dad. His sharp tone drove a rusty stake into my heart. "If you don't behave, we will stop this vacation right now. We will go back home! How would it make you feel, to ruin our family time together?" The child cried.

Every father has lost his cool; I did it myself—more often than I want to admit. But this guy had gone too far. I wanted to grab him by the chest hairs and tell him, "You idiot! Do you realize that child is your greatest treasure? You have the luxury of hugging your son, telling him that you love him and buying a hot fudge sundae for him. That is your privilege, not your right. Do not take it for granted!"

Instead, I mounted the bike and pressed on, trembling with anger and hoping to ride it off. I had planned to travel south on Interstate 25 for nine miles between Socorro and the hamlet of San Antonio. But after a mile of grappling with the wind-wash of trucks zooming past at 75 miles per hour, I decided the deserted frontage road would be safer. So with great effort, I dragged the bike through a washed-out area under a six-foot wire fence, snake-crawled under myself, carried the bike up a hill through the brush and headed off ... for a lousy two miles until I encountered a "dead end" sign. I walked sadly back toward the interstate; the bike wouldn't fit under fence at this place, so I lifted it over. I nearly set it down on a thorn about the size of a tine on a pitchfork, which caused me to utter quite a muscular vulgarity. Construction workers who were patching the road nearby smiled and signaled thumbs-up. No doubt I had spoken their language.

Like the Pie Town restaurant, the Owl Bar and Grill in San Antonio was for real. San Antonio's hospitality comes naturally: hotelier Conrad Hilton was born here. In fact, Hilton's carved name ("C Hilton 1903") can still be seen in the wall of a barn that was once the town's school.

Nicki and I walked into the Owl, where our eyes took a while to adjust. Happy country music—there's an oxymoron for you—filled the cozy building like water in a fish tank, and seeped into our receptive souls. "Kiss an angel good morning, and love her like the devil when you get back home." Patrons had written messages on dollar bills and tacked them on the dark-paneled walls. Every booth and table was full. Nicki and I patiently waited our turn, then devoured the specialty of the house: green chile cheeseburgers.

As I sipped my 85-cent root beer, I looked across the wooden table at Nicki and admired the dignity with which she bore the tremendous burden of sadness. She cried every day. Every single day. I had been around world-class athletes and talented musicians, but I had never seen anyone work as hard at anything as Nicki was laboring to find something resembling a normal life. I wanted to help her, but I didn't know what to do except keep loving her, keep listening to her, keep letting her know that I was crying myself.

The waitress brought our check—a bargain $8.25 for the two of us—and we stepped back into the bright world outside. The spicy lunch sat surprisingly lightly in my stomach on the climb out of the Rio Grande Valley. I feared that the road ahead would be an uphill battle of Yarnell Hill-like proportions, so Nicki drove ahead to scout the route. As I pedaled slowly up a hill, wondering if the blue moth waited at the top, she returned with an ear-to-ear grin like nothing I had seen on her face since the crash. "This is the last hill," she said. "There's another big flat stretch ahead, like the San Agustin Plain!" So, as storm clouds gathered in the west again, I rode into the Jornada del Muerto with a spring in my figurative step.

Andie, when I began the bike ride, big trucks frightened me, like they did the man by the road today. But then I learned to trust the drivers. Probably more than 300 cars and trucks passed by me most days. I had to believe that they wouldn't whack me. I know what you're thinking—my daddy trusted that airplane, and it crashed. That is true, but we have to live, and it is trust that binds us all together.

Journey of the Dead

The Jornada del Muerto—which roughly translates to "journey of the dead"—is a flat 90-mile valley dotted with yucca, honey mesquite, prickly pear, and sand sage. The valley lies among stark brown mountain ranges. There's little water. No McDonald's. Few tourists.

A curious juxtaposition of ancient and modern death, the Jornada was the hottest, driest segment of El Camino Real, the 17th-century Spanish colonial road from Mexico City to Santa Fe. The area earned its name in 1680, when Pueblo Indians drove the Spanish from northern New Mexico. More than 2,000 fleeing Spanish colonists and loyal Indians attempted to walk 300 miles south to El Paso; almost 600 of the exhausted refugees died on the journey. (Of course, Nicki and I were on our own journey of the dead. Riding my bicycle through a vast, seemingly endless place so aptly named was almost too coincidental.)

In modern times, what might have been the world's most horrific journey of the dead began in the heart of the Jornada. On July 16, 1945, the first atomic bomb was tested at a spot known as the Trinity Site. It was just a few miles from where I rode. That test concluded the Manhattan Project, the frantic arms race between Adolf Hitler's scientists and America's. The bombings of Hiroshima and Nagasaki followed within days of the test at Trinity. The deep fog of grief that swept the world then, encompassing all the deaths of World War II, still seemed to hover there between the jagged walls of the Jornada del Muerto. It was shocking that a lovely, almost fragile piece of geography could represent such horrors. Remembering the fathers of all those war casualties made my grief seem less significant; I knew the blue moth had been very busy during those days.

On that summer morning of 1945, scientists exploded a hunk of plutonium the size of a tennis ball. Until then, no one knew whether The Bomb would actually work. It did.

Observers six miles away saw a flash of light brighter than the sun, then, seconds later, heard the sound echoing off the mountains. No one had warned the few area ranchers. One thought a locomotive had blown up. Another assumed it was a volcano and said, "I ran to my bedroom window expecting to see a flow of lava. When I didn't see any lava, I went back to sleep." The MacDonald ranch house, commandeered by the government as the final assembly point for the bomb, survived the blast intact. Amazingly, scientists secretly stationed all over New Mexico reported safe levels of radiation, although the hair turned white on the exposed sides of area cattle near the blast.

Not everyone celebrated the success of Trinity. On July 17, 1945, scientists at the Chicago Metallurgical Laboratory sent the following petition to President Truman:

"If after this war a situation is allowed to develop in the world which permits rival powers to be in uncontrolled possession of these new means of destruction, the cities of the United States as well as the cities of other nations will be in continuous danger of sudden annihilation. All the resources of the United States, moral and material, may have to be mobilized to prevent the advent of such a world situation."

DAY 13

STILL CHERRY CIDER

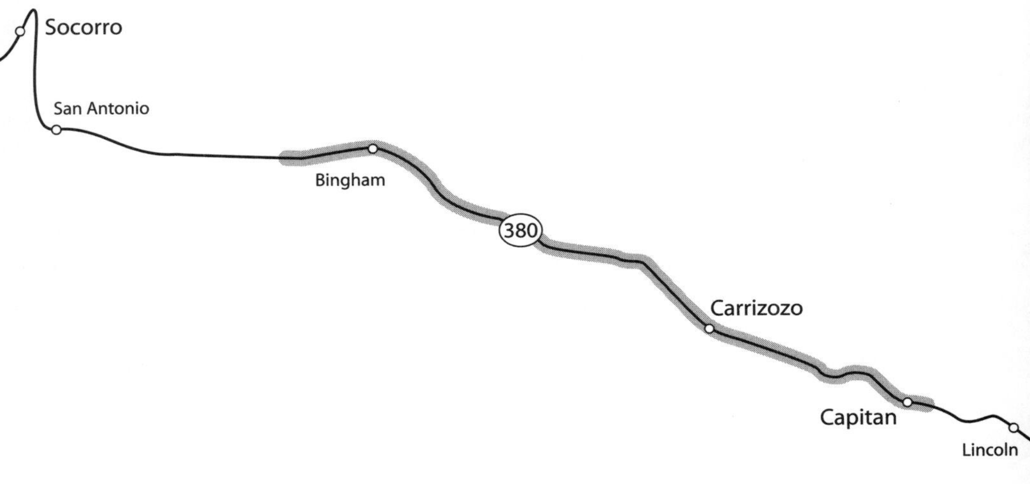

Date: Saturday, July 21.
Distance traveled: 67 miles in New Mexico, from 22 miles east of San Antonio to two miles east of Capitan.
Total miles completed: 923.
Starting time and temperature: 66 degrees at 5:45 a.m.
Finishing temperature and time: 85 at 1:45 p.m.
Food: breakfast—toast, banana; lunch—Vienna sausages and 12 Cheez-Its; dinner—nachos, tacos, enchilada and two margaritas.
Additional fuel: three quarts of water, three quarts of Gatorade, one root beer.
Health: Just fine, except for numb hands.
Song stuck in my head: "I got a gal in Kalamazoo-zoo-zoo-zoo-zoo-zoo-zoo-zoo...." ("I've Got a Gal in Kalamazoo," most famous recording by Glenn Miller, 1938.)
Overnight: Little Creek Campground near Ruidoso.

The rain storm we experienced in Socorro last night—a rare occurrence, judging by the sparse foliage—brought new life to the high desert. Millions of insects appeared in the morning dampness. An army of frogs had trained in the flooded ditches and several made the mistake of conducting maneuvers on the highway. A small one perished under my front wheel. Ground fog obscured the mountaintops, and the rain drew out the aroma of the desert sage, cedar and mesquite—the world's largest flower shop. There was that metaphor again: new life springs from desolation.

I stopped to look at a coyote carcass because his eyes, open in rigor mortis, seemed to plead with me for help. Initially, I did not notice a fuzzy, chocolate-colored scorpion that crawled between the bike wheels, under my right pedal. I told myself the scorpion was more scared of me than I was of her. "Yeah, right," my scared self answered.

While I fooled around with animals—dead and alive—Nicki visited the Bosque del Apache National Wildlife Refuge on the Rio Grande. She had been surprised to find the large wetlands park, home to cormorants, blue herons, coots and other birds, in the middle of a massive high desert. Mystery waited around every bend and intrigue beyond every hill, all free for the taking—my only obligation was to stay awake. The lure of the unexpected was as scintillating as a blind date. More importantly, it sparked my curiosity about our own futures; it was the first time since the crash that I cared what might happen to us.

DAY 13

Carrizozo was the first real town since tiny San Antonio 66 miles before. East of town, I negotiated a nice climb to the last Rocky Mountain pass—not really a pass but rather a junior summit known as Indian Divide. The rest of the journey to the Atlantic Ocean, I told myself, would be downhill. Reaching the crest of Indian Divide should have warranted a celebration, but I threw no party because I didn't realize that I was actually at the top. It is sometimes difficult to know when the worst is over. Or *if* it is over.

Memories flooded back when Nicki and I visited a plywood fruit stand among the cottonwood trees in Capitan. In our family's carefree summers of the 1950s, my dad took us to Ruidoso and he always bought Carrizozo cider from roadside vendors. Since then, I seldom passed a chance to enhance the economic welfare of a highway entrepreneur. Like Nicki's kisses, the cider tasted as sweet today as it had in my youth.

We had planned to stop for the day in Capitan, after visiting the Smokey Bear museum (and gift shop). Smokey—and one of history's most brilliant advertising campaigns—originated in 1944 when the National Forest Service, with help from the Advertising Council, authorized artist Rudolph Wendelin to create a poster to symbolize fire prevention. The bare-chested Smokey, wearing jeans and a ranger's hat, soon became a national fire prevention icon.

The Smokey Bear museum is in Capitan because life imitated art after humans started a forest fire nearby in 1950. During the blaze, a firefighting crew found a tiny bear cub in a tree. His feet and buttocks were badly burned, but the cub survived and found a new home in the national zoo in Washington, D.C., where he became a real-life hero to match Wendelin's eye-catching poster.

And now the gift shop in Capitan sells all things Smokey: the Smokey Bear board game, Smokey hats, watches, dolls, canteens, Viewmaster reels, and plenty more. As the museum's sales information points out, "six thick scrapbooks trumpet Smokey's achievements as if he were a high school athlete."

I was enchanted with Smokey and his accoutrements, but soon decided to take advantage of a rare tail wind and rode on. A lightning bolt ricocheted off the bluffs north of Highway 380 and seemed to roll down the valley like the giant boulder that threatened to steamroll Indiana Jones in *Raiders of the Lost Arc.* Nicki pulled the van alongside the bike and looked at me as if to say, "You're not going to cause trouble, are you?" She needn't have worried; the lightning scared the rebellion out of me, and I hopped into the van just before a thunderstorm devoured us. Within minutes small hailstones covered the ground like grits on a Southern breakfast plate.

After the storm passed, we drove up the mountain to Ruidoso in search of someone who could fix the six-day-old screech in my bike. Matt, an earnest, pony-tailed bike mechanic, rode the Cannondale around the block and could hear no squeak. Why do the symptoms vanish when we visit the doctor? Matt wanted to know all about my trip, and so I obliged him while he removed and greased the pedals for $20, which silenced the bothersome wheel.

Matt was unable to repair the expensive bike light, so we bought a cheap one at Wal-Mart, somewhat dismayed by the disharmonious presence of a bustling, cut-rate megastore in an idyllic mountain hideaway. After we left the Wal-Mart, a minor miracle occurred: We found the tiny cluster of log cabins where my family stayed during those peaceful 1950s vacations. I figured that a Holiday Inn Express or a moccasin shop had long since replaced them, but no—a very real cornerstone of my distant happy past still remained.

In those innocent days forty-plus years ago, I loved to sit in a swing under a tall pine tree near the cabins, wearing my Davy Crockett coonskin cap and calling play-by-play while counting license plates of passing automobiles. "Oh, my goodness, ladies and gentlemen, there's Louisiana; we haven't seen many of those! Texas still leads here in the Ruidoso License-Plate Championship." Back then, I could not have imagined that I would ever own a radio of my own, much less manage the Final Four, or marry someone as lovely as Nicki, or have two beautiful blond sons who would later produce their own play-by-play accounts of computer football games. The pine tree was still there and so was a swing, which was now occupied by a young couple who were locked in a heavy embrace.

Because the food service was slow, Nicki and I were obligated to sip too many margaritas on the shady patio of a Mexican restaurant. Two skunks frolicked in the grass within tortilla-tossing distance, but scentlessly ignored the diners. I played with Nicki's knees and got my hand slapped. We laughed until we felt guilty because sad parents aren't supposed to giggle; then we drove back to the RV park. Maybe we were beginning to learn that living was acceptable.

Nicki ducked inside Roci while I relaxed beside a campfire under the stars, talking to a stranger about University of New Mexico football. A huge motor home arrived, shattering the quiet evening like the *Close Encounters* space ship. It was the crème de la crème of RVs: the legendary Prevost. RV-park denizens whisper of the Prevost as if it were a Stradivarius violin or a Hasselblad camera. Our pop-up trailer looked like a pup tent in comparison. Although a Prevost retails for $850,000, we met one man who bought a used one for a song—$500,000. Okay, so perhaps the song was Barbra Streisand performing "People" in his living room, accompanied on the piano by Elton John.

As I squinted into the beguiling lights of the arrogant Prevost, Nicki ran through the night down the gravel road. She was sobbing. CNN had carried a story, based on a report by the National Transportation Safety Board, speculating about the cause of the Oklahoma State plane crash—a malfunctioning inverter combined with pilot error. I held her as the embarrassed stranger dug into the gravel with his toes.

As the hills had strengthened my body over the last two weeks, so too had they given me a modicum of defense against the wretched blue moth of grief. But the innocent Nicki had not acquired similar resolve. I was never more angry than when the moth attacked her. Its game was grossly unfair. Neither Nicki nor I could ever really win.

Andie, I bought a quart of cherry cider, then put it in the refrigerator to drink later. While I was waiting for "later," the cider turned to vinegar. Enjoy sweetness when you get a chance.

5
Homeward Bound

DAY 14

ALIENS

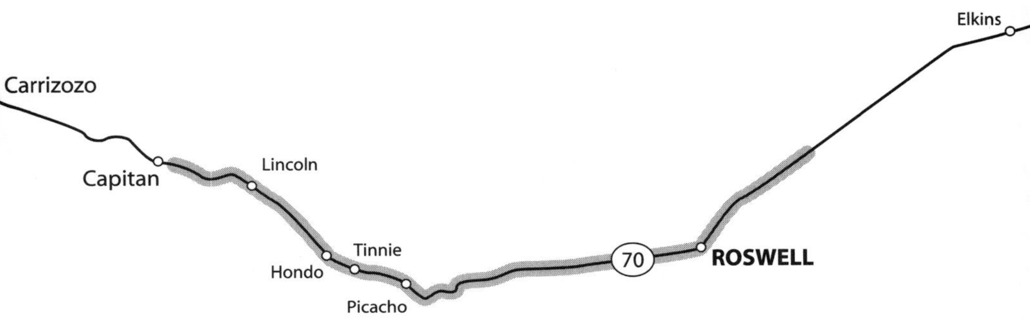

Date: Monday, July 23.
Distance traveled: 85 miles in New Mexico, from two miles east of Capitan to 15 miles northeast of Roswell.
Total miles completed: 1,008.
Starting temperature and time: 56 degrees at 5:30 a.m.
Finishing temperature and time: 103 at 1:45 p.m.
Food: breakfast—toast, banana; lunch—cheese crackers; dinner—Rice-a-Roni, carrots, broccoli. (No Vienna sausages!)
Additional fuel: 21 chocolate-covered pecans, 18 Fritos, seven quarts of water, one gallon of Gatorade, one root beer.
Song stuck in my head: "You fill up my senses ... like a mountain in spring time, like a walk in the rain, like a storm in the desert." (For the second time, "Annie's Song" by John Denver. I always thought of it as Nicki's song.)
Overnight: Town and Country RV Park, Roswell.

Being ahead of schedule, Nicki and I used a perfect mountain Sunday in Ruidoso—the second built-in catch-up day in the schedule—to replenish our souls by reading, napping, watching the daily thunderstorm, avoiding CNN, and wishing our lives could include more sweet cider and less National Transportation Safety Board. Together, we shoved the sadness toward the back of our brains.

I was chomping at the bit to ride again on Monday morning, and two curious deer rewarded me by running alongside me for a quarter-mile. A thunderstorm had cleansed the world overnight, and there wasn't a car in sight; the fresh pine smell clung to my clothes like strawberry jam on a child's pajamas. I rode downhill through a forest, past green pastures, and beside orchards of apples and peaches, chilled by the spray from the gurgling Rio Bonito River. As Shoeless Joe Jackson asked in the movie *Field of Dreams*, was this heaven?

When Will and I watched that baseball love story together one perfect May afternoon in 1989, both of us were hooked. I cried when Ray Kinsella asked if his father wanted to have a catch—but hid my tears from Will. I remembered the night my own father, William Ransom Hancock, Sr., wept when a visitor performed Chopin's *Butterfly Etude* in our living room on the Baldwin grand piano that my dad had spent half his annual income buying for me. In the movie theater, I caught a glimpse of my son, William Ransom Hancock III, shielding his own tears in the seat next to me. Here in the New Mexico Rockies that I first explored with my dad, I hoped that Andie had inherited the gene for appreciating beauty—and I hoped that she would be moved to tears by music or movies, and not by the blue moth.

The daydream ended when I arrived in the historic little town of Lincoln, where, in 1881, Billy the Kid escaped from jail to avoid a date with a noose. Running to escape death—or fleeing the blue moth— certainly was not something invented by the Hancock family in 2001.

Bidding farewell to Lincoln, I raced downhill and was soon in flat country, cutting into waves of heat like a bride and groom slicing into a wedding cake. The cool peaks of the mountains were in my rear-view mirror, but a honeymoon in a treeless plain awaited my arrival on the horizon. The sight of the massive Rockies behind me raised chill bumps. Of course, I knew there were more hills ahead, but this was a moment of excitement to be cherished—a mission accomplished.

Fun was the only mission for a giggling gaggle of high school girls in an icily air-conditioned gas station-cum-Taco Bell in Roswell. The girls fired comments and questions at me like a baseball pitching machine gone haywire.

"We're from Lubbock!" declared one girl. "That's our youth-group leader over there at the hotdog counter."

"Do you know Bobby Knight?" asked another. "My dad likes him, but my mom hates him."

"You rode your bike from Ruidoso!?" pondered a third girl in amazement. "My dad rode his horse to Hurlwood."

"You're, like, riding across the country? Where do you sleep?" wondered another. "If I rode two blocks, my legs would, like, fall off. And you're old! Oh, I didn't mean that."

"Yes, she did," giggled her friend. "Bye-bye, sir."

We had planned to stop for the day in Roswell, but once again I felt strong, and so I rode ahead while Nicki set up Roci in a campground.

Near the Pecos River, a genial construction flag man shared his water with me. "You are the first person who ever stopped to talk," he said. "I born in Mexico. I live in the United States 14 years. It best country. This is nice road, no? We make it better for you. Good luck."

Better or not, on the shoulder of that nice road three miles later, a highway worker had written one word with leftover tar: "SEX." The creativity made me smile.

Grinding down the highway with the sun directly overhead and the temperature reaching 106, I nearly ran afoul of BST—Bike-Sucking Tar. Highway crews used the rubbery black goop to fill cracks in the road; the BST "hardened" to the consistency of Play-Doh. I probed into the tar with my finger; it went in clear to the middle knuckle. The inch-wide cracks could easily swallow a bike tire, so it was necessary to pay attention every minute. Bike accidents—and the disgusting blue moth—await those who let down their guards.

My old nausea and blurred vision returned as the temperature climbed. Still, I fought through it to finish the day 15 miles ahead of schedule. After I medicated the nausea and performed optic correction with Fritos, Nicki and I visited the UFO Museum and Research Center in an old movie theater in downtown Roswell.

"It's the Lourdes, the Jerusalem, the Mecca of UFO-dom," local journalist Peter Farley told the *Albuquerque Journal* in July, 2000. "When you think of UFOs, what do you think of? There's only Roswell. People are drawn here."

Roswell gained fame when, on July 3, 1947, rancher Mac Brazel discovered strange debris in his sheep pasture. The U.S. Army Air Force cleared away the wreckage and then issued a press release identifying the debris as a crashed flying saucer. It was reported that the Air Force had purchased a baby-sized coffin, possibly for an alien. The next day, the government backtracked and said the rubble was actually nothing more than a weather balloon. The controversy remains after all these years. Was the press release an honest mistake by an over-eager public relations person, or had the Air Force performed the mother of all cover-ups?

Thousands of people trek here each year seeking the answer. The Roswell museum outdraws the more stately visitors center at nearby Alamogordo, which features dignified exhibits about real space exploration. The Roswell UFO museum is more than an American institution; it has received e-mail from Turkey, Indonesia, Belgium, the Philippines, Iran, New Zealand, England, Malaysia, India, China, Canada, Brazil, and South Africa.

"It strains the imagination to think of anything extraterrestrial," former Roswell mayor William Brainerd told the *Journal*, "but I know the UFO museum is good for business."

"It's like a natural resource—you take it, you manipulate it, you add value to it, you sell it," said Charlie Walker, director of economic development for the Roswell Chamber of Commerce.

Nicki and I took our doubts with us to a cool swim and to dinner in Roci. Then we sat under the mesmerizing sky watching for space ships piloted by little green men. All we saw was lightning leaping from cloud to cloud. Or was it really lightning?

Andie, I don't know whether people live on other planets. But I'm pretty sure there's another world called heaven, and your dad is there. An old baseball coach said to me, "Will is in a place so fabulous that you wouldn't take him back, even if you could." I must admit that I would take him back quicker than you can say, "Granddad, you are silly." I'd rather he'd visited that fabulous place sometime later.

DAY 15

Hon-yoks

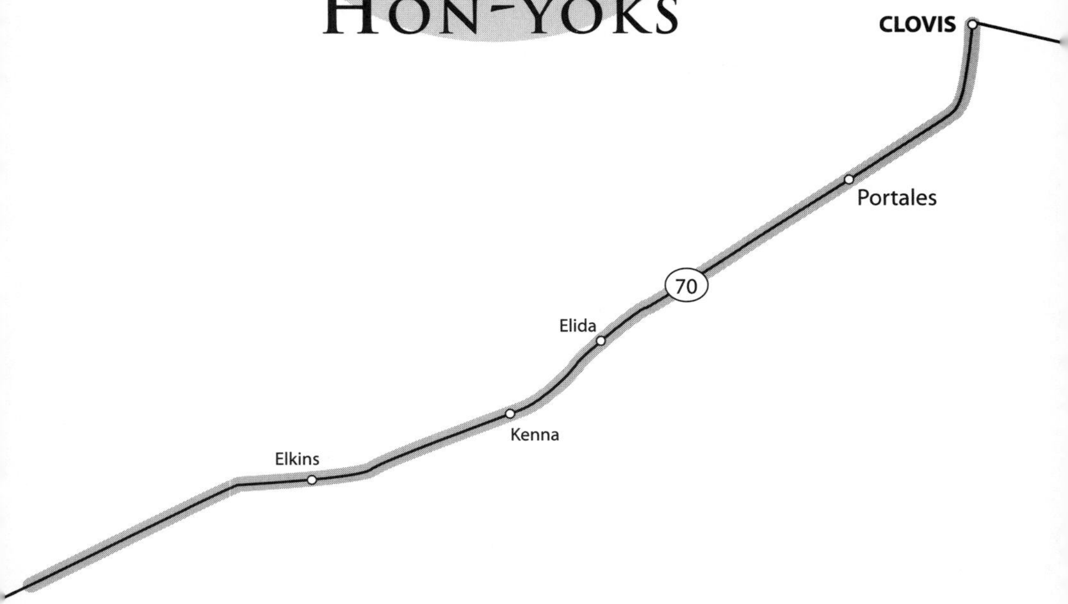

CLOVIS
Portales
70
Elida
Kenna
Elkins

Date: Tuesday, July 24.

Distance traveled: 89 miles in New Mexico, from 15 miles northeast of Roswell to Clovis.

Total miles completed: 1,097.

Starting temperature and time: 73 degrees at 5:15 a.m.

Finishing temperature and time: 101 at 1:15 p.m.

Food: breakfast—toast, banana; lunch—hamburger; dinner—quesadilla, broccoli, carrots.

Additional fuel: 22 Fritos, six quarts of water, three quarts of Gatorade, one root beer.

Song stuck in my head: "...and parked in a rickety old garage is a brand new, shiny red super stock Dodge." ("Little Old Lady from Pasadena," popularized by Jan and Dean, 1964.)

Overnight: Travelers World RV Park, Clovis.

Today, along with a haircut, I received a lesson in hand-me-downs. But first, a rancher shared some history with me in the one-building town of Kenna.

"The winter here is tough," he said. "A man has to check his cattle twice a day to make sure snow hasn't blown up their noses." Later in the day, when the temperature hit 99, an icy wind would have been welcome.

According to the rancher, the Kenna store was built in 1906 as a bank. It later became a service station and was handed down from owner to owner. Now it no longer sold gasoline, but disbursed snacks, ice, pop, the U.S. Mail, and conversation. The rancher collected his supply of each and left for his 12-mile drive home.

This was the fabled prairie, the Llano (YAWN-oh) Estacado—*staked plain* in English—that rolls from the base of the Rocky Mountains to the middle of the Texas Panhandle. If buttermilk pancakes were a place, this would be it—flat, golden, and sweet. Historians disagree about the origin of the name. Some say "estacado" refers to the geological formation known as the Caprock, an escarpment which serves as a natural boundary between the high plains of northeast New Mexico and the lower plains of west Texas. The Caprock meanders almost the width of the Texas Panhandle—a miniature Mogollon Rim. Others believe the Coronado expedition of 1541, when crossing the sea of grass as perilous as the uncharted ocean between Spain and the Americas, placed stakes along its route as a guide for the return trip.

Francisco Vasquez de Coronado was leading a party of 350 Spaniards and perhaps 900 Indians northward from Mexico. Coronado had a cause: gathering riches from the fabled Seven Cities of Cibola. He was 31 years old, the same age as Will when he stepped onto that airplane in Colorado. Why did fate grant Coronado and his crew safe passage on a journey to "terra incognito"—at a time when most Europeans never ventured more than a few miles from their homes—when Will and the others were not able to survive a routine 90-minute airplane trip? Coronado knew he was risking his life and the lives of his men. Did he deserve better than the cautious Will, who was simply traveling home from work? Any time I dared to question why, I was a flame to the blue moth, which now dived down to peck mercilessly at my left ear.

The moth departed when I saw the following words painted on the pavement west of the town of Elida: "WE … ARE … SO …

PROUD ... OF ... YOU." I envisioned eight effervescent cheerleaders dashing between passing trucks to write on the highway in celebration of a returning football team, but I pretended they were honoring me. After seeing the size of Elida, I changed my fantasy to four-cheerleader football.

My U.S. Olympic Committee friend Bob Condron called on the cell phone, just to check on me. Bob seemed to have a permanent videoconference with my heart; he sensed when I was lonely, often before I knew it.

"Mornin'," Bob said. "What's that sound?"

"The wind," I replied. "I'm riding downhill, about 30 miles per hour."

"Is it legal to talk on the phone while you're riding a bike?" he asked.

"Probaby not. Sure is fun, though."

Life is easier when it's downhill and friends are connected.

Soon I became connected to a sign reading, "Student of the Week: ROBERT" that was posted outside the Little Red Caboose Day Care Center in Portales. It made me cry, which probably puzzled nearby motorists as I stood over the bike at a faint stoplight bumper-to-headlights with a pickup truck and an SUV. Losing Will took one of the few people totally devoted to me, unquestionably loyal, astoundingly trusting. That love, that rare commitment, that reverence—all were irreplaceable. I hoped Robert's dad knew how lucky he was.

My father died when I was 23; my mother, when I was 28. I could now smile when I remembered them. Logic said that I would eventually be happy when I thought of Will, but my heart replied, "no way."

However, in nearby Eastern New Mexico University's splendid museum, I found something to be happy about. It was Clovis Man—believed to be the earliest human to inhabit North America—whose remains were discovered in Blackwater Draw near here in 1932. Clovis Man is said to have walked across the Bering Strait from Russia to North America 11,000 years ago. Too bad he didn't have a Cannondale R600 bicycle to transport him.

The temperature was 99 degrees in Clovis when I rode past two young boys soaking their clothes with a garden hose, then making water angels in their cement driveway—like kids make snow angels in the north country. Amarillo had set an all-time record for the most consecutive 100-degree days in July. I was headed that way.

The scorching sun made my neck tingle, so I scanned the yellow pages to find a barber who'd give me a summer haircut.

"I'm sorry, but I'm all booked up this afternoon," said the first one I phoned. "You could call my brother at his shop, or my uncle at his shop." I selected the uncle, who provided a $9 military clipping and a $200-per-hour analyst's philosophy.

"I got those two hon-yoks started in the barbering business," he said. "I'm proud of both my nephews."

I smiled to hear a down-home term. "Hon-yok" is a 100 year-old ethnic slur that originally referred to immigrants from Central and Eastern Europe. Now it is best used by a big brother to describe every potential beau who arrives to court his little sister. What initially meant "careless," "sloppy," and "derelict" has now become a light-hearted term of endearment.

"Do they steal any business from you?" I asked.

"Nah, they don't compete with me. They have a different group of customers," he replied. "That's what life is all about: young people growin' up."

If he had asked, I'd have poured out my life story. Barbers and bartenders—in a three-way tie with old printers—are the best listeners. But he didn't ask. So I inquired as to what I should do in Clovis.

"If you're around Allsup's at about 10 o'clock tonight, you can watch them defrost the freezer. I ain't kiddin', that's about it."

The barber could have told me about the Norman Petty Studios on 7th Street. Petty was a fine piano player, but earned fame as a recording engineer. It was in his studio that Lubbock's Buddy Holly recorded "Peggy Sue" and 18 other hits. Holly, of course, died in an airplane crash at age 22, thereby ensuring his fame. Would Buddy Holly have been a star at age 40? At 50? How about Will Hancock, what would he have become if given the opportunity?

In the evening, Nicki and I drank root beer—a sweet memory from my childhood and now my stomach-soothing evening staple—at a picnic table and enjoyed a breeze that carried the fragrance of cow manure. We didn't object to the smell; it was earthy and genuine, a fitting conclusion to the day. Being outdoors for both sunrise and sunset was a rare privilege. It was as if we were living an entire life, from birth to death with natural portions of joy and sadness in-between, in one day—with more lives coming tomorrow and the day after and the day after that.

Andie, that barber in Clovis understood the rhythm of life: old folks move aside and make way for young ones like you. Also, I was surprised that he didn't know or care about the musical history in his town. Sometimes we don't see the wonders right under our noses. There's magic in your own backyard—I know you'll go find it.

DAY 16

THE LAST PICTURE SHOW

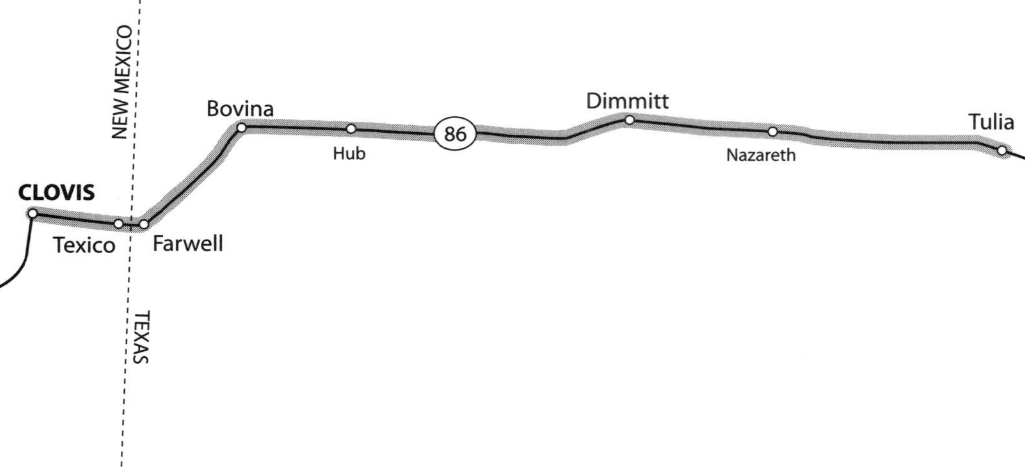

Date: Wednesday, July 25.

Distance traveled: 86 miles, from Clovis, New Mexico, to Tulia, Texas.

Total miles completed: 1,183.

Starting temperature and time: 74 degrees at 5 a.m. Mountain time.

Finishing temperature and time: 98 at 1:45 p.m. Central time.

Food: breakfast—toast, banana; lunch—cheese crackers, Vienna sausages; dinner—nachos, taco, enchilada.

Additional fuel: 12 Fritos, one apple, two gallons of water, two quarts of Gatorade, one root beer.

Song stuck in my head: "...I ride through Texas to enforce the law. And people look at me and say, 'oh-roh, oh-roh, is you the law?'" ("Long Tall Texan," recorded by the Beach Boys, among others, in 1964.)

Overnight: Select Inn Motel, Tulia.

The route of my 2001 trip across the country covered 2,746 miles, from the Pacific Ocean to the Atlantic.

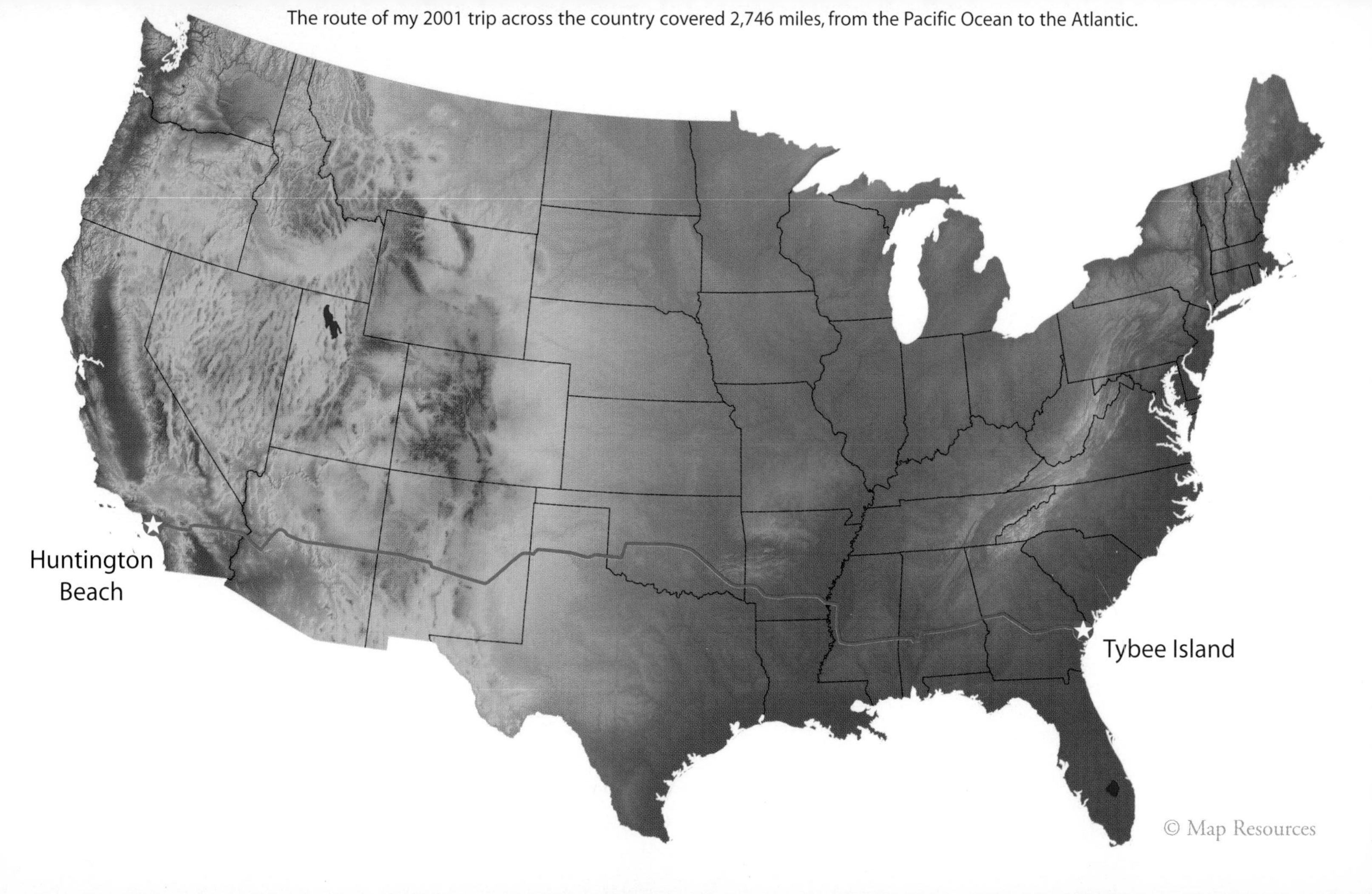

Photo by Chris Theisen

My sons—Nate (left) and Will (center)—and I enjoyed being together at the Final Four, such as in 2000 at the RCA Dome in Indianapolis.

Andie listened to some advice from her granddad.

My wife, Nicki, and I are pleased to be together again at our home in Kansas City.

Before sunrise in Huntington Beach, California, was a perfect time to mark the ride's ceremonial beginning by dipping my back wheel into the waves of the Pacific Ocean.

The 100-mile journey across the Mojave Desert east of Twentynine Palms, California

The six-mile climb up Yarnell Hill in Arizona required nearly two hours of labor; but the view from the top was worth every sweaty minute.

Among Ponderosa pines in Arizona's Sinkhole Campground, Nicki—my support and guidance on this journey—relaxed outside our camper, which we dubbed "Roci."

The lovely Indian Divide west of Capitan, New Mexico, was the last Rocky Mountain pass of my trip.

Sturdy cattle and squeaky windmills, like these outside the small community of Nazareth, were common in the Texas panhandle.

My hometown folks of Hobart, Oklahoma, staged a small celebration when we arrived. Nicki and I were happy, too; our journey was half complete.

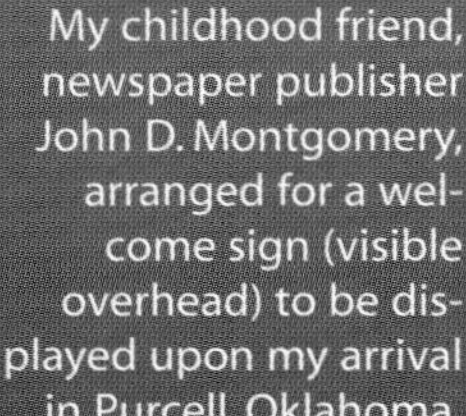

My childhood friend, newspaper publisher John D. Montgomery, arranged for a welcome sign (visible overhead) to be displayed upon my arrival in Purcell, Oklahoma.

The third flat tire of my trip occurred near Ozan, Arkansas; number four happened just two miles later

History came alive at the Pettus Bridge (in background) near the flower-lined downtown of Selma, Alabama.

Outside McRae, Georgia, the "Peach Angel" taught me the trip's finest lesson: "Accept what you're given with grace." Here he prepares to unpack his peach stand from the bed of his truck.

Two police officers provided a surprising—and quite helpful—escort as I neared the finish line in Savannah, Georgia.

On a warm August morning, I dipped my front wheel into the Atlantic Ocean at Tybee Island, Georgia. The odyssey was over, but the lessons learned would remain with me forever.

At 5 a.m., as I sat on a sidewalk among the June bugs and flattened old chewing gum outside a Clovis convenience store, five sweaty people in dirty jeans spilled out of a Toyota. One said to another, "Hey, remember who you (bleepin') talking to, you (bleepin') bitch. I can (bleepin') beat the (bleep) out of you any time I want to. Don't (bleepin') forget it."

The blue language made my head spin.

The speaker—a greasy, cigarette-thin young man whose sleeveless t-shirt revealed a rat's nest of deep purple tattoos—glared at me and then stumbled into the store. A young woman remained alone in the Toyota's back seat. I should have asked if she were in danger. But cowardice prevailed. I took his departure as my cue to get the (bleep) out of Dodge.

I rode into Texas—my fourth state—and realized that I had become emotionally attached to my two-sided Arizona-New Mexico road map. I had studied it every hour for nearly two weeks. Because I had handled it with sweaty hands, it looked like it had been dropped in the creek, and then re-folded. That map had been read hard and put away wet. Texas offered a fresh start, but I would carefully save the old map forever. It was a worthy metaphor for life after Will's death: start over but cherish the past.

West of Bovina, a sign reading "Watch for Dust on Highway" proved prophetic. Indeed a brown cloud—and a stench like a locker room after a 10-day basketball tournament—hung over the valley like Los Angeles smog. The odor and haze came from a feed lot the size of 500 gymnasiums where thousands of cattle shuffled their hooves, swatted flies with their tails, and grazed at half-mile-long troughs. I stopped to watch the awesome scene, using my bandana to cover my nose and mouth against the dust. I imagined the doomed beefs as junior executives crowding for space at the corporate spigot, totally oblivious as to how their lives were perceived by outsiders.

Down the road, I thought I heard a monster truck ahead. Then I decided it must be a small airplane preparing to land on the highway. Or, maybe the devilish blue moth coming back to roost. It turned out to be a series of irrigation pumps, each feeding a long pipe pivoting around a center post and resulting in a circular field of green cotton. The sprayers were positioned just over the tops of the plants, to decrease water loss due to evaporation. Conserving water is an important topic in West Texas because of the rapid depletion of the Ogallala aquifer, a primary source of ground water for the region.

I dropped my bike beside the road and walked into a corn field, half expecting to spot Shoeless Joe Jackson and his teammates from *Field of Dreams*. After 10 steps, I was in a different world—like the Amazon rain forest. No machete could create a path. If not for the sun in the eastern sky, I would have become lost. I don't know about an elephant's eye, but the corn was so high that I couldn't reach the top with arms outstretched. After finding my way back to the bike, I rode past a vivid field of sunflowers, their bright yellow faces turned to the sun. The sunflowers smelled sugary, like a candy store.

As I neared Dimmitt, a pickup stopped on the shoulder in front of me. The driver, wearing a uniform, stepped out. My heart skipped four beats before I realized it was Ray Cragar, who grew up with Nicki and me in Hobart. Ray was part of our e-mail support crew and had been following our journey. He interpolated the route across the Panhandle and drove 100 miles from his home in Lubbock to see Nicki and me. And he didn't show up empty-handed. Bless his heart, Ray brought me a cold bottle of water and a candy bar. For an hour, we sat on the tailgate of his pickup in the shade of an elm tree enjoying the late-morning breeze. Ray had turned his Oklahoma State University education into a nifty job as a silviculturist for the Texas Forest Service; his job was to convince landowners to plant trees in order to create wind breaks to help prevent another Dust Bowl.

His hobby was charting rural cemeteries. I imagined the 10-year-old Ray, the type-A youngster with a blazing fastball, and then remembered the high school Ray who drove a friend's automobile on the railroad tracks. And then I looked at the mature 50-year-old man sitting next to me. I was proud of his career and hobby of preserving the past. I didn't want our conversation to end. But I was getting no closer to Tulia, and the temperature was climbing. We shook hands and I rode east.

In Dimmit, I was greeted by a smiling convenience store clerk whose platinum hair was piled as high as the Matterhorn. She said, "I would like to go with you on your bike adventure. Where you going from here?"

I told her I was heading home, to Hobart, Oklahoma.

Her manner changed abruptly. "Oklahoma?" she said, now scowling. "Well, cancel my reservation. I ain't got no desire to go to Oklahoma. Nothin' good ever happened there." Sometimes the grass is not greener.

Just west of Tulia, I inhaled a live fly; it buzzed around in my throat for a few harrowing seconds before succumbing. Nicki had a similar experience. A black mass of flies invaded the van when she stopped next to a cattle pen. It took her six hours to extract them all from the van.

The weather was blast-furnace hot. Linotype hot. So hot that I could barely breathe. The stifling air wrapped around me like the cloak of death. Yet each morning I looked forward to the heat and then reveled in its consistency each afternoon. I grew comfortable with it. Comfortable, that is, until I stepped inside a cool store or restaurant. Then it was necessary to acclimate myself all over again. This was no different from our grief. The worst times were right after a brief exposure to happiness. So I found it easier to avoid cool places—and steer clear of joy.

But there was joy in what West Texas native Bob Condron said about Tulia: "It's the most nondescript town in the world. The whole town is a typo. It was supposed to be Tule, named for nearby Tule Lake, but the postmaster misread the form and it came back Tulia. Before they built the interstate, I remember as a kid going through the middle of all the towns from Canyon to Lubbock: Canyon, Happy, Tulia, Kress, Plainview, Hale Center, Abernathy, New Deal, and Lubbock. All the great-looking farm girls of this region go to Texas Tech to make that school the 'wife capital of the universe.'"

In the deliciously lazy afternoon, downtown Tulia was nearly lifeless. Even the buildings seemed to be sleeping. We did find the town's museum, which was dark, but a woman came to the door. "Yes, sah, we're open," drawled the matronly docent, turning on the lights. "We are tryin' to save electricity. Our town is in trouble. We rely on agriculture, and so the drought and the low prices for farm products are hittin' us real hard."

This could have been a snapshot from Larry McMurtry's novel-turned-movie, *The Last Picture Show*. Was that Cybill Shepherd or Cloris Leachman walking across the street? I recalled that Ben Johnson's character in the movie said, "I remember when this land didn't have a tree on it." In fact, almost all the trees in the Texas Panhandle and Western Oklahoma were carefully hand-planted by human beings, an army of unpublicized Johnny Appleseeds who knew the value of trees in a wind-blasted prairie. For centuries before humans arrived, a few trees occasionally took root along creek beds. But they never grew to maturity because of the frequent fires that ravaged the plains—and nourished them at the same time by exploding pods of grass seeds that then grew with a flourish in the rich soil. Again, that metaphor: new life from ashes.

Now, a modern-day tree phenomenon played out which was remarkably similar to the one that occurred 3,000 miles away among the giant sequoias of California. Often in the Sierra Nevada, tiny saplings grew from the roots of an old giant, eventually forming a ring of smaller sequoias around the mother. After centuries the big tree died and rotted away, leaving the circle of now-mighty clones as a legacy.

It also happened in the plains, except in this case the life-giving nucleus was a house constructed by a farm family. The family carefully planted hardy trees—usually cedar, but sometimes elm or bois d'arc—around their home as a barrier against brutal winter winds. When life became too harsh and the family moved away, their little house either slowly fell apart or was loaded onto a truck and hauled to town. The ring of trees remained, a reminder of a life that once existed.

Andie, we all have road maps for life. Sometimes we enter a new state and must switch to a different map. Don't be afraid to change. When you do, remember the old days and be glad for them. Your mom, uncle, grandmother, and I were determined to find the new map for our journey through the rest of our years without your dad.

Two Rhode Islands

The bike carried me across the former XIT Ranch, which originally covered three million acres running east from the Texas-New Mexico border—about twice the size of the state of Rhode Island. According to H. Allen Anderson in *The Handbook of Texas,* the ranch reached its peak in the late 1880s, when its 150 cowboys rode 1,000 horses and branded 35,000 calves in one year. The Texas state legislature created the XIT from unsettled territory in

1879, intending to sell the land to finance construction of a new state capitol building. The state organized a syndicate to operate the ranch while it was being sold piece by piece. Texas got its ornate capitol building—where Governor George W. Bush later presided—and the construction of ponds, windmills, and roads slowly tamed the raw country. The last of the land was sold in 1963. Today, practical brick farmhouses with neatly kept outbuildings are sprinkled across the old XIT.

A man in Bovina offered his explanation on how the XIT got its name. "It stands for Ten in Texas," he told me, because the ranch originally covered ten counties. That's a rural myth, however, said Nicky Olson, director of the XIT Museum.

"Although the counties had been drawn up in Austin, they were not yet established when the ranch was named," she explained. "In fact, there were no towns in Dallam and Hartley Counties. 'Ten in Texas' just came up sometime later.

"It really happened this way: In 1885, when the first herd of cattle was delivered to the ranch, a brand had not been chosen. The ranch ordered 20 flat iron branding irons the month before. Ab Blocker, who delivered the herd, scratched out a pattern in the sand that could use the irons already on hand. He designed XIT, because it was easy to use but hard for rustlers to change."

In a 1999 column in the Amarillo *Globe-News*, Dave McReynolds wrote that the syndicate used many legal tricks to sell the land, including delivering potential land buyers from the Eastern United States to the Panhandle at night. "This was done to make sure the prospective buyers would be kept apart as much as possible from those who already made their homes in the area," McReynolds wrote.

Likewise, Nicki and I had been delivered to the other side of the fence at night, with no chance to investigate the landscape. But the parallel ended there because those who were already in the territory when we arrived—those who had experienced a tragedy of their own—were our most comforting allies. From them, we received information and reassurance. In any case, we were all irrevocably branded.

DAY 17

Six-man Football Palace

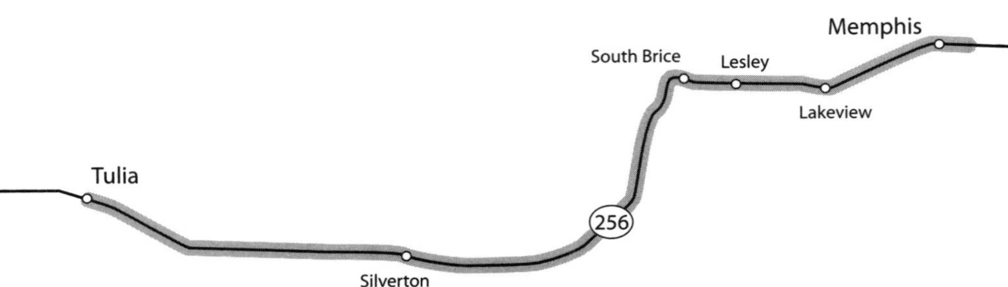

Date: Thursday, July 26.

Distance traveled: 90 miles in Texas, from Tulia to just east of Memphis.

Total miles completed: 1,273.

Miles to go: well, fewer than yesterday.

Starting temperature and time: 79 degrees at 4:55 a.m.

Finishing temperature and time: 101 at 1:30 p.m.

Food: breakfast—toast, banana; lunch—cheese crackers, Vienna sausages; dinner—chicken livers, salad, apple, broccoli, baked potato, rolls, gravy.

Additional fuel: 21 Fritos, two gallons of water, three quarts of Gatorade, one root beer.

Song that wouldn't leave my head: Nothing. Just didn't happen today.

Overnight: Executive Inn Motel, Memphis.

I had discovered that the two hours between first light and sunup was the best time of the day because of kaleidoscope sunrises, silence, and the smell of wet grass. Perhaps, as the song says, the darkest hour is just before dawn, but certainly the coolest hour is just after sunup. I had the road to myself and the world between my handlebars. To me the solitude was like the Elixir of Egypt. Life hardened and got noisy when it woke up.

I rode fast; the stars blurred into ribbons of light when I glanced up at them. Each time an oncoming vehicle popped over a hill, it was as if someone had turned on a light in a dark room. The iris of my eye had adjusted and grown comfortable with the darkness; in the suddenly bright light, I could see nothing. All I could do was trust that my path was clear. Paradoxically, after the vehicle passed, I went back into darkness and could see again. I was more at home in the gloom.

Just before dawn, I stopped at a tiny high school football field, home of the six-man Silverton Owls. The dinky concession stand, steel-pipe fences and cinder-block restrooms were painted a cheery crimson and white. A sign by the entrance proudly listed the Owls' championships. A burly brown dog reclined at mid-field, which was the 40-yard line on the 80-yard gridiron used for six-man football. The field's green grass, which obviously had been watered heavily, was ostentatious amid the burned-up brown of the surrounding countryside—it was an oasis. A lone figure ran sprints on the smooth asphalt track. Her footfalls were the only sound piercing the stillness as the town slept. I timed one of her 200s: 35 seconds.

"Ah'm gonna be a sophomore," said the rail-thin, long-legged athlete, hands on hips, smiling through braces. "Ah'm a distance runner, just doin' some speed work this mornin'. We're a football town, but we're gonna have a good cross-country team. We have two little freshman girls who're pretty good. Last year, we got third in district.

"Well, I gotta go do more sprints. You wanta run with me?"

I considered getting off the bike and hammering a few 100-yard dashes. There was no way I could match her pace, but her vulnerable teenage optimism was charming, and I thought perhaps I could acquire some of her cheerfulness by osmosis. Instead, I hopped back on the bike and took off, hoping that she would never be poisoned by the blue moth.

After 35 flat and treeless miles, a sweet smell wafted toward me from the east. Soon, the road dropped off a long escarpment into rolling red hills covered in red cedar and mesquite. It was the Caprock. The aroma of the cedars—portending an unexpected change in terrain—was an omen eerily similar to my nightmare that foreshadowed Will's death, a warning of what was ahead. I had tried without success to determine whether the nightmare had a deeper meaning. Surely it had not been an accident; I wished for the wisdom to understand.

East of the Caprock, two cowboys on horseback were moving a herd of cattle across the highway in front of me, almost like a person would sweep checkers off a board with his right hand. I got off the bike and walked, uncertain how the hoofed creatures or their owners would react to me and my blue helmet. But everyone was well-behaved. One cowhand adjusted his glasses, grinned and said, "I think this is the first time my horse has ever seen a bicycle."

After the cattle crossing, the road descended to one of the forks of the Red River that spread across this land like varicose veins—Prairie Dog Fork, Salt Fork, Elm Fork, North Fork. Today, none of them actually carried water. Grasshoppers the size of frogs bounded onto the road, hitting my bicycle spokes and making little "tink" sounds that were as pleasing to the ear as plucked violin strings. When I ran over them, the grasshoppers crunched like drum snares. Riding over the hot, wet asphalt created "pops" like the cannon in the "1812 Overture."

I loved the natural symphony. The sweet "Bob White, Bob White" call of a quail rolled across the land. Then larks sang, and I heard another bird whose call was exactly like the factory-set ring tone of a cellular telephone—BRRRRRRRRIIIIINNGG. Cicadas played a rhapsody in the air. Like on almost every day of the ride so far, a rooster crowed. What a privilege to be in Texas on a bike, smelling and hearing the country!

The landscape, burned by the relentless sun, was the color of vanilla pudding. The grass crackled under foot, and even the Siberian elm trees—chosen by pioneers 100 years ago because they survived in dry weather—had given up their quest for life this year. They dropped their tiny brown leaves, as if they were leaving a wake-up call for next spring. The irrigated plots of farmland stood out like an Augusta National golf green that had been dropped onto the North Pole. Cool air spread from the few watered lawns of ranch houses. Still, I found the hot, dry noontime soothing, like time spent at an expensive spa.

The Great Plains serves as a fence between East and West. Most think of the plains as Kansas, Nebraska and the Dakotas. But an arm extends south into Texas and Western Oklahoma—sort of a Baja Great Plains. Environmental psychologists Rachel and Stephen Kaplan determined that people prefer pastoral country such as Texas and Oklahoma. They theorized that perhaps it's because our species evolved from the African savannah, which offers access to game, plenty of water, and big-sky scenery.

As I tried to dial Nicki on the cell phone from the Texas savannah, I lost control of the bike and rolled right off the highway. A 70-year-old cyclist had once told me that most crashes are caused by riders overreacting. So, like an 18-wheeler on a runaway truck ramp in the mountains, I simply continued straight into the ditch and came to a halt in the sand and chest-high Johnson grass. As I maneuvered the bike back to the road, I wondered what triggered the calm reaction. Did an animal instinct for survival save me, or had I intuitively recalled the old-timer's lesson?

Similarly, although my fitness level at the start of the ride wasn't sufficient to get me across a small county—much less the continent—I had fallen back on a base of conditioning from all my years of long-distance running. Enough fiber remained in my leg muscles, enough oxygen-carrying capacity in my lungs, enough toughness in my brain. My body was like a bank account; I withdrew what I had deposited earlier. Did our emotional banks contain similar deposits—perhaps a long-forgotten Sunday school lesson or an encouraging word from a friend—that Nicki and I could use to construct a new path in life?

Today's path led to the town of Memphis, whose Texas-tough residents deal regularly with would-be humorists looking for Elvis and Graceland. I was surprised to read about my bike ride in the local weekly newspaper. Later, I learned that a high school pal had told his mother, who told a friend, who told the Memphis Chamber of Commerce manager, who told the editor of the Memphis *Democrat*. It was one of four "local" stories in this week's paper.

"You're Bill Hancock, right?" said a man in the DeVille restaurant. "We read about you. We have a Billy Hancock here in Memphis, and we all gave him a hard time about it. He ain't no bike rider."

Funny—three weeks ago, neither was I.

Andie, when my bike went off the highway, I remembered what I had learned: think clearly and don't overreact. Learn from your lessons; you'll need that knowledge if trouble ever comes.

The Growing E-Mail Crew

More people were reading my daily e-mail journals, which were being forwarded on by recipients. Yesterday a query arrived from a stranger who had learned of the ride from another stranger, who got his information from a high school friend of mine. I was spending 45 minutes each day just reading the messages; it was a good problem to have. I also was spending an hour on NCAA business most days—clearly failing at the "no-work" vow.

Do you ever have real music on your ride or only those tunes you can't shake from your head? There's no real music, unless you count meadow larks, owls, coyotes, and cicadas.

I hope the ride is helping you heal. I'm not sure I will recognize "healing" if it ever comes. I do know that I am enjoying the solitude—and the root beer.

Aren't you bored? I think I would go nuts, out there alone all day. Oh, no. Foremost, I'm never truly alone; I see Nicki two or three times each day. I spend time thinking, or just daydreaming. Sometimes I entertain myself by inventing stories about people who pass me in cars and trucks. Yesterday, after a woman in a Ford pickup scowled at me, I decided that she had won a beauty contest but was forced to renounce the crown after she shoplifted cat food from the feed-and-seed store.

That's not too exciting. I'd be very bored. There is plenty to observe, from historical markers to people to bugs, birds, and cattle. To come all this way without learning would be like performing a solo rather than playing in a symphony. The music that plays in my head each day is always a surprise. I also do mathematical calculations. Did you know that I pedal approximately 254 times per mile on flat ground? That would result in 635,000 pedal strokes across the country—if the country were flat, which it isn't, and assuming I never coast, which I do. As you can see, boredom is not an issue.

Are you losing weight? Yes, I lose six or eight pounds a day, but put most of it back on by eating each evening like Arnold the Pig. Overall, I'm 10 pounds lighter than when the ride began.

Do you use a cell phone to connect to the Internet to e-mail us, or do you find a local connection in each town? I use land lines. Most private campgrounds have special lines for e-mail. If not, the campground owners let me use their private phones. Of course, state parks and national forests don't have phones, so I don't send journals on those nights.

Do your toes get numb in addition to your hands? Mine do when I ride a stationary bike. Yep, they do. Every half hour, I wake them up by pretending a wad of chewing gum is on the toe of each shoe and trying to shake it off.

I don't think that I could handle all those bugs. Do they bother you? Only the ants. Every time I sit down to rest, ants decide to hold a convention.

You haven't said a word about your, er, tail end. If I ride more than five miles, my tail is sore for a week. That's a rather, er, personal question, isn't it? Actually, I haven't been sore at all. I give credit to the Cannondale's split-style seat, which spreads the burden.

Do you just snack all day long, or do you eat at regular meal times? I eat toast and a banana at about 4 a.m. Then at around 7 a.m., there's a "second breakfast" which may be a biscuit or a donut that I purchase from a little store. I usually don't eat anything else until I finish for the day, when I'll have Fritos or Cheez-Its. For supper, I eat all that I can hold.

What does Nicki do all day, while you're riding? She spends more than an hour taking down Roci. She shops for food and Gatorade, then often visits a museum or a bird sanctuary, or she goes for a hike. She finds scenic spots to take photos of me on the bike. She's glad to have so many chores.

Why didn't you just stay in Ruidoso until September? But then I'd have missed Tulia!

And this, which doesn't speak well about the public's perception of big-time sports, but made me chuckle nonetheless: Y*ou're on the take, aren't you? How much is Gatorade paying you? Are you riding an orange-and-green bicycle?*

DAY 18

SHORTGRASS

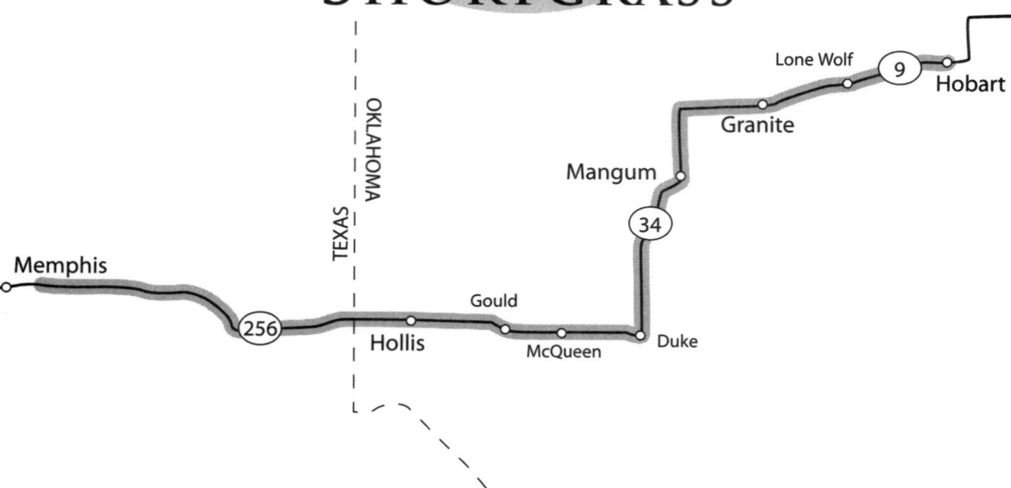

Date: Friday, July 27.

Distance traveled: 103 miles, from four miles east of Memphis, Texas, to Hobart, Oklahoma.

Total miles completed: 1,376.

Starting temperature and time: 77 degrees at 4:45 a.m.

Finishing temperature and time: 101 at 1:30 p.m.

Food: breakfast—toast, banana; second breakfast—cinnamon roll; lunch—cheese crackers, Vienna sausage; dinner—Big-a-Burger, hotdog, onion rings, tater tots, peach cobbler.

Additional fuel: six quarts of water, three quarts of Gatorade, one root beer.

Song stuck in my head: Today's lyrics—known only to true aficionados—popped into my mind in the pink pre-dawn, just after I crossed into my home state: "Gonna give you barley, carrots and potaters, pasture for the cattle, spinach and tomaters. Flowers on the prairie where the June bugs zoom. Plenty of air and plenty of room. Plenty of room to swing a rope, plenty of heart and plenty of hope." (Title song from *Oklahoma!*, Rodgers and Hammerstein, 1943.)

Overnight: mother-in-law's house in Hobart.

Today was the six-month anniversary of the plane crash. In some ways, the past six months had seemed like only an instant; in other ways, a lifetime. Nicki and I had moved from disbelief to shock to deep sadness to paralysis to hesitant steps forward. Fittingly, I was headed to my hometown Hobart, and the rich, life-giving farm country of Southwest Oklahoma—for the anniversary.

As I rode this morning in the dark, I wasn't certain what creatures might inhabit the black ditch next to the road, so I sat down to rest on the dotted white center stripe of a highway that held yesterday's warmth like a grudge. Before the ride I hadn't seen the Milky Way in years, and now it was a constant companion, an icy lace veil draped over the immense black bowl that covered the world. Drinking in the blackness and the silence, I knew that the light and music, when they came, would have more meaning. We demand illumination and noise and activity when often the best balm is boredom. Herman Melville wrote in *Moby Dick*, "To insure the greatest efficiency in the dart, the harpooners of this world must start to their feet out of idleness, and not out of toil."

As I swigged water idly on that dark ribbon of welcoming asphalt, a coyote howled, sending chills racing down my spine. Then another answered. Soon several were singing like banshees. I must confess, I have never heard banshees, but these sounded like movie banshees, at least. Then the howling choir drew closer. A coyote attacking a human was news to me. But then again, many facts about the world had escaped my notice. So, I hopped on the bike and fled—someone else could do the research on coyote dietary habits.

Day had broken by the time I paused at the granite "Welcome to Oklahoma" marker west of Hollis. I was home. My father was born in Indian Territory before Oklahoma became a state and my mother's family migrated here in 1918. That big piece of pink rock seemed to grow soft arms, cuddle me like a baby on a January morning and say, "You're back in the Shortgrass country now; everything will be okay." Tears flowed, but the wind—already whipping warm and dry—quickly turned them to salt on my cheeks.

After I parked the bike and stepped into a fragrant donut shop in Hollis, three ranchers—a father, son, and friend—asked what I was doing. My response sent them down an inquisitive path and they spent the next 15 minutes asking more questions. As they left the donut shop, the father put his warm hand on my shoulder and said, "Good luck, boy."

I asked the donut-shop owner for directions to the football field, so that I could again see where Darrell Royal played high school ball. Royal was an All-American at the University of Oklahoma and a legendary coach at the University of Texas. Despite his success and worldwide acclaim, Darrell and his wife, Edith, were not immune to tragedy; they have lost two children in accidents. When Will was killed, Edith sent a warm letter to Nicki which helped us cope. Edith and Darrell had locked the blue moth in a room somewhere and successfully rebuilt their lives. Perhaps we could, too.

"The field where *who* played?" the donut woman asked.

"Darrell Royal."

"Who's that?" she inquired.

Someone in Hollis not knowing of Darrell Royal is like a New Yorker unaware of Rudolph Giuliani. Darrell laughed when I told him about it later. Anyone seeking a role model should look no farther than Darrell. Small towns have a way of keeping good people humble. For example, the story is told that Coach Royal visited his brother in Hollis during the winter of 1970. Darrell's Longhorns team had just won the 1969 national championship, so he was the most famous person in college football, and arguably one of the 20 most-recognized men in America. But one of the old boys in a Hollis café said to the coach, "Oh, yeah, Darrell, I remember you. You still in ball?"

Red Tiger paw prints in the street led me to the Hollis football field. A jeans-and-boots-wearing man, Marshal Dillon in the flesh, said, "Glad you didn't ask those guys watering the field about Coach Royal. Two of them are convicts, and the other is new to town and doesn't know anything. It takes an old-timer like me to remember that several boys from here played ball up at OU."

The football stadium is not named for Darrell Royal. Instead, it carries the name of Will Husband, the fatherly physician who ushered the newborn Royal into the world in 1924 and was Hollis's version of the hero from the movie *Field of Dreams*, Dr. Archibald "Moonlight" Graham. Dr. Husband died in 1947, en route to watch Royal play for the Sooners against the University of Detroit. Hollis preferred to honor the teacher, not the student.

The day turned sour in a café in Duke, where a sign at the city limits read: "Home of the 1998 State Class B Girls State Basketball

Champions." Eight patrons were assembled at what surely was their regular table, parishioners at caffeine mass. When I smiled and said "howdy," they glowered as if I were an alien carrying the "I Love You" virus. Clearly, I was unwelcome. I left Duke with a heavy heart and rode hard to escape the aggressive blue moth.

Kindness drove the moth away south of Mangum when I passed a sign reading, "Inmate Work Crew Ahead." Sure enough, a dozen orange-clad men unenthusiastically swung scythes at chest-high weeds. The burly black supervisor smiled at me, saying the Hobart radio station declared the temperature was 95 but that it felt much warmer inside his pickup. He let me fill my bottle with icy water from the inmates' cooler. None of the workers returned my hearty "Good mornin'." People who were forced to be out in the hot weather showed little respect for those who did it on purpose.

North of Mangum I crossed the site of the railroad tracks where, in 1940, my grandfather's car was hit by a train. Josiah Nathaniel Gardner—Brother Gardner, they called him, a hale fellow if ever one existed—sold groceries wholesale to owners of the one-room stores that dotted the countryside in those days. A quick-witted man, he supplemented his meager income by giving comical homespun speeches to the delight of Kiwanis Club members, Rotarians, and school groups. But his life after the accident was pure agony because of a leg injury that didn't heal properly. Humor and pain were fighting a similar cage match in our lives; right now, pain was winning.

The Shortgrass country of Southwest Oklahoma—so named because the native grasses were only knee-high as opposed to the hip-deep flora elsewhere in the plains—is home of the ancient Wichita Mountains, which lay like ginger-pink pearls in a general east-west direction across the flat landscape. Tucked into a tree-lined elbow of the mountains is the charming community of Granite. I sat alone in the town's little baseball park in the shadow of the granite hills, remembering when little Will played imaginary baseball games behind the dugouts while I chronicled Granite Panthers games for the Hobart *Democrat-Chief* 25 years ago. Tears rolled down my cheeks when I realized that Will wouldn't be able to watch Andie play ball. I reviled the persistent blue moth for having the nerve to follow me home.

Most residents of Granite are employed either at the state reformatory or at one of the two companies that make tombstones and other monuments. My beloved Uncle Nathan, a good-humored

Okie who married a girl from North Carolina and spent most of his life there, loved that Oklahoma granite so much that he had his gravestone made of it. Among the dark headstones in the North Carolina cemetery where he is buried, his pink marker stands out like a beam of light.

In the town's bright new convenience store, a barrel-chested farmer—whose fingers were like Vienna sausages with knuckles—struggled to open a small salad-dressing packet. He finally did what comes naturally in rural America: he pulled a pair of pliers from the pocket of his overalls and used them to rip open the packet. Etiquette wasn't an issue. The point was to extract the salad dressing.

Just east of Granite, only 16 miles from Hobart, an enthusiastic welcoming committee awaited me: my sister, mother-in-law, niece, Nicki, Karen, and Andie. Okie, my sister's ferocious-looking but friendly boxer—she was the only dog on this trip that I was happy to see—wore a sign around her neck that read, "I Love You, Uncle Bill."

Yes, baby Andie found tears of happiness in my eyes when she grabbed at my sunglasses. In sharp contrast to the trail of tears that I had followed since January 27, I was in familiar territory now. I knew where the old beer joint once stood, who rolled his car on which dirt road, and who had farmed most cotton patches. A field of blooming alfalfa hay smelled like 1,000 lilacs. I filled my lungs with the scent, wishing that I could bottle it up for later.

I rode past Little Elk Creek, where a friend of mine found a giant catfish encased in ice in 1962. It was also near where I swigged my first beer in 1966, and along the road that Nicki and I drove down on our first date. This was my home, and I could have loitered forever, protected by its shell built with love and loyalty. I thought back to the advice of Pop from Pie Town: "this ole stuff of gettin' in a hurry just ain't no good." But home was not the end of the road for me; I would eventually have to move on.

The Hobart water towers popped into view and another greeting party waited at the city limits. A Hobart police officer offered to lead me into town. Embarrassed, I asked the officer if he would please just quietly return to the police station; I did not need a police escort. "But the city judge asked me to meet you," he said. "Here, we do what the judge says." Someone thrust an American flag into Nicki's hand, and we posed for photos. I was sweaty and salt-encrusted as I said "cheese," but happy to be home.

My sister had moved to Pennsylvania, and Nicki and I had taken our young family to Kansas City. But brother Joe stayed in Hobart to publish the *Democrat-Chief*. Joe is our family's hero and anchor, and he keeps us connected to a hometown that we left in body but not in spirit.

In Hobart, we baby-boom children were a tribe that was raised together under the loving guidance of adults. If we sinned—such as the night that a friend and I painted "Seniors '68" on the concrete dam at Hunter Park Lake—our parents knew within minutes. Our high school reunions today are held by the decade, not by the year. There were only 68 students in my graduating class.

As I rode toward Nicki's mom's 1907-vintage farm house on the edge of Hobart, I followed my old paper route and pretended that it was 1962 all over again and a newspaper bag hung on the handlebars. I moved quietly, passing where my childhood friends once lived. They had moved away, grown up. But as the shadows lengthened on this afternoon, the homes remained theirs. I could describe every room in those houses, though I hadn't set foot in them for years. It was a pleasant ride down memory lane.

Andie, there is no substitute for the warmth of home and friends and family. Your grandmother and I consider ourselves fortunate to have Hobart, which is like a cozy resort where we find a kind of comfort that we can't get anywhere else. Put your roots down some place—or better yet, two places, like your grandmother and I did—and cherish every moment that you're able to spend there.

The Blue Moth at Home

My father, Ransom, lost his dry-goods business during the Depression. Embarrassed, he found a job selling advertising for the *Democrat-Chief*. He walked to work every day because the family could not afford an automobile. He worked hard and moved up the ladder, eventually becoming publisher. Later, he and my brother Joe borrowed money and purchased the paper.

Daddy was a violin player who also directed the Methodist church choir and the Hobart men's chorus. My mother, Annie B., gave piano lessons. I did not know them as energetic young people; they were 47 and 40 years old when I was born. I might not have been born at all if the blue moth had not attacked them.

When my brother was a college sophomore and my sister was a junior in high school, my mother became pregnant. My parents' outrageous fortune drew good-natured slings and arrows from their friends, but they quickly became enamored with the prospect of another baby in the house. Sadly, little Anne Ransom died when she was 14 days old. Their doctor told mother, "You can try again." My dad wasn't sure; I'm told my mother may have tricked him. If it was inter-uterine deception, it worked and—eight days after my brother's wedding and one day after my sister went away to her freshman year of college—I was born.

The death of my sister was never discussed at our house; nor was the fact that I probably wouldn't be here if she had lived. Once I found a cedar chest full of condolence cards; I read them by flashlight, feeling like a burglar invading someone's privacy. Some day we will show Andie our own box of a thousand such cards.

When my family visited the cemetery on Decoration Day, I always saw the baby's tiny gravestone, but nobody ever said a word about it. My dad was a no-nonsense Scotsman who did not suffer fools well but gave me everything that I ever wanted, including plenty of love. But I was too frightened to ask about Anne Ransom, my sister. That chapter in their lives was closed for good. After Will's death, however, I needed to know more, and so I asked one of my father's friends how Anne's death affected my father.

"Your dad was devastated, but he did not let anyone know it. His role was to be strong for your mother, who was heartbroken at the loss of the baby. But one day, he asked me to drive him out into the country. I stayed in the car as he walked into a field, fell to his knees and sobbed. He curled up into a ball, like a child. After five minutes, he came back to the car, wiped the dust from his knees and the tears from his eyes, and said, 'I'm ready to go back to town now.'

"He was reluctant for your mother to get pregnant again, because he didn't think she could survive another bout of grief if she lost another child. And he wasn't confident that he could survive it, either. That's one reason they raised you so carefully. Your dad lived 24 more years after Anne Ransom died, but he was never the same. I will say this: having you grow up healthy and happy was a real tonic for him."

The blue moth had lived at my house while I was growing up, and I hadn't even known it because my mother and dad built a protective barrier of love around me. Only now did I comprehend the crisis which my parents endured 50 years ago, and—in the most terrible irony—the positive effect it had on my own childhood. I traveled with my parents all around the country, attended hundreds of football, basketball, and baseball games and never wanted for anything—including discipline. I was showered with education and praise. It was as if I were living the life that should have been Anne Ransom's. In a strange way, I had been George Bailey, given another opportunity at a wonderful life.

DAY 19
GOTEBO

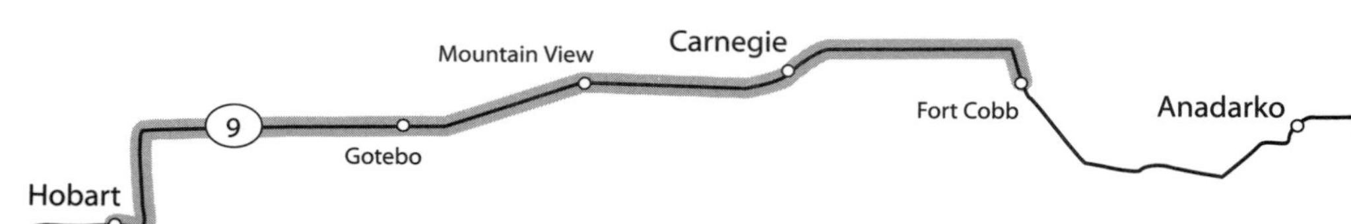

Date: Sunday, July 29.

Distance traveled: 43 miles in Oklahoma, from Hobart to Ft. Cobb Lake.

Total miles completed: 1,419.

Miles to go: perhaps 1,300.

Starting temperature and time: 78 degrees at 5 a.m.

Finishing temperature and time: 91 at 9:30 a.m.

Food: breakfast—toast, banana; second breakfast—biscuit and gravy; lunch—KFC, pea salad, cantaloupe; dinner—veggie salad, pasta, peach cobbler, chips and avocado dip.

Additional fuel: one gallon of water, one quart of Gatorade, one grape slush.

Song stuck in my head: "And when I kissed a cop down at Thirty-Fourth and Vine, he broke my little bottle of Love Potion No. 9." ("Love Potion No. 9," The Searchers, 1965.)

Overnight: Ft. Cobb Lake State Park.

Nicki and I re-energized ourselves on Saturday with a day off in Hobart, spending time with Andie, Karen, and Nellie—all four generations enjoying the soothing Oklahoma wind. Everyone was asleep when I left on Sunday morning. The streets were deserted and I detoured to drag Main Street on the bike, under the yellowish glow of street lights.

Riding a bicycle would have been unthinkably geeky on the fragrant summer nights of 1967 when Nicki and I put as many as 100 miles on my father's Buick Electra 225, honking to friends and crooning along with such anthems as "Georgy Girl," "Daydream Believer," and "Somethin' Stupid." Today the Cannondale was the only vehicle in the dim light except for the red 1965 Pontiac GTO and yellow 1967 Plymouth Satellite that were cruising in the bustling streets of my mind.

Our old two-story brick high school building was gone; a low-slung new model stood two blocks away. The movie theater was closed; a video store was down the block. The Dairy Queen was boarded up, but the lights of a new Sonic attracted hundreds of June bugs nearby.

New replaces old, that's the natural sequence. Will's death fouled up the order, and I had that pesky moth looming overhead to remind me. I couldn't shake him from my trail.

I had been on Highway 9 east of Hobart a thousand times or more, almost always in an automobile. Yet I had never experienced the road as I did from the bike today. Being in the open air made it seem as if I could see each blade of the Johnson grass, smell the dirt, and caress the air. One December morning during my marathoning days, I ran the 16 miles from Gotebo to Hobart, but the world was frozen that day. The temperature was four above zero; ice formed on my eyebrows and crystals glistened on the tops of my shoes. Today the lights from thousands of yesterdays twinkled in my mirror as I bicycled into the future.

That rearview mirror, about the size of a quarter, attaches onto the side of my helmet. Objects are small and shaky, and it's difficult to see what's behind, so I spent little time looking into the past. Riding—like life—is healthier that way. But when I really needed to see what was back there, lurking in the ground I'd already covered, the mirror was available.

The silhouette of a critter loomed ahead on the shoulder. I figured it was a dog and prepared to implement my experimental canine-avoidance procedure: Step No. 1—try to make myself invisible; Step No. 2—if that fails, then try to make myself look very large; and Step No. 3—if that fails, too, then pedal as fast as I could. In this case, the villain was worse than a dog—it was a skunk. I skipped directly to Step No. 3 and dashed to the town of Gotebo.

To us natives, the name Gotebo (pronounced GO-tee-bowe) sounds no more unusual than Piscataway or Islip or Secaucus to a New Yorker. Gotebo, a Kiowa Indian chief, was among those who gave up land when this section of Oklahoma was allocated to lucky white settlers in 1901. After the chaotic first-come, first-served giveaway of land in the fabled Oklahoma land run of 1889, the government chose a more humane random-selection process for the southwestern section of the state. The great Southwest Oklahoma land lottery was civilized, I thought—for everyone except the Indians.

People in Kiowa County were accustomed to bikers because of the annual 50-mile Tour de Gotebo, a bike race through the scenic Wichita Mountains. I proudly finished last in it one year.

Until today I had yet to see the state mammal of Texas—the armadillo. Today I spied two, and began to search for a live version of the accordion-shelled, snout-nosed animal that has become the unofficial road kill of the American Southwest. The armadillo's claim to fame, besides being a frequent victim of the automobile, is that its young are of the same sex, always quadruplets developed from the same egg. So plenty of young clones are available to replace those that perish. The thought of lost youngsters—even armadillo youngsters—opened the door to my spirit and the revolting blue moth bolted right in.

Another winged friend soon came to my rescue. A miniature stealth bomber—a swallow, actually—flew over my head like a guardian angel for 10 miles; its flutter-glide, flutter-glide flight pattern caused me to laugh out loud, driving the blue moth away.

In the shady little town of Mountain View, its stately elms contrasting with the surrounding treeless prairie, I thought that I heard someone call out my name. But no one was there. Was it my imagination or the swallow or Will calling from heaven? Four blocks later, a woman pulled her late-model Chevrolet into a convenience store parking lot and introduced herself. She was the editor of the Mountain View *News*, the daily newspaper. A polite woman, she had called out from her driveway as she saw me ride past; then she gave chase in her car. Someone had forwarded one of my e-mails to her, and she wanted to write a news story about my journey.

The newspaper is also the local Internet provider, sort of a SAG for rural computer owners. "You have to diversify to survive in small towns," said the editor.

In a convenience store, I got so caught up in conversation with three men about old basketball players that I left without filling my water bottles. I returned sheepishly after riding a half-mile.

"You back already?" said one fellow.

"I understand," said another, "I've been trying to get out of this town for 30 years, and I can't do it, either."

Andie, that newspaper editor from Mountain View knew that in small towns it's important to have many different interests and skills. It's true in life, also. So, I hope you will be able to enjoy music and sports and science and literature and gardening—and occasionally go for bike rides with your granddad.

6
The Road to Hope

DAY 20

HUMP DAY

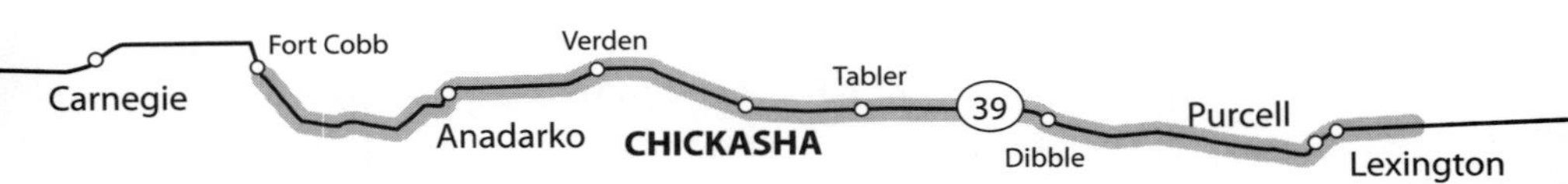

Date: *Monday, July 30.*

Distance traveled: *82 miles in Oklahoma, from Ft. Cobb Lake to 10 miles east of Purcell.*

Total miles completed: *1,501.*

Starting temperature and time: *81 degrees at 5 a.m.*

Finishing temperature and time: *99 at 2 p.m.*

Food: *breakfast—toast, banana; lunch—cheese crackers; dinner—pasta, boiled shrimp, salad.*

Additional fuel: *19 Cheez-Its, 47 Chili Cheese Fritos, five Oreos, two gallons of water, one gallon of Gatorade, one root beer, two Budweisers.*

Song stuck in my head: *none.*

Overnight: *the home of John D. and Gracie Montgomery in Purcell.*

I went on full dog alert as I neared a church camp in a wooded hollow west of Anadarko. Back in 1971, early in my conversion from nerd to outdoorsman, I was attempting to ride the 120 miles from Norman to Hobart on my three-speed Schwinn, when a monster dog bounded out of the woods and nipped at my heels. A little girl ran out of the church screaming, "Wolf, don't eat that man!" I had been thinking the same thing. Wolf persuaded me to telephone 20-year-old Nicki and say, "Please come pick me up. I'm done." Thirty years later, she was still picking me up.

While celebrating the absence of Wolf or any of his progeny, I was stunned by a sunrise that could have been lifted straight from a Bible painting. On second thought, no mortal artist could have conceived such majesty. Perhaps Will Hancock, the lover of Monet, had a hand in it. Purple clouds hung in front of the orange sky and white sun rays shot like lasers in all directions. Then the clouds changed to peach, the sky went blue, and the lasers faded. It was a live cosmic PowerPoint presentation. Once again, nature provided a glimmer of hope for the future.

An American Indian in a crimson "OU Sooners" baseball cap meandered down Anadarko's Main Street with a plastic bag of bottles and cans slung over his shoulder.

"Good morning," I said.

"People throw away too much," was his only reply.

He was correct. So far, I had seen enough goods along the highway to start a decent second-hand store: toys, televisions, mattresses, lawn chairs, easy chairs, high chairs, director's chairs, sofas, stoves, refrigerators, every article of clothing (outerwear and underwear) imaginable, a toilet, and a half-dozen sets of keys. There were plenty of abandoned buildings, too: liquor stores, shells of old motels, and even a couple of shuttered Wal-Marts—left empty when goliath Wal-Mart Supercenters were built a few miles away. I had also observed dozens of forsaken people. Each discarded article—and human being—once was a shiny new treasure, laden with promise. The remains of such promise—homeless persons living under bridges and wordly goods rusting in ditches—left me with a heavy nugget of sadness.

East of Chickasha (CHICK-uh-shay) I encountered a geographical barrier as significant culturally and meteorologically as the Rockies had been physically. A Berlin Wall of sorts dissects Oklahoma; pioneers found a virtually impenetrable mass of hardwoods, live oak, post oak, and hickory running from Kansas to Texas and dubbed it "crosstimbers." West of the wall, the land is flat, arid, open, and free. To the east is a little Appalachia, closed in by trees. I know westerners who become claustrophobic when traveling east of Interstate 35.

The first half of the ride was over two days ago near Hobart, but the crosstimbers served as a symbolic gateway. To paraphrase Winston Churchill, "This is not the end; it is not even the beginning of the end. But it is the end of the beginning." In our race against the blue moth, Nicki and I were in a land without time; there was a beginning to our sadness, but no end in sight and few discernable mileposts. On the bike, I was thankful for measurable progress. Today I would slice through the crosstimbers.

I was somewhat saddened to arrive at the hump in Oklahoma because it marked the end of the remote West. Although not as precarious as the South Col of Mount Everest or the Roaring Forties seas around Cape Horn, the mysterious West did evoke a spark of delicious danger. I enjoyed the risk, not in a suicidal fashion, but as a challenge faced down. Cycling across the West was a rare victory in our world of loss; I wanted to drive back to Los Angeles and do it all again.

In the West, the air was dry, and the people few. The mountains had summits. Even the road kill was bearable. Beginning at Chickasha, the humidity and endless hills made the riding more difficult, but there was a tradeoff; after the sparsely populated West, what seemed like throngs of people east of the crosstimbers gave the trip a heartbeat. As if to celebrate my symbolic crossing to the other side of the nation's fence, dozens of white egrets rose from a muddy pond and flew in unison over my head like a flock of snowy angels.

Friends later counted 54 hills in the 27 miles of Highway 39 west of Purcell. There was no shoulder and much traffic. Self-discipline and a sense of humor were vital on this ribbon of fright. I remembered the silly pun about the favorite "wine" of a bicyclist: "Oh, I don't like these hills; this wind is so awful and the traffic is terrible. I wish I had stayed home."

"Stop your whining," I told myself. "Take what you get and put one foot in front of the other." I remembered the "Ten Commandments for Success in Baseball," that were written by Joe McCarthy, the old New York Yankees manager. My favorite was No. 6, an admonition to take responsibility: "Do not alibi on bad hops. Anybody can field the good ones."

In truth, there was so much traffic on Highway 39 that I was forced to stop the bike and step off the pavement a half-dozen times to let vehicles pass. One pickup driver gave the "you idiot" honk. I was happy to arrive at the home of John D. and Gracie Montgomery, who publish the dandy Purcell *Register*, a weekly newspaper full of up-to-date local news and advertising. John D. and I grew up together in Hobart and worked together at the University of Oklahoma in the 1970s. Members of our families have known each other almost as long as Oklahoma has been a state. Nate and John D.'s two sons could continue the relationship into its second century, but half of my legacy was gone. Will was the family genealogist; the laptop computer containing his records was lost in the crash. We could re-create that data. But not the heritage.

John D. suffered as much as anyone from Will's death and was determined to make my life—and the bike ride—as pleasant as possible. He arranged a welcome ceremony nearly as happy as the one the Lullaby League and the Lollipop Guild gave Dorothy when she arrived in Oz. A 25-foot banner strung over the highway in Purcell announced "Welcome Bill Hancock." Several people called the Chamber of Commerce asking, "Who in the world is this Bill Hancock?"

It reminded me of one NCAA tournament in Seattle's Kingdome, when comedian Bill Cosby sat in the courtside press section and cheered happily for his beloved Temple University Owls to the chagrin of journalists who were trying to write stories. I asked him to return to his seat in the stands. He was quoted in the next day's newspapers saying, "I had fun until the NCAA sent some lackey to make me move."

Andie, just when you think you're hot stuff, there's always someone to bring you back down to earth by saying, "Who are you, anyway?" Stay humble; the meek are blessed.

DAY 21

REFEREEING A DOMESTIC DISPUTE

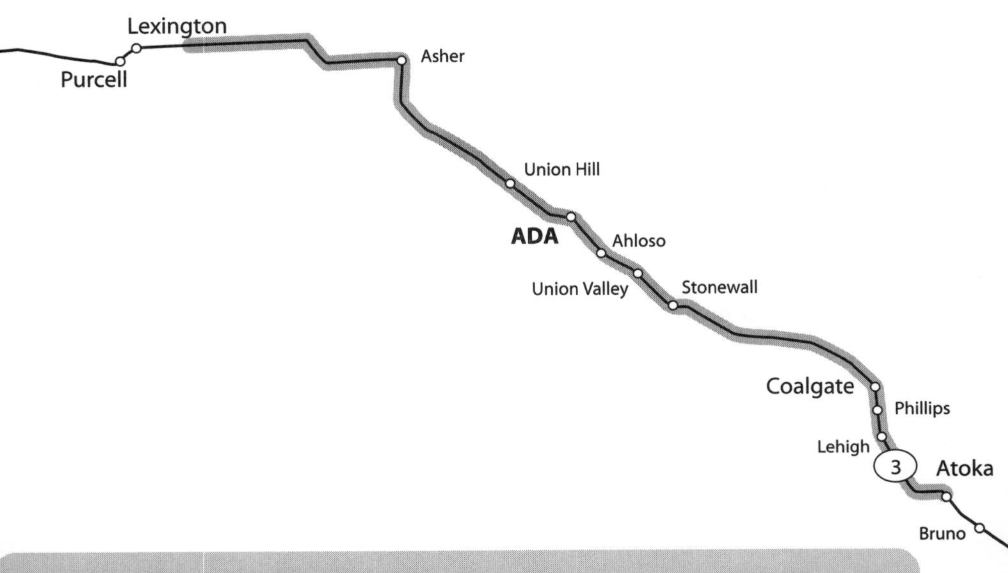

Date: Tuesday, July 31.

Distance traveled: 85 miles in Oklahoma, from 10 miles east of Purcell to Atoka.

Total miles completed: 1,586.

Miles to go: still a whole bunch.

Starting temperature and time: 79 degrees at 4:20 a.m.

Finishing temperature and time: 98 at 12:45 p.m.

Food: breakfast—toast, banana; lunch—cheese crackers, Fritos, little tacos; dinner—tamale, enchilada, beans and rice, and nachos.

Additional fuel: six quarts of water, three quarts of Gatorade, one root beer, one margarita.

Song stuck in my head: "In the sky, the bright stars glittered. On the bank, the pale moon shown. And 'twas from Aunt Dinah's quilting party, I was seeing Nellie home." ("The Quilting Party," traditional, 1912.)

Overnight: Best Western, Atoka.

The rising sun carried a rare easterly wind, a remnant of tropical storm Barry. Riding into the 20-mile-per-hour gale felt like pulling a parachute. We are seldom prepared for headwinds; life is going along the way we expect, then all of a sudden a blast of hot air hits us. The world looks the same, but it isn't. Even highways are often not what they seem. Today, on what I thought was flat land, I just couldn't get going. I thought something was wrong with me: too many Vienna sausages, perhaps? Then I glanced in my rear-view mirror and noticed that the terrain actually wasn't level. I had been proceeding gradually up and up and up. Bikers call them "false flats."

The hills of east-central Oklahoma are packed with mighty white oaks and pin oaks. I decided every branch was a miniature water cannon spraying humidity into the air, like fire boats in New York City's harbor on the Fourth of July. Three white cows stood up to their armpits in a muddy pond. I wanted to join them.

In Coalgate, the heart of Oklahoma's small coal-mining territory, Nicki joined me for lunch across the street from the Ol' Coaly, "the largest rodeo mural west of the Mississippi." A young man and woman with an untamed 16-month-old daughter waged a fierce domestic dispute in a booth next to ours.

"Your mom and dad give Bobbie Jo and Larry Don fifty dollars, and they didn't give us nothin'," said the chesty wife.

"I cain't change my momma and daddy," responded her fuzzy-cheeked husband in his local dialect. "I ain't gonna try no more. You cain't make me."

Nicki and I were embarrassed to be in the middle of such personal intimacy and tried to break up the quarrel by talking to them about the bike ride. The young husband was interested, but the wife rolled her eyes, filed her purple fingernails, and bellowed at the child.

"There's a bar in the next town," said the husband. "An old man runs it, but he's a good guy. He'll give you water."

Then, looking wistfully at his watch and speaking with a voice of experience, he added, "He don't open 'til one o'clock, though."

We had done all that we could for the couple—which wasn't much—so I headed south toward Atoka, waging a 13-mile battle against a warm but fragrant headwind. At the edge of town, I was reminded why I love this state—Atoka's golf course is adjacent to the rodeo arena. Where else but in Oklahoma?

Andie, remember those false flats; when you're struggling, there's a reason. Look upon the bad times as an opportunity to be silent. If you make no excuses and ride through trouble with your head up, you will set an example for others.

DAY 22
HOBO AND THE COACH

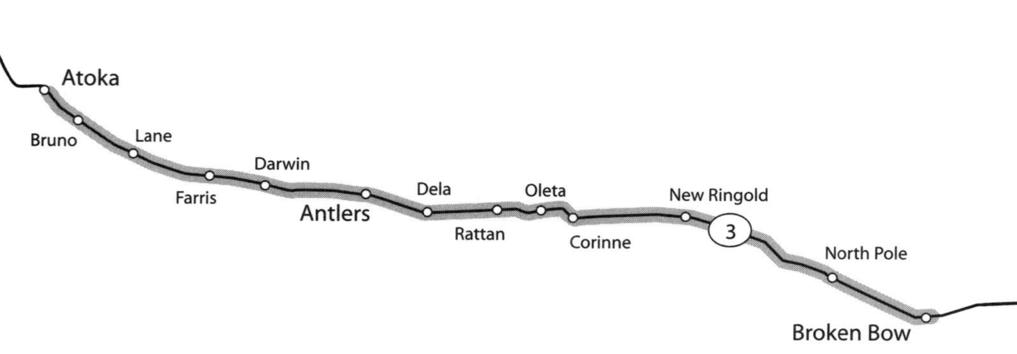

Date: Wednesday, August 1.

Distance traveled: 89 miles in Oklahoma, from Atoka to Broken Bow.

Total miles completed: 1,675.

Starting temperature and time: 77 degrees at 4:50 a.m.

Finishing temperature and time: 96 at 4:50 p.m.

Food: breakfast—toast, banana; lunch—cheese crackers, orange juice, 14 Cheez-Its; dinner—apple, Rice-a-Roni, cherry snow cone.

Additional fuel: two gallons of water, three quarts of Gatorade, one root beer.

Song stuck in my head: none today.

Overnight: Beavers Bend State Park.

A family of raccoons crossed the road ahead as I coasted down into a foggy glen just before dawn. They marched along in a convoy, two big ones—the mom and dad?—followed by five miniatures in a straight line, all wearing tiny bandit masks. The last little guy was still in the road when I arrived. He panicked, fell down, scrambled to regain his footing like Buster Keaton on ice skates, and then dashed off the pavement to safety, surely much to the relief of his siblings and parents.

After crossing Muddy Boggy Creek, I found myself in a green tunnel of Southern pine, oak, hickory, walnut, pecan, and sycamore trees, broken only by an occasional lake or a pasture or clear-cut area. The lumber company Weyerhaeuser owns a large chunk of Southeastern Oklahoma. Granola-eating liberals (and also some of us who dine on Vienna sausages) want to confront the loggers and demand that they put the forest back the way it was. On the other hand, Western Oklahoma farmers cultivate wheat and cotton; here, in the eastern part of the state, the crop is trees. As the wheat farmers busted sod that had lain untouched for eons, eastern lumbermen "busted" the forest's old growth and replaced it with new trees that would be ready for harvest in 13 years. What's the difference?

I was now at the confluence of the Jack's Fork Mountains and the Kiamichi Mountains, in the heart of the Oklahoma Ozarks. The hills created an endless roller-coaster. "Why go down if you're going to go right back up?" I asked myself, in a burst of anger. Riding up and down these Oklahoma hills was like grieving: struggling hopelessly one minute, flying happily the next, struggling again. Always looking ahead for a consistency, but finding none. Wandering near the road's edge sometimes, as if I might just fall into total despair, then catching myself. But being close enough to peer into the chasm of gloom, to feel out of control—worried that I could fly off the road in an instant.

I wanted to shoot a steel cable from one hilltop to the next and ride on it like a high-wire circus performer instead of dipping down to each brown creek and then climbing out again. I almost got my wish near the logging town of Antlers. The state was laying a new road, the expensive kind that smooths the hills. The existing road looked like a wrinkled old woman—the new one, a cherry-cheeked prom queen.

The new road wasn't open to traffic, but it was paved. So I rode on it for six miles in hill-free bliss, then slammed on the brakes when the pavement ended at a creek. Construction workers waved kindly through the hazy steam of hot asphalt as I toted the bike back to the old highway and continued eastward.

In the town of Antlers, near majestic magnolia trees and crape myrtles as big as houses, I saw a man sitting on a downtown bench. He resembled a statue with a fuzzy ball on top. Atop his full, fluffy white beard was an equally downy head of hair, on which was perched a hat reading, "Stay Off Drugs." He had Carolina blue eyes, peppermint pink cheeks, and cracked purple lips.

"I don't do any biking," he said crisply, in a surprising East-coast accent. "I backpack and ride the freights from Joplin to Shreveport."

"Why?" I asked.

"To get there," he replied.

As I got back on the bike to ride away, he said, "There are many hills ahead of you. Are you prepared?" Before I could answer, he continued, "Nobody's ever really prepared. You just roll the dice, man, take what you get, and do the best you can."

I stared into his sapphire eyes. They told me that somehow he knew about our family's tragedy, although I had not spoken a word about it. I pedaled away.

A few blocks later, I encountered another local denizen, who said to me, an obvious outsider, "I like it here, but it's a poor town. You can have a person killed for $10." That statement convinced me that it was time to head down the road. I preferred hills to homicide.

Log trucks were my companions all afternoon. In 20 miles, I saw perhaps 50 of them chugging over the hills. Some of them were going my way, but others, still loaded with trees, went back the other direction. What were they going to do, I wondered. Replant the trees?

Out of water and tired of the hills, I spied a man tossing minnows out the door of a small shack near a store called the Little Oklahoma, miles from anywhere except Pine Creek Lake.

"Dead...dead...dead," he said. Then he spotted me. He did not smile. He picked his words carefully, pausing between each one. "Why. In. The. World. Would. A. Grown. Man. Be. Riding. A. Bicycle. In. This. Heat?"

He hobbled on two smooth wooden crutches into the store and found a Gatorade for me. I told him about the ride, and he began to talk. And talk. And talk.

"I'm a high school history teacher. Some day I'm gonna go up yonder to that Louie and Clark Trail. I want to see where they started and where they ended. Louie and Clark, they were strong men. My students like hearing stories about them. Them students like stories better than memorizing facts."

He paused to catch his breath. I sat, transfixed, as he continued.

"After the divorce, I got them two boys. Me and them boys follow the big three—football, basketball, and baseball. But we been likin' what we hear about that bicycler Lance Armstrong. He must be your hero. It's somethin' for an American to go to Europe and win that Tour Dee France. I ain't never been over there, but my friend told me them people ride bicycles more than cars.

"Them boys are both baseball players. The young 'un is a senior in high school; the big 'un is a senior over at Southeastern (Oklahoma State University in Durant). I used to pitch to 'em for hours. Pitched with my right arm 'til it got tired, then switched to my left arm. Drank a little beer while I was doing it."

Eventually, the conversation turned in my direction.

"What you do for a living, mister?" he asked.

"You're not going to believe what I do."

"Let's give 'er a try."

When I said that my job was director of the NCAA Final Four, it was his turn to sit in amazement. It was as if Lewis and Clark themselves had paddled their keel boat into the lake next to his Little Oklahoma store.

"You wait right here a minute, I'm gonna take your pitcher. Me and them boys, we love that NCAA tournament. My name is DeWayne Lindley; I'm honored to meet you.

"I read in the *Daily Oklahoman* that they changed the way they're gonna do the bracket for that NCAA tournament. What do you call it, the Pods Plan? I think I like it, but they better not do it just to take care of the Dookies and North Carolina. They's basketball in other places besides North Carolina, you know. OU and OSU cain't get them North Carolina schools to come out here and play, because you bring your team to play at Norman or Stillwater and you ain't gonna win. Them fancy teams are good, and they're on teevee all the time, but they ain't brave enough to come to Oklahoma to play."

He paused to change gears.

"Weyerhaeuser owns everything north of this road. They do clear cut, but they're required to leave the trees within 100 feet of streams. I guess the greenies don't like it. There was a proposal to dam the Glover River, and that lake would have brought a lot of jobs here. But the environmental people said we had to protect something called the snail darter. I like the outdoors 'bout as much as anybody. But who in his right mind would choose a fish over a man's life? We gotta have a balance between the environment and jobs."

He saw the look on my face and must have known what I was thinking.

"I do talk a lot," he admitted. "My parents own this store; I mind it for them in the summer. School will start soon, and I'll go back to coaching baseball and teachin' kids about the travels of Louie and Clark."

Outside the store, he took my photo, then let his eyes linger on mine. The silence would have been awkward had it not been so magical; it was as if we were communicating in an unspoken language.

Finally, he said, "You be safe, now. Just a minute; 'fore you leave, you need to know somethin'. I'm 47; I had polio back when it was sweeping the country. Three years later, I'da been safe because of that vaccine. There's a reason for things that happens. Some day we'll learn the reason. We're not supposed to know right now, but we'll find out when it's our time."

I hadn't told DeWayne about Will's accident, but, much like the fuzzy gentleman in Antlers and Pop back in Pie Town, he seemed to know—perhaps better than I did—that I needed help. A half-mile down the road I stopped and sat with my back against a pine tree to write down DeWayne's words and ponder their meaning. Then I rode on into the sleepy afternoon.

A sign on a side road proclaimed, "Road Ends in Water," which made me chuckle. Mine, too, I thought, if I could actually make it to the Atlantic Ocean. Today's journey ended instead in the Mountain Fork River, where Nicki parked Roci under a canopy of cypress trees and oaks in Beavers Bend State Park. We swam in the frigid river and dried off before a storm rumbled past, sending thunder bouncing off the mountains. After the storm, fog rose from the water like the mists of Scotland. It was the perfect ending to a meaningful day.

Andie, we'll learn the reason when the time is right. I know another man whose son died. He told me, "I trust God, and I'm comfortable that things happen for a reason. But the first day when I get to Heaven, I'll be sitting on the front row with my hand in the air, saying, 'I have a question.' My question for God will be, 'Why have you been so good to me?'"

DAY 23

Up and Down in Arkansas

Date: Thursday, August 2.

Distance traveled: 85 miles, from Broken Bow, Oklahoma, to Hope, Arkansas.

Total miles completed: 1,760.

Miles to go: fewer than 1,000!

Starting temperature and time: 77 degrees at 5:15 a.m.

Finishing temperature and time: 96 at 3:45 p.m.

Food: breakfast—toast, banana; second breakfast—McDonald's breakfast burrito; lunch—cheese crackers, two gnats; dinner—Burger King chicken sandwich, strawberry milkshake, onion rings.

Additional fuel: one apricot fried pie, seven quarts of water, five quarts of Gatorade, one root beer.

Song stuck in my head: "Cheer, cheer for old Notre Dame. Wake up the echoes, cheering her name." (Notre Dame fight song, 1909.)

Overnight: Hope Fairgrounds campground.

I was already drenched with sweat just 45 minutes into my ride. It was a polite introduction to the humidity of the South.

Just inside Arkansas, mist floating over the lowlands resembled a long gray battleship at anchor against a hillside. A coyote loped like a ballerina across the highway, as the sweet aroma of lumber mills wafted across green pastures. I celebrated arriving in State No. 6 by relaxing for a second breakfast at the McDonald's in DeQueen. It was so cold in the restaurant that I swore they must be anticipating the arrival of a busload of penguins, so I ate my burrito outside—sitting on the curb next to the drive-up lane—where I was comfortable. A threatening ant gladly accepted a tiny tortilla crumb as a peace offering.

In truth, I understood the artic air of McDonald's, because keeping cool was important in Oklahoma and Arkansas. Almost every town had a snow-cone stand where a solo proprietor, normally an elderly gentleman, sold shaved ice drenched with cherry, strawberry, or grape syrup. A party of ants usually staged a hoedown in the sticky parking lot. I did my best to keep the snow-cone operators in business, since I did not see a single child's lemonade stand. Perhaps all the entrepreneurial kids were inside, in front of the air-conditioners, playing *Metal Gear Solid 2* on their PlayStations.

The ditches in one brief stretch were full of litter, as if a garbage bomb had exploded. I decided the person who invented the Adopt-a-Highway program should get a medal, or even be made a knight. The idea was genius, but the execution sometimes was lacking. On the entire trip, I never saw anyone actually picking up trash.

In Arkansas—or so it's been said—"alcohol, tobacco and firearms" equals groceries. But the state did not fit its redneck stereotype. Everyone that I saw had shoes *and* teeth. Yes, there were pickups with camper shells, but not as many as in Arizona. Admittedly, chickens cackled in the front yards of a few mobile homes, but not more frequently than in Oklahoma. My time in Arkansas was like a ride through a long national park; its quiet woods and green pastures beckoned me to return soon.

Abundant wildlife in Arkansas resulted in more road kill. Raccoons were No. 1, with armadillos trailing closely. I paused to examine one highway stain that resembled the face of Alfred E. Newman in *Mad* magazine, complete with freckles and oversized ears. I still had not seen a single live armadillo. No married live ones, either. (Ba-da-bump!)

Roadkill was easy to spot and simple to dodge. That was not the case with the other thorn among the Arkansas roses—dogs. It's time for a few words about them. Dogs injure 4.5 million people per year, send 334,000 to the emergency room, and kill about a dozen. Of course, humans injure and kill *each other* much more frequently. But dogs are part of a biker's life. If you can't handle them, don't take up biking.

I preferred the dogs with high-pitched barks—the sopranos. They were cocky little divas who seldom chased and, when they did, always stopped abruptly at the end of their front yards. They reminded me of the old joke: "How many sopranos does it take to change a light bulb? One: she just holds on and the world revolves around her." In the canine choir, the bass dogs were also safe. Those lumbering, droopy-jowled characters reclined regally in the shade. It was the baritone dogs, as macho as Tom Jones, who were the trouble-makers. Those testosterone-charged juvenile critters, show-offs auditioning for the lead, would go anywhere for a bite of biker.

My pulse went to *prestissimo* when three baritones leaped out of a garage in Lockesburg and bobbed for apples at my heels. I was grateful for a flat stretch of road. Anger and fear fueled a quick sprint and, as I left them behind, I decided that evolution would take care of the dog problem—eventually the entire species would become smarter because the dumb ones all would be killed by trucks on the highways. After 10 or 12 generations, truck- (and bike-) chasing dogs should be extinct. I realized how low my dog-esteem had sunk when I smiled at the sight of two dead mongrels by the road. Then I grew ashamed. After all, that hyperactive Fido may have been a little girl's best friend, or a lonely grandfather's last remaining companion. CBS commentator Andy Rooney said, "The average dog is a nicer person than the average person." It isn't the dogs' fault that nobody taught them not to chase.

I remembered how one sports writer related to our family's grief. "I know what you are going through," he told me. "This may sound inappropriate to you, but I was heartbroken when my dog died." His sincerity was touching. I thought of Will's hand-raised Staffordshire Terrier, Scully, who would gleefully lick the salt from our legs when Will and I returned from sweaty summertime runs in Stillwater. For weeks after the crash, Scully waited patiently by the door for Will to come home. After a few months, a saddened Scully gave up the vigil.

The blue moth sensed my moment of weakness and swooped in for an attack. I resolved to think more kindly of my four-legged adversaries in the future.

Down the road, two jolly, Elizabethan women joined Nicki and me in a store under a rhythmic ceiling fan. The store's owner told the women about our bike adventure, and they stood in open-mouthed amazement. Did they think I was crazy? "No," said one. "Hay-ell yes," said the other.

I met a happy five-year-old girl whose first name was MacBeth. Little MacBeth was as innocent and cheery as early Beatles music. Her hair was pulled back and tied with elastic entwined in four white marbles; her smile shone like a harvest moon. It was clear that I was a mystery to her. In wonderment, she rubbed the white hair on my arms until the woman with her told her to stop. I smiled; MacBeth smiled. I winked my left eye; she closed both of hers. I tugged my ear; she grasped hers. When it was time to go, I gave her a high-five and her little hand felt as cool as a popsicle. MacBeth's eyes lingered on me as if she were looking for guidance. "Keep smiling, young lady," I whispered.

* * *

At midday on my trek toward the second town called Hope on my trip, I went into an amazing series of ups and downs.

Up: I enjoyed a lunch of cheese crackers in a restful city park in the town of Nashville, watching a bare-chested man mowing thick, green grass. I noted that my trip had taken me through San Antonio, Memphis, and now Nashville. None of them are home to the Alamo, Elvis, or the Grand Ole Opry.

Down: I ran over a sharp stone on the shoulder, causing my third flat tire of trip—all on the back wheel.

Up: The flat happened near a side road with a shade tree. I remained remarkably calm, zen-like, and Yoda-esque with a new understanding that all things happen for a reason. After all, changing a tire is not sprocket science.

Down: Nicki was waiting five miles ahead. I wanted to tell her that the flat would delay me, but I couldn't reach her on the cell phone. Two highway patrolmen sped past without stopping.

Up: Two citizens stopped to offer water and sympathy. Then the local game warden volunteered to drive ahead to tell Nicki of my progress. I gratefully accepted. He also suggested that we rest in a store in the historic little town of Washington, and he drove ahead to tell the owners that we were coming. They prepared a special surprise.

Down: I changed the tube, rode two miles, then had another flat in the same tire. This time my serenity was forsaken. All the balls and bats came out of the dugout. I don't know whether it was a hissie fit or a conniption fit, but I threw it. Thankfully no one was around to hear. When a new tube goes flat that quickly, it's either: (1) the tube was bad; (2) the tube was the wrong size; (3) the careless biker over-inflated tube; (4) the clueless biker failed to remove whatever caused the first flat from the inside of the tire; (5) the dumb biker crinkled the new tube when installing it, and the crinkle turned into a wrinkle which ruptured under pressure; (6) the inept biker didn't see the spoke protruding through the wheel into the tube; or (7) some other stupid darn thing.

Up: I convinced myself that the flat was a good thing, because I needed practice in removing the difficult back wheel—and more practice in self-control.

Down: The balls and bats came out of the dugout again when I realized that I had forgotten to get a replacement tube from Nicki; so, my choices were now: (1) patch the tube; (2) walk to where Nicki was waiting; or (3) cry.

Up: I seriously pondered choosing Door No. 3 but decided that the one-mile—I hoped—walk to Nicki would exorcize my anger. After I pushed the bike a half-mile, Nicki appeared, having sensed that something was amiss. For this she will win the coveted SAG-of-the-Year trophy. She was even clever enough to have met me beside a shady driveway where I could install an entire new rear wheel. I decided to apply a Scarlett O'Hara solution: worry about the cause of the flat tomorrow.

Down: Two lion-sized, territory-protecting baritone dogs stormed down the driveway toward me, barking from deep within their angry dog diaphragms, spitting through immense yellow teeth, and churning up gravel with bulldozer paws.

Up: I petted the dogs and sweet-talked them into happiness by explaining the intricacies of bike-tire changing to them while replacing the wheel. My new canine friends reclined in the shade like teddy bears and watched me hand-pump air into the new tube.

Then, when I hopped on my bike and pedaled down the road, the dogs resumed their hostility and gave chase again, like World War I British and German soldiers resuming their shooting after the famous Christmas truce near Laventie in northern France.

More Up: The ride continued, albeit two hours behind schedule. In a comfortable store in the peaceful town of Washington—site of the Confederate state government from 1863 to 1865—Nicki and I received good directions from a friendly truck driver who was waiting for his horses to be shod. We also ate delicious fried pies provided free of charge by the pleasant sisters who ran the store. While in town, we also saw a magnolia tree that was planted in 1839 and was now as tall and wide as a Chicago hotel.

"Up" won in overtime.

* * *

Later, I wanted to know more about that 1914 World War I incident. As reported by Anthea Hall in the *London Daily Telegraph* in December, 1966, it began when a German soldier sang the Welsh hymn, "All Through the Night," then other voices joined in. The British soldiers responded with "Good King Wenceslas." Private Harold Diffey recalled: "We came out of our trenches, shook hands with the Germans, swapped fags (cigarettes) and had a good smoke together. Of course, we realized we were in a most extraordinary position, wishing each other Happy Christmas and shooting each other the next day. After 30 minutes, a major appeared, yelling, 'You came out here to fight the Huns, not to make friends with them!' So our lads reluctantly returned to the trenches, followed by a salvo from our artillery which ended the episode."

The dogs and I were at war, but there was similar honor in the combat.

* * *

On the road into Hope, I saw no signs proclaiming it as the birthplace of Bill Clinton. It reminded me of the way the Oklahoma town of Hollis seemingly ignored the legacy of coach Darrell Royal. Nicki and I finally found our way to the president's understated boyhood home. Later, we spotted a large Clinton sign on the interstate.

I decided that President Clinton and football coach Barry Switzer may have been brothers separated in childhood. I considered myself knowledgeable on the matter because I once worked with Barry and twice voted for Clinton. The coach and the president are both good ole Arkansas boys with humble beginnings, an amazing ability to relate to people at all levels of society, and world-class charisma. They are also, considering their status, remarkably human. Coach Switzer, who is as loyal as anyone I have ever known, was a hero of Will Hancock's. In the eulogy, when I jokingly said that Will could have used his 1,400 SAT score to qualify twice to play football for the Sooners, Barry held up three fingers and winked. "Three times," he mouthed to me. I needed a smile at that moment, and the coach delivered it. Barry also took time to track down Nate Hancock on the telephone, which gave Nate immediate comfort and instant celebrity status at his workplace after it was announced over the intercom: "Nate, Barry Switzer is on the phone for you."

I wished for a similar VIP resume when I arrived at the Hope community swimming pool precisely at 5:01 p.m. Unfortunately, the pool had closed precisely at 5:00 and the manager wouldn't let me swim because the lifeguards had gone home. (How they got out of there so fast, I'll never know.) I explained to her that I had ridden my bicycle 85 miles and needed only three minutes of cool therapy for the legs. I offered to wade only up to my waist, to waive the city of all liability, to give the manager free Gatorade. She politely but stubbornly refused, saying the pool would be open again tomorrow. The balls and bats nearly came out of the dugout again when she asked, in a sweet drawl, "Where y'all from?" I was in no mood for politicking. But Yoda carried the day.

Five 80-year-old women were doing what appeared to be ballet in the pool. I should have joined their water aerobics class, because doing so might have shooed away the stalking blue moth, which now camped on my shoulder, hoping to feed on my impatience. I rinsed the moth away with a hot shower at the Hope Fairgrounds, where campers gathering in preparation for the upcoming watermelon festival reminded me of vendors arriving early for the Final Four.

The watermelon festival is as important to Hope as the Final Four is to a host city such as Atlanta—local citizens are energized, friendships are nourished among pilgrims who return every year, and hotels and restaurants profit handsomely. One of those Atlanta people, Hyatt hotels vice-president Tim Lindgren, gave us the support we needed after the crash. He climbed to our side of the fence in a 1981 tragedy. He was general manager of the Hyatt Regency Kansas City when two skywalks collapsed in the hotel lobby, killing 114 people. When I thanked him for his thoughtful deeds, he said, "NCAA people were very kind to me back in 1981. I'm just passing it along."

Tim, who spent his college days in a humble way as student-manager for coach Jack Hartman's Southern Illinois University basketball team, was a member of the bike-ride e-mail corps. On this hot night in Arkansas, I couldn't have imagined the treat that Tim had in store for Nicki and me when we made it to Georgia. But more about that later.

Andie, I hope you enjoyed the silliness of the ups and downs today. Laughing made me feel guilty; I thought it was okay to appreciate a sunset, but I was worried that humor was inappropriate because your grandmother and I were in such a sad world. Oh, but your dad was funny, too. He inherited it from his two grandmothers. Judging from your happy smile, I believe that you received the same gene.

7
The Road Ahead

DAY 24

DOG DAYS

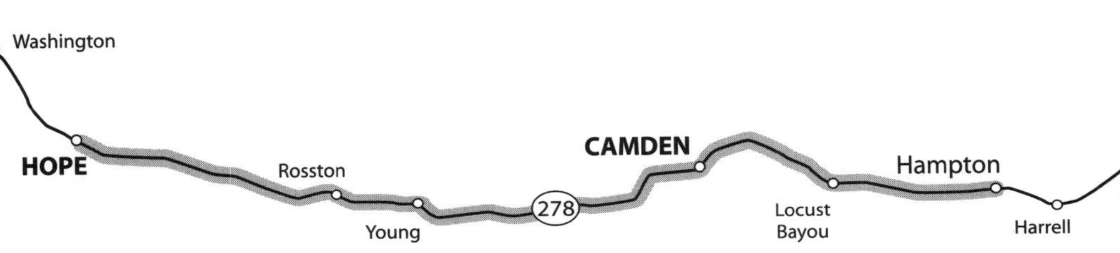

Date: Tuesday, August 7.

Distance traveled: 77 miles in Arkansas, from Hope to Hampton.

Total miles completed: 1,837.

Starting temperature and time: 78 degrees at 5 a.m.

Finishing temperature and time: 96 at 12:30 p.m.

Food: breakfast—toast, banana; lunch—ham sandwich; dinner—chicken livers, baked potato, salad, snow cone.

Additional fuel: cheese crackers, Pringles, one gallon of water, two quarts of Gatorade, one root beer.

Song stuck in my head: "Smile, and the world smiles with you, sing a song. Don't be weary, just be cheery, all day long. Whenever your trials, your troubles and your cares, seem to be more than you can really bear, smile, and the world smiles with you, sing a song." ("Smile," written by James O. Scott around 1910; recorded by Lewis James, 1918.)

Overnight: Silver Eagle RV Park, Hampton.

We drove back to southwest Oklahoma for four days, to attend the celebration of Hobart's 100th birthday. My dad had been there for the town's 25th and 50th anniversary parties, and my brother Joe and I had helped plan the 75th. There was no way I could miss gala number 100. Nicki and I enjoyed being with old friends, saw a dandy a parade, and, best of all, spent quality time with Nate.

We hadn't seen Nate since May, when he stopped in Kansas City en route to Colorado where he and Karen visited the site of the airplane crash and thanked the local people who had helped out on January 27. That night, he had been given a lousy battlefield promotion to Son No. 1, and it had not been easy for him. But he was coping as best he could—just like the rest of us.

We were sad to send Nate back to Connecticut after the festivities in Hobart, but it was with fresh legs and a renewed soul that I returned to the biking adventure on a bright morning in Hope.

DAY 24

"I told a triathlete about your ride," e-mailed Tim Lindgren, our friend from the Atlanta Hyatt hotel. "He is concerned about your shoes. Cycling shoes with clip-on pedals are a must. He thinks you should buy some. Also, he feels you need to eat more fruit. He hates your diet, especially the Vienna franks! He says to raise or lower your handle bars to stop the numbness in your hands. He thinks your clothes should be tight-fitting. He's looking at the pictures you've been e-mailing, and he thinks anything that lowers wind resistance is a plus."

The triathlete was right on all counts. My diet was, indeed, lousy. But I was having so much fun. The hours on the bike each day were a perfect excuse to gorge myself on comfort food. And besides, all the exercise was keeping the pounds off.

Today was the dog-iest day of the ride so far. The more houses, the more dogs. And dogs seemed more common than mailboxes in this part of Arkansas. I refined my canine-defense system, opting to remove my helmet and talk to them in soft, Jimmy Stewart tones. That approach seemed to be succeeding. Perhaps I was becoming the Dog Whisperer.

I was now cycling through a part of Arkansas where the blacks nearly outnumbered the whites. In the Two Bayou Country Store, I asked a white woman about race relations: She said, "We all do just fine out here in the country. In town, there's trouble. Town people can't get along. Country people can."

In one pasture near Rosston, a dozen cattle clustered in the shade, swatting flies with their tails. One mule stood all alone under another tree. It was hoofed-animal segregation. Human pettiness was nearby, too. Spray-painted in the highway were these words: "A Thief 500 Yards Ahead." Then, "A Thief Here" with an arrow pointing to a house. A woman wearing a powder-blue bonnet sat in the yard, shelling peas. She bore no resemblance to Bonnie Parker. I wheeled over to her, said "howdy," and asked about the message in the road.

She glanced up at me, nodded, and then lowered her eyes and calmly returned to her shelling, as if lanky bikers in tight shorts rode into her front yard every day. Her only visible reaction came from her pointy cheekbones, which seemed to turn pink.

All she said was, "Don't know nothin' about no thief."

An awkward silence followed, and it was clear that the conversation was over. I decided that she may have been cousins with those taciturn Connecticut Yankees from back in the California desert. Perhaps *CSI: Arkansas* could investigate the alleged thievery, but not *CSI: Biker*.

People were stirring. A man ran a chainsaw. Another rode a horse. A third repaired a fence. But by noon, a Tom Sawyer sleepiness blanketed the world. The sky disappeared in a haze. Even the cicadas seemed to be on siesta. Horses lay on their sides. Floppy-eared dogs raised their heads and woofed half-heartedly as I rode past. Maybe my legend as Dog Whisperer was beginning to precede me? More likely, it was the weather. Englishmen may go out in the midday sun, but not Arkansas mad dogs. Myself, I was tranquilized by the calmness.

Our directories listed no campgrounds in Hampton, today's destination. The only motel was as musty as Scrooge's vault. We didn't expect the Ritz Carlton, but hoped for better than the Pits Charlatan. Two cheerful women in a convenience store laughed with us.

"I sure wouldn't stay there," said one about our prospective lodging for the night. "Oh, Lawdie, me neither," said the other. Nicki and I sadly considered driving to a motel in Fordyce, 28 miles north.

"Wait, do you have an RV?" said the first woman. "I think Mister Larry takes overnighters at his place just north of the snow cone stand."

North of the snow cone stand sounded like an ideal place for relaxing. Indeed, we found an oasis—an RV park on a shady hillside, with sparkling showers, an e-mail connection, laundry, and even cable television. The two employees, a 35-ish man and a spry older woman, were uncommonly kind. Their warm hospitality reminded me of the response which we received after one newspaper story mentioned that Will had been preparing a CD of college fight songs for his dad when the plane crashed. Within a week, we received seven cassette tapes of fight songs. Hail, I thought, to the victors.

I didn't feel so much like a victor on this evening, though. Tomorrow morning, I would lose my Support And Guidance. Nicki, my invaluable SAG, was heading back to Kansas City for the start of the school year and taking Roci with her.

Before the airplane crash, she and I were accustomed to separation, as my NCAA schedule kept me away from home 100 nights each year. But this was different, because we had been such close teammates on the bike ride. Each day after the dawn spilled over into morning, I began to look forward to her pulling alongside me in the minivan, rolling down the passenger-side window, and giving me a smile and a wave. Usually she would say, "Great news, I found the NPR station!" I eagerly anticipated our picnic lunches and the stories about her day.

We were about to be apart for the longest time since the airplane crash. The road ahead would be different without her. But, like Will, she would be in a good place (home), and I would see her again soon (she would fly to Savannah for the finish, if there was to be a finish).

In addition to life without Nicki, the trip would be different without Roci. I had become accustomed to turning off the air-conditioner, unzipping Roci's tent and sleeping to the cool rhythm of the night. The rest of the way, I would be staying in antiseptic motels. To wean me from the lip-smacking meals that Nicki prepared in the trailer, we decided to eat out for our last night together. The dinner of chicken livers—with a snow cone for desert—was a fitting farewell party.

Andie, we saw the best of human nature after your dad died. You will hear much about the national parks and oceans wide and blue, but God's greatest creation—by far—is people.

DAY 25

RICE PADDIES

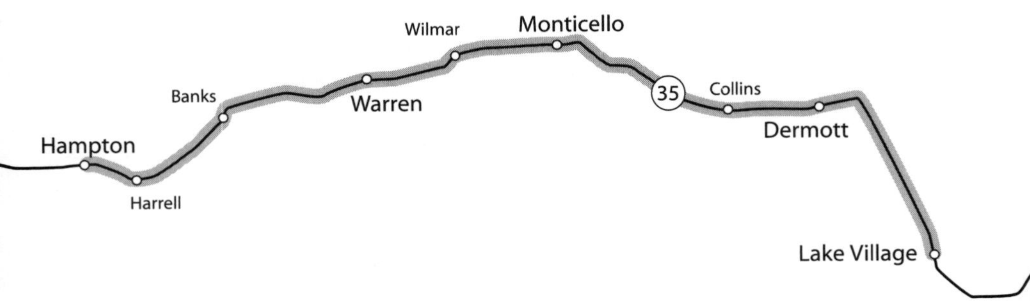

Date: *Wednesday, August 8.*

Distance traveled: *87 miles in Arkansas, from Hampton to Lake Village.*

Total miles completed: *1,924.*

Miles to go: *fewer than yesterday.*

Starting temperature and time: *79 degrees at 5 a.m.*

Finishing temperature and time: *95 at 2 p.m.*

Food: *breakfast—toast, banana; lunch—"taco roll"; dinner—sweet and sour chicken, fried rice, egg roll, Tootsie Roll Pop.*

Additional fuel: *cheese crackers, chocolate milkshake, popcorn, two gallons of water, one gallon of Gatorade, one root beer.*

Song stuck in my head: *"Arkansas, Arkansas, I just love ole Arkansas. Love my ma, love my pa, but I just love ole Arkansas." ("Arkansas," from the musical Big River by Roger Miller, 1985.)*

Overnight: *Ramada Express, Lake Village.*

After a tearful goodbye with Nicki, I departed for the day's ride. Nicki handed the SAG baton to 71-year-old Jim Gantert, a retired printer from Kansas City who would be with me the next three days. Gantert's lovely wife, Joanne, had recently lost a heroic five-year battle with cancer, so he was on our side of the fence.

Jim wasn't around to come to my aid this morning when three dogs erupted into a frenzy of barking as I rode past. They had been sleeping near the road's shoulder; the bike startled them. Although the full moon illuminated the countryside like Yankee Stadium ready for a night game, I had not seen the dogs. I screamed in terror, which frightened the canines and sent them yelping and scurrying in the other direction. The furor awakened two more dogs in the adjacent yard, and they dashed to the roadside to examine the situation. Those dogs woke the neighbor dogs in succession. The dog domino effect continued for a mile.

Further down the road, a peaceful cemetery guarded by a huge magnolia in front of the stately Ebenezer Baptist Church seemed to cry out, "Stop and recharge your batteries here," as I passed. So I screeched to a halt and walked across the dew-covered grass to a tombstone from the 1850s, where I sat and tried to enjoy a snack. But the sound of crunching cheese crackers was utterly incompatible with the silent surroundings. I put the crackers away, relaxed, and talked to Will for the first time since the climb up to the Mogollon Rim back in Arizona.

"Your mom is driving back home right now," I whispered. "She will go through Little Rock, which will make her cry because she'll remember that you lived there when you met Karen. She'll remember when we visited the both of you and saw that you were in love. I'm not sure that I can make the rest of this trip without her. She's been gone only two hours, and I already miss her like crazy—just like we miss you.

"Did you ever drive down here from Little Rock? You would like it. The trees are beautiful and it's peaceful. Time moves slower, and slow time is good.

"You know, this cemetery reminds me of the one outside Reidsville, North Carolina, where my great-grandmother is buried. You found her when you were doing that genealogy work, remember? Did I ever tell you that she committed suicide? She was 51 years old; golly, I'll be 51 next month. I think the blue moth got the best of her. I guess she and all of our other ancestors are with you today. Man, I wish I could interview them. But I guess there'll be time for that later."

There was no sound except my voice. But the dew, the grass, the white church, the slate tombstones, and the trees seemed to creep closer to me. I relaxed in their warmth and went to sleep. Soon a truck scooted past on the highway and woke me up. I knew it was time to move on.

A mousy little man—barely thicker than a pencil, really—was directing traffic around a construction site near the Saline River east of Warren. He bade me to stop while a yellow Caterpillar road grader smoothed the surface.

"I shore hope today is better than yestiddy," he said. "I spilt my Gatorade and went four hours without nothin' to drink."

Before I could ask why he hadn't asked other workers for water, he drilled me with laser eyes.

"Sir, are you a Christian? Those big guys pouring concrete back at the bridge laugh at me because I am a Christian. I tell them, 'Would you like it if I physically dragged you to hell? Dragged you kickin' and screamin' to hell? Well, you're doin' it to yourself if you ain't a Christian.'"

I wanted to ask if he thought that non-Christian people with good hearts could also find eternal peace, but decided that I didn't have time for the graphic and lengthy sermon that was sure to follow. The Cat' rumbled past, and I followed in its protective cloud of dust.

On the bike I enjoyed the freedom to strap my feet to the pedals and ride away. Although I was more grounded than in months, focused on nature and in the simple process of moving from point to point each day, on the other hand—and I regretted this—I was not attached to humanity. I was free to flit from person to person like the governor at a cocktail party, not truly involved in any life except my own. I could talk to someone for five minutes, then move on if the conversation became even mildly oppressive. Others' problems were not mine; I was an island, merely an observer of life and not a helper or confidant or teammate.

I hadn't helped that diminutive flagman, and I thought about him for a long time. He was reluctant to ask the big guys for water and yet unafraid to promise them hellfire. I had been inhibited myself before running gave me strength; he had found his own muscle in rock-solid Christianity.

Just past the Seven Devils Swamp east of Monticello, an assisting tailwind propelled me down onto the Mississippi River delta—a thousand-mile billiard table with the big river snaking through the middle—to the town of Dermott.

"Don't put your foot down in Dermott," a man had told me yesterday.

"It's a bad town," a woman had also said. "I'd ride 30 miles out of the way, if I was you, rather than going through that nasty Dermott."

"Why?" I asked.

"It's a black town," was her reply.

"How long since you were there?" I wondered.

"I ain't been over that way in quite a spell. It ain't no place you want to visit."

In protest, I put my size-13 feet all over Dermott, almost dancing as I met cheery people and, yes, a few others who wanted nothing to do with me. Dermott was poor but clean, small but lively, tree-lined and rustic—in short, pretty much like all the other charming Arkansas towns I had visited. I enjoyed a 98-cent "taco roll" for lunch (a small tortilla wrapped around beef and deep fried), read a church bulletin, smelled the barbeque, drank the water—and tried to understand the local dialect, laughing with people as they tried to comprehend mine and celebrating together when we finally communicated.

"Whaccha gawn be haffin' foh draynk wiccha tawccho roll?" asked the shopkeeper.

"Uh, I'll have water, please," I responded.

"Hain't gawt nooh eeysse."

"That'll be fine, I don't like ice anyway."

Leaving Dermott, I committed myself to getting a handle on the relationship between blacks and whites in the rural South. I decided I would tackle Jerusalem later. Then Auburn versus Alabama. Then Itchy and Scratchy. I had always tried to be a peacemaker at the NCAA; maybe I could work on it with strangers as well.

If whites stand out from blacks hereabouts, one thing is certain: all bikers look alike. At least a dozen people mistook me for someone they knew. "Don't you remember me, from the Mini-Mart last spring?" one woman pleaded today. "You was real nice to me, and I showed you to the Gatorade cooler."

I had never been near Southeast Arkansas before, much less to the Mini-Mart. She refused to believe me. Her confusion was understandable because there were plenty of bikers on the delta. This road seemed to be the Piccadilly Circus of bicycling.

Near Monticello, a construction flagman said, “Oregon come through here yesterday on bikes.” He seemed perfectly comfortable with the three rings of sweat discoloring the armpits of his shirt. “A half-dozen of ’em. Had a bunch of vans following them. Headed for Florida.” A woman said a solo biker passed through Dermott last week, bound from California to Florida. “But he was a lot younger than you.”

Bikers used this route because it led to the U.S. 82 Greenville Bridge, one of only four that span the Mississippi River in the 500 miles between Baton Rouge and Memphis. I would cross it tomorrow. Now I was in flat country, making good time. For the first time since West Texas, I stayed on the big front chain-ring all afternoon.

Cypress trees, their knees resting in turgid swamps, lined the lowlands. Frogs leapt into the black water. The cotton was chest high. A rice paddy—I’d never seen one before—drew my attention, and I strolled off the road to inspect it. As I walked in tall Bermuda grass on what I thought was a solid dike, I suddenly plunged into muddy water up to my right knee. Again, there was the roller-coaster: we swing happily along and then abruptly fall into intractable muck.

I slogged back to the bike and felt like an idiot, riding down the road with one white leg and one muddy brown one. At the end of the day, after showering away the muck which had dried into a chocolate-colored cast on my leg, I slid happily into the Ramada Express swimming pool in Lake Village, joining two ninth-grade Baptists who were part of a youth group ministering to the local church kids. I’d seen so many Baptist churches in the area, I decided they were preaching to the choir, like Mormons sending missionaries to Salt Lake City.

One of the youngsters was interested in the bike ride. “Where do you go to the bathroom?” he asked me.

“Anywhere I want to,” I replied.

They were shocked.

So was I, by the quiet dignity of the little town of Lake Village, which is located on the shore of Chicot Lake, an oxbow that was left behind thousands of years ago when the Mississippi River changed courses. It was now the county seat—sort of by default. Two earlier county-seat towns had been swallowed by the muddy waters before the 1830s, when the commissioners wised up. They moved the village to higher ground, away from the capricious river. I understood. I was trying to ride my bike to safety—away from the similarly unpredictable blue moth.

Tomorrow I would cross the Mississippi and begin a trek across the heart of the old south. Everything I had done to this point—the desert, the Rockies, the Oklahoma hills—was in preparation for the heat and humidity of Mississippi, Alabama, and Georgia. "You cannot imagine it, you cannot prepare for it, you cannot live normally in it," a friend from the Southeastern Conference office in Birmingham had told me before the ride. When I protested that I was from Oklahoma and knew hot weather, he said, "Believe me, you do not understand *this* weather."

Andie, those people didn't like the town of Dermott because they didn't understand the people who lived there. Hate and ignorance go hand in hand. You may encounter people who don't like you, but usually it will be because they don't know you. Let others into your heart, and in doing so you will conquer their negativity.

DAY 26

THE GREENVILLE BRIDGE

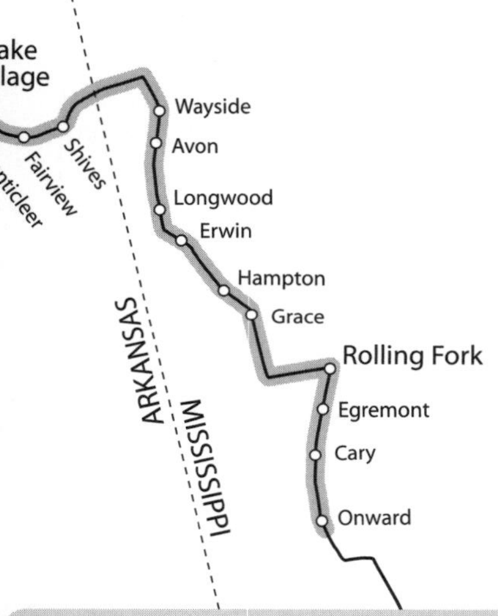

Date: Thursday, August 9.

Distance traveled: 74 miles, from Lake Village, Arkansas, to near Onward, Mississippi.

Total miles completed: 1,998.

Miles to go: we're gettin' there, slowly but surely.

Starting temperature and time: 79 degrees at 5:15 a.m.

Finishing temperature and time: 94 at 1:15 p.m.

Food: breakfast—biscuit, dry waffle, banana, gnats; dinner—broccoli, carrots, cottage cheese, peaches, salad, pizza, one-half Miller Lite.

Additional fuel: 13 Fritos, two gallons of water, four quarts of Gatorade, one root beer.

Song stuck in my head: Man: "He rides for days on end with just a pony for a friend." Woman: "I sure am feelin' sorry for the pony." ("Farmer and the Cowman," from Oklahoma!, Rodgers and Hammerstein, 1943.)

Overnight: Motel 6, Vicksburg.

A surly layer of gray clouds swept low over the delta at first light this morning; the air was damp and breezy, reminding me of Huntington Beach. A more threatening blanket of fog hovered down near ground level, as I rode through a cloud of gnats, getting a mouthful. Later, when I glanced at myself in a mirror, my face looked like someone had splattered black paint on it.

I had slipped out of the hotel room before SAG Jim awakened. I wanted to cross the Rubicon alone. Day had barely broken when I arrived at the Greenville Bridge, a mile-long span 10 stories above the brown, gurgling Mississippi River. I shifted into granny gear, hunched over, and started up the old two-lane structure as the wind howled. Keeping the bike upright was as difficult as walking across a creek on a fallen oak.

There was barely room for two cars to meet, and no shoulder outside the white line. The bridge surface was waffle-iron rough and the pitch so steep that I could barely see anything behind or in front of me. I was like a soldier crawling on his belly up a hill. The lack of visibility was a metaphor—the past was gone, the future uncertain. I was trapped with only one place to go: forward, one pedal stroke at a time. As fast as possible.

A vehicle's headlights popped into view behind me. I gritted my teeth, held my breath and guided the bike to the white line, fearing my right elbow would scrape the superstructure that formed a cage up and over the pavement. The car slowed to a crawl and then gingerly zipped past me. Seven other cars and seven trucks passed me during the 10 minutes that I spent on the bridge, each going my way, each veering cautiously into the left lane to skirt what they probably least expected to see: an orange-and-yellow bicycle wobbling in the traffic lane. By what could only have been divine intervention, no other vehicles were approaching when they passed. One truck driver gave the extended "You idiot" honk. Come to think of it, I *was* an idiot to be riding alone on that bridge. When it opened in 1940, the bridge was considered an engineering marvel, but over the years cars and trucks had outgrown it. Vehicles—like people—are wider today.

I will always carry a love-hate relationship with that grandfatherly bridge; I regret that it will be torn down after a new version opens downstream in 2007. New replaces the old, that's the proper rhythm. Maybe I'll come back and ride across it again before it vanishes. Nicki suggests that maybe I won't.

The fearsome Greenville Bridge symbolized the blissful ignorance that I brought to the bicycle ride. Had I known how narrow the bridge would be, how steep, how rough, I'd have ridden in fear every day since California. Perhaps I would never even have left Huntington Beach. Likewise, our lives would have been stunted if we had worried every time Will or Nate boarded an airplane. The root of inner peace is accepting what you don't know.

With great relief I surfed down off the bridge and into the seventh state on my journey. I sat on a concrete pad beneath the "Welcome to Mississippi" sign to let my heart rate settle. The sign creaked and groaned in the stiff wind.

"People in Miss-ippy won't help you none," a tiny white-haired Arkansas woman had told me. "I broke down on Highway 1 over there, and no one stopped. They sorry people." Other folks also had little use for the land of Elvis, William Faulkner, and Archie Manning. "Be careful," a gentle-faced man had said over biscuits early this morning. "There's crazy people in Mississippi."

Those folks were like the Texas woman who warned me to steer clear of Oklahoma. Some people look suspiciously at those across a state line or across a racial barrier or beyond the fence that separates those touched by death from those merely observing. Strangers watching Nicki and me in the months after the crash would have judged us to be odd—but they could not have understood unless they had climbed that fence themselves. So I ventured on into Mississippi with an open mind.

The morning headwind whipping through a dry cornfield sounded like a thousand starched Easter dresses on parade. When studying the map yesterday, I had envisioned Mississippi Highway 1 to be an idyllic path through pastoral fields and small towns. Instead, it was Times Square in a hurricane. Traffic was bumper to bumper on the sliver of highway between the tiny communities of Wayside and Avon. Four times, I was certain that pickups were going to hit me, and once I bailed off the road to avoid a big truck with a passenger-side mirror that stuck out like one of Alfalfa's ears. When three yellow buses lumbered past, I finally understood why there were so many vehicles in this rural land: school had started.

The parking lot of the Mattox Store near Avon High School was jammed with young people. They goosed each other, danced, hugged, kissed, and laughed like—well, like high school kids. Nearly every one sipped a Coca-Cola. Some smoked cigarettes.

Most of the girls' shirts, like the Grinch's heart, were three sizes too small. The youngsters darted around like euglena on a petri dish, enjoying the warm breeze, the excitement of the first day of school, and each other.

Shoppers at the pleasant Mattox Store could purchase everything from hardware to canned goods to ribs, sausage, and boudin. Uncertain what the latter was, I bought a Gatorade, then took it outside to watch the bedlam from a creaky wooden bench while playing keep-away with a brown ant. I spotted one grownup among the beehive of students and asked him about boudin (pronounced BOO-dan).

"Gotta be a coon-ass to make it right," said the 30-ish man with a belly that made him look eight months pregnant and a smile that suddenly seemed too friendly. "It's peppers, onions, and meat wrapped in pig intestine. They make it right down in south Loosiana. This stuff here in Mississippi ain't worth shit."

While I considered purchasing a sample of the Cajun specialty just for the experience, the man gave me a long look that chilled me despite the toasty morning air. Then he asked, "Are you carrying a gun?"

"A gun? Excuse me?" I was certain I had heard him incorrectly.

"No gun, huh? That's good," he replied. "Come ride with me for a while. I'll show you some things."

Tiny geysers of sweat erupted from my forehead. I'm pretty sure my heart stopped. My thumbs tingled as if pricked; something wicked was coming. The word "Deliverance" chased everything else from my brain. But then I did some quick thinking and explained that, while I certainly appreciated the kindness, my 71-year-old friend was driving along the highway and would be looking for me.

Scratching his ample sides, the man wouldn't give up, "Com'on, you'll enjoy it. I'll show you old cotton gins and freakin' awesome vacant farmhouses and nice country down by the river where you'd swear you were the only man alive."

His intentions could have been honorable, but his manner said not. Thankfully, I felt safe and snug in the midst of the squirming school kids. As they jived and spat and giggled, none of the young people had any idea of the drama playing out on that weathered bench, but they were safeguarding me like a squadron of fighter planes around a World War II bomber.

"You're gonna miss a good time, but have it your way. I guess I'll git on down to work," he said. Then he climbed into his pickup and drove off.

I saddled up and rode away from the comforting chaos of Avon, expecting Pregnant Man to pull alongside any minute. I formulated an elaborate battle plan that involved my water bottles, cell-phone antenna, and spare tire tube. Thankfully—for him, I said to myself with a fool's swagger—he never reappeared. I continued southward, plunging ever deeper into the warm, fertile, sleeping delta.

Major problems—such as large men with cloudy purposes—have a silver lining; they overshadow smaller challenges. When the house is on fire, bugs on the rose bushes become inconsequential. Now, with the threat of Pregnant Man behind me, I noticed the headwind again. Despite the flat terrain, I could manage only 10 miles per hour.

"Wind only blows here when it's time to spray the cotton or rice," said a smiling, cigar-chomping man as I caught my breath in the quaint, little Grace Farmers Store. "We get up at 4 a.m. to avoid it."

I responded, "Well, I was up at four yesterday, and I seen five 'coons crossing the highway back yonder."

Good grief, my grammar had gone South. English-teacher Nicki would have been shocked. But despite the scare from Pregnant Man, I found this particular South to be a lovely place. At one point, I passed within a half-mile of the Mississippi River. I couldn't see it because of tall, protective levees, but a damp, fishy aroma gave it away. The pink flowers on the crape myrtle bushes looked like candy ready to be plucked. It was a green land of plenty.

The soaring cotton was impressive, but not to everyone.

"Too tall," a farmer said. "Machines won't be able to get into it right."

"Surely a tall crop is a good sign," I said.

"Hay-ell, yes, it's a good crop," he said in agreement. "That's because the gub-mint promised us all $600 per acre if we didn't make no cotton crop this year. So we just kinda half-assed planted cotton and, look here, we got ourselves a bumper crop. It don't pay to cheat. Or even think about it."

I dallied in the cool store and pondered cheating. I had once been a world-class crook myself. When I was in fourth grade in

1959, schools in Hobart dismissed for "cotton pickin'." Children slung burlap bags over their shoulders and trooped to the fields to help farmers pull the puffy cotton from the plants. When classes resumed, teachers asked students how much cotton they had picked.

"Sixteen pounds," I said. It was a lie. Being the son of a town-dwelling publisher, I never pulled a boll in my life; I used cotton-pickin' week to play football tournaments alone in my front yard while most of the other kids labored in the dirt. But I wanted to be a part of the group, and so I invented a farmer's life for myself. The teacher phoned my father, an old school chum, to congratulate him on finally putting his son to work in the fields. My embarrassed dad didn't spare the rod that evening. Nonetheless, even into adulthood, I continued occasionally to use small fibs when cornered.

However, since the crash, I had been burdened by a heavy sense of honor, perhaps because I thought Will might be watching. Nicki—a woman of Victorian ethics before—was even more of a fanatic for honesty and for treating people kindly.

It wasn't kind of me to have left without waking SAG Jim this morning. I knew he would be worried, and it turned out that he was now criss-crossing this corner of the delta, looking for me. He put 150 miles on his Civic and even filed a missing biker's report with the county sheriff. Jim finally located me relaxing on the russet earth near a cotton patch. I had been lulled to sleep by the wind blowing through the fields, which now sounded like elderly patrons applauding politely for a matinee opera.

I rested again at noon in the tiny community of Onward, Mississippi. Old gentlemen sat on benches on the wide, shady front porch of the Teddy Bear Store, picking their teeth and allowing the hot breeze to fend off the suffocating heat. The building's wood floor, high ceilings, and dusty shelves seemed little changed from 1902, when Theodore Roosevelt had visited the store on a hunting trip. The hunting wasn't good that day, so locals tied up a bear for Roosevelt to shoot. But Teddy refused to kill the defenseless animal. The *New York Times* picked up the story, and the *Washington Post* ran a cartoon of the president and the bear; later someone created a stuffed animal and called it Teddy's bear. Now a couple of token teddy bears—the state toy of Mississippi, by the way—were on display in the store, but any real, live ursine Mississippians were long gone from the wide patch of woods lining the hills that shimmered in heat waves above the delta.

SAG Jim drove the Civic with the air-conditioner turned off in order to share the full experience with me. "You know," he said, "like those people in Spain who used to whip themselves." Later, when we fellow flagellants toured the Civil War battlefield in Vicksburg, I thought about all the parents who lost sons in the fight. Their all-consuming sorrow reached across the years to penetrate my defenses, and the blue moth swept in.

After the pain eased, I compared those Civil-War families to ours in 21st-century America and decided that we lead remarkably good lives. Our family had taken its good life for granted before we lost Will. I wanted to shout "Don't make the same mistake" to everyone I saw.

Andie, today's lesson is simple. No matter how lonely or tired you are, nor how hot it is outside, never get into a car with a stranger. Period.

The Boll Weevil

Since I crossed the Texas Panhandle, I had been seeing strange contraptions that resembled green plastic soda bottles on sticks. Actually, these were the final weapons in a battle against one of the most destructive natural predators in American agricultural history. Throughout the cotton belt, farmers celebrate a victory that their grandparents had considered an impossibility: the eradication of the boll weevil.

Boll weevils entered the United States from Mexico in the 1890s, well before NAFTA was signed. They're tiny pests—four would fit on your thumbnail—but, with the ease of an army of Poulan Weed Eaters, they destroyed nearly every inch of cotton in their path. How? The weevil poked a hole in the cotton pod, or boll, with its snout. Then it laid an egg in each boll. The eggs became larva, which ate the bolls. King Cotton was history.

Boll weevils wiped out entire family businesses. Not only were cotton farmers victimized, but so too were the people who worked for them. And the people who owned shops patronized by those farmers and workers. And the sales people who called on those stores. And so on down the food chain.

Some cynics believed that the government could have eradicated Mr. Weevil sooner, but didn't because the plague benefited certain important constituents. Among the non-urban myths were these:

• Oil producers wanted the weevils to survive because they devoured whole cotton crops, rendering the land virtually valueless. Beleaguered farmers then sold their land to oil men—cheaply.

• Cattlemen treasured the bugs for the same reason.

• Big farmers loved the weevils because they could afford to use poisons such as arsenic, which were not economical for small farmers. Every time a small farmer sold out, an ambulance-chasing corporate operation was there to take over.

• Farm-chemical manufacturers, applicators, and dealers wanted to strike a balance—kill a few of the weevils, but not all of them. That way the farmers would buy more chemicals the next year.

The conspiracy theories weren't true—I hope—but they flourished just as the boll weevil did. In the meantime, farmers tried everything to kill the weevils. They set traps, imported weevil-eating bugs and, of course, sprayed insecticides. Those poisons also killed other kinds of bugs and more than a few people. Oklahoma farmer Uriel Dempsey wrote in his book, *Boll Weevil Alley*, "Oh, they killed a few [farm] hands with poisons, but they just gave them quiet funerals and replaced them."

Finally, in a terrific show of unity in the mid-1990s, cotton farmers agreed to wage their version of jihad against the insects. State by state, they voted to tax themselves and to fight the weevils by applying insecticides approved by the Environmental Protection Agency. The Oklahoma Boll Weevil Eradication Organization (OBWEO) used a sophisticated computer program to monitor the status of the insects. Those green pop bottles on sticks were actually boll weevil traps. Unlike earlier weapons in the war, these traps weren't designed to wipe out the population. Instead, weevils found in the bottles indicated that they were living in the adjacent fields, and the crop-dusting airplanes were hustled back into action.

By end of 2001, thanks to the coordinated, multi-state spraying program, boll weevils had been eradicated in most counties across the cotton belt.

DAY 27

THICK GREEN SYRUP

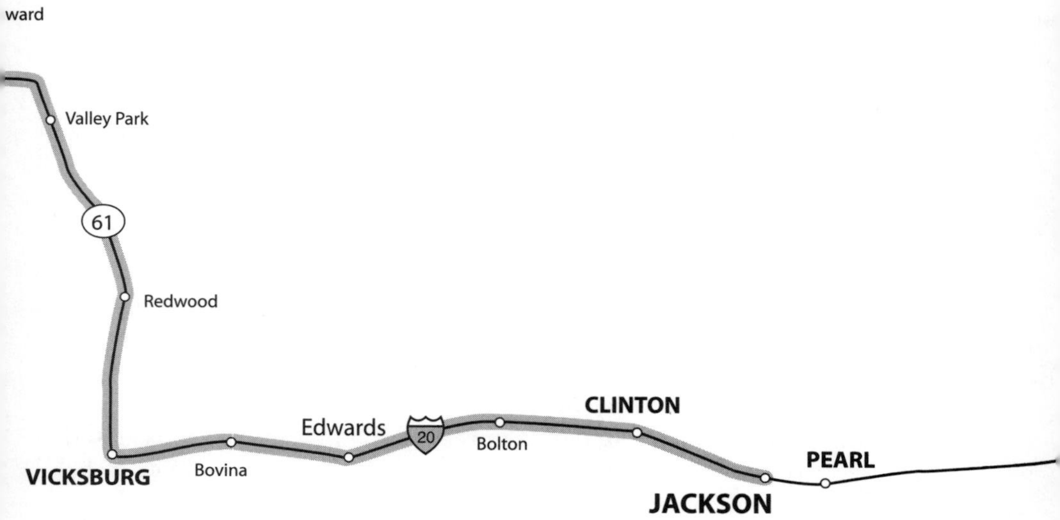

Date: Friday, August 10.
Distance traveled: 78 miles in Mississippi, from near Onward to Jackson.
Total miles completed: 2,076.
Starting temperature and time: 72 degrees at 4:45 a.m.
Finishing temperature and time: 85 at 1 p.m.
Food: breakfast—toast, banana; second breakfast—sausage biscuit; dinner—pizza.
Additional fuel: three gallons of water, cheese crackers, five quarts of Gatorade, 37 Fritos, one root beer.
Song stuck in my head: no song today.
Overnight: Ramada Inn Express, Jackson.

After my experience yesterday, I was leery of any bridge. Any crossing—over a river or over a fence to another world—portended danger. And so I worried about crossing the Yazoo River. But it turned out to be a dud, like Y2K. Besides, SAG Jim was determined that I not cross this bridge alone, so he puttered along behind me in the Civic, which reminded me of walking behind little Will as he tried out the training wheels on his red bicycle. The blue moth sat on my handlebars and hissed through its mean little lips.

Later, Jim explained the cross-country bike ride to a hollow-cheeked, chain-smoking young man. "Gaw-uh-ud day-umm," said the man, scratching himself. It took him five syllables, but we got the message: he was impressed by the ride.

East of Vicksburg, I wheeled through a batch of kudzu, the vine imported from Asia for erosion control. It has spread across the Southern states like an evil fungus from a horror movie, covering barns, creeping up electric poles, and even engulfing roads. Jim suggested that a giant had poured thick green syrup over the world. An elderly gentleman in Bovina urged me not to leave my bike on the ground because the kudzu might grow over it. The thought gave me a laugh, but in reality the mighty vine possessed a hefty dose of symbolism. Sadness was like kudzu for Nicki—if she sat still for more than a minute, its vines overwhelmed her, binding her to the ground like Gulliver.

A coyote loped into a cotton field near the one-building village of Redwood. It was as graceful as a figure skater, but a Mississippian told me, "They're a nuisance. They came up here from Texas and Mexico. I kill every one I can."

A shiny black and white police car sat in the parking lot of a convenience store in the little town of Edwards, population 1,347. "That's our chief of PO-lice, behind the counter," said a patron. "He works here when he ain't police-chiefin'."

A whirlpool of life spun in that sweltering parking lot, but no one appeared uncomfortable—including me. One man labored under the hood of a minivan while two others consulted. A mother scolded a toddler in a small Chevrolet, its back seat packed with old tires. Six men with glistening ebony skin sat on a guardrail like robins on an electric wire, solving the world's problems. I shot the breeze with them about soft drinks, football, tomatoes, and the weather. I fit right in with the drumbeat of life; it was as if I had lived in Edwards forever.

"Your Kansas City Chiefs gonna be any good this year?" one man asked.

"Yes, they are," I replied.

"Lots of money in pro ball," he said. "Lots of money. I heard they charge $10 for parking. I remember when a feller could buy two tickets, four hotdogs, and two bags of popcorn for $10. I 'spect the rules have changed."

He was right; the money game in pro and college sports is different. Nothing stays the same.

My own rules for getting along with people—whether they were the owners of the joint or just there to clean it—were simple: smile, wave and speak. All across the country, people treated me well. I was not a threat. Being a sweaty, solitary middle-aged biker was a great equalizer. I was Everyman. It might have been different if I were six foot six, weighed 250 pounds, wore flashy jewelry and had braked my Lexus in front of these country stores. Then again, maybe not.

Time after time, I entered a small store or restaurant, and the locals eyed me with curiosity. Then one brave soul would find the courage to ask me where I was going. The others would subtly lean forward to hear the answer, while nonchalantly pretending they didn't care. Then, within a few minutes, they would all be gathered around, eagerly relating their own lives' adventures and giving me advice about the road ahead. I did not tell anyone my name, nor did I mention the Oklahoma State airplane crash. Frankly, once the locals would start to talk, I could seldom get a word in. I preferred it that way.

Always, there was advice. Sometimes, arguments.

"Take this here road a quarter-mile, then turn right," one would suggest.

"Don't send 'im down there; ol' Jake has a new dog and she'll chase 'im," another would counter.

"Yebbit that main road is full of trucks. Which do you choose, Mister Biker? Death by truck or death by dog?"

Today I chose old U. S. Highway 80, once the "mother road" for this part of the South. It had been the Dixie version of Route 66, connecting Savannah with Louisiana and points west. In the cotton country east of Vicksburg, the highway had been reduced to a frontage road along Interstate 20 and was not even listed on maps. It was a sad demise for a proud lady. Now too narrow for a highway, the old girl found a nice new identity for me as a wide, peaceful, and comfortable bike path.

Long before Highway 80 was constructed, the Jackson Road ran along basically the same route to Vicksburg. During the Civil War, the Union Army advanced from Jackson on the road, whipping the Rebels near Bolton, which shut off the South's supply lines and led to the fall of Vicksburg. Now there were great contradictions on rural U.S. 80: a mansion and grounds like the fabled Tara set back in the woods, then a dilapidated trailer with a trampoline and six automobiles in the front yard, then a gated housing addition surrounding a lake, then a place yearning for an adopt-a-yard program. Everyone, rich and poor, shared splendid pine trees and the soft summer morning.

Riding past the wrought-iron opulence made me ashamed of my own obsession with work and well being. Indeed, while I loved managing the NCAA tournament, I also treasured the perks that came with it—nice salary, fancy dinners, and travel to all parts of America.

John de Graaf, David Wann, and Thomas H. Naylor may have said it best in their book, *Affluenza: The All-Consuming Epidemic*. "Affluenza," they wrote, is "a painful, contagious, socially transmitted condition of overload, debt, anxiety, and waste resulting from the dogged pursuit of more." The illness itself is not difficult to diagnose. There are twice as many shopping centers as high schools in America. Many modern garages are larger than the size of a 1950s starter home. They have to be so large to shelter our living rooms on wheels. Our priorities are fouled up.

I desired not only poison for the blue moth but also an antidote for my own greed and ambition. My biker's life was a remedy, but it might be gone with the wind if and when my front tire met the Atlantic Ocean.

As we entered Jackson, SAG Jim asked if I wanted a Honda Civic escort. I declined and asked him to meet me at a motel on the other side of town. Jackson was the biggest city since the suburbs of Los Angeles that I would negotiate on the bike, and just as I had done with the deserts of California, I wanted to ride across it alone. A friend had suggested that I take leafy Northside Drive across Jackson. Instead, I opted for industrial Highway 80 through the heart of the old city. I knew the Northside Drives of the world. I grew up on a Northside Drive. I live on a Northside Drive today. I wanted something different.

I got plenty of something different. Bubba's Barbeque. Quality Lifts. Hubcap Heaven. The shell of the formerly luxurious

Tarrymore Motel. Broken glass. A toothless woman in a 1973 Cadillac deVille with the cloth top worn away. Pickups with white fronts but red backs. A white-shirted Indian behind the barred windows of a store that smelled of urine. Cigarette butts piled up like miniature snow drifts on the roadside at stop lights. The Mid-South ("Air-Conditioned") Motel. A city park with bald ball fields. The "IRS Rebate Special" at the tire shop. A sign reading "We take paychecks and hold 'em." A starving mother dog with purple teats dragging the ground.

It was a brutal domain, yet refreshing for me in a voyeuristic fashion. Many of those wanderers along U.S. 80 had never seen the fertile, innocent side of the fence. I felt sad for what they had missed. Their existence, like mine, was in disrepair. But at least I had memories.

Past the heart of Jackson, I decided to use a truck-stop shower. As long as I was going for "real," I would go all-out. I was as apprehensive as a ballet dancer at a goat ropin'. Were the showers only for truckers? Would they be clean? Private? Must I bring my own soap and towel?

The shower cost $10, with $5 of that refundable if I didn't steal the towel. I paid my $10, was assigned control number 366, and soon heard the woman on the public-address system say, "Shower number 366 is now ready." It was trucking high tech. My private little room contained an immaculate shower, sink, and toilet. Rolled up on a little bench were two towels, two washcloths, a bar of soap, and a paper floor mat. There was plenty of hot water. Surely, I thought as I rummaged in my Ziploc-bag shaving kit, this would be the first time Coeur d'Alene Resort shampoo would be used in this truck stop.

After the shower, I dashed off to the Jackson airport to catch an airplane to Connecticut for daughter-in-law Kristin's graduation from Quinnipiac College. Then I would spend a day attending NCAA meetings back in Indianapolis before continuing the ride. I was worried about what to do with the bicycle while I was away, but a stranger in Jackson, Jules Michel, came to the rescue. I had mentioned in the e-mail journal that I needed help, and an Oklahoma friend forwarded my e-mail to Jules. He met Jim and me at the airport's departure area. There, among vacationers happily dragging bags into the terminal and frenzied businessmen scurrying to their flights, we loaded the bicycle into the back of Jules's pickup. He would store it for four days in his garage at home.

After he put me on the airplane, SAG Jim headed south to explore the Natchez Trace. Although we got separated from each other on all three days, we were a fine team. I can only hope to be as fine a SAG for some young person when I'm 71 years old.

* * *

Nicki flew east to meet me in Connecticut, where we had the pleasure of sharing in the life that Nate and Kristin had made for themselves. We had visited several times before, driving on the lovely Merritt Parkway up from New York. But this time we saw a different Nate. His adjustment to Son No. 1 was still full of bumps and bruises, but he was different—stronger and more at peace. Nate's method of dealing with his emotions was to gather his friends around. He and Kristin had not known anyone when they moved to Connecticut, but now they were part of a veritable commune of students and professionals. Oh, how we loved those young people—and how we loved watching Nate interact with them.

Nate was four difficult years younger than his brother. As a child, there was no way that Nate could keep up in anything—sports or school or music. Will was patient, though, and kind with his little brother until the gap naturally evaporated as they grew up and their interests meshed. One of my fondest memories is from when they were 24 and 20 years old, and we hiked the Grand Canyon together. Like always, I was the tortoise—they had gone ahead. I began to hear Simon and Garfunkel's "The Sound of Silence," I thought, in my head. But I rounded a bend in the North Kaibab Trail and there they were—my sons sitting under an overhanging rock in a two-person amphitheater singing a duet from the sixties. Their dad's sixties.

Only as I watched Nate interact with his Connecticut friends and tried to imagine what Will's death meant to him, did I grasp the complexity of my sons' relationship to each other. Of course. I cursed my own blindness. Nate had seen, in those early days, how easy life came to Will. In our fanatic determination not to compare the boys when Nate was small, Nicki and I must have overdone it. Nate might have filled in the blanks, made his own comparisons, and ranked himself in second place. It was so elementary that at first I rejected it. Nate, a typical little brother measuring himself against the seemingly perfect big brother? Goodness, I should have seen it because I had failed that same test myself. As a youngster I felt that I could never measure up to the standard set by my own older brother, Joe, and worried about it until I realized that it didn't matter. Each of us carries our own strengths and weaknesses.

Nate had certainly proven himself a hero after the crash, giving comfort beyond measure to his mother, Karen, and me. He researched facts that were too intense for Nicki and me to think about. He took care of himself and his bride. He was a stalwart protector of Andie; I think it was no coincidence that one of her first words was "Nate."

Now, spending time together, Nate and I shared our pain. Parallel careers in sports had made peers of Will and me. This awful tragedy had done the same for me and Nate.

Andie, something told me to leave my comfort zone today and ride through the rough part of town. It was a good lesson, as it reminded me to appreciate the good life your grandmother and I have. It also reminded me once again that I should never judge what I do not know. For example, that truck-stop shower turned out to be in far better shape than I expected. Don't be afraid to take risks; you'll learn from them. But not silly ones, like getting into cars with strangers!

DAY 28

DOG STATUES

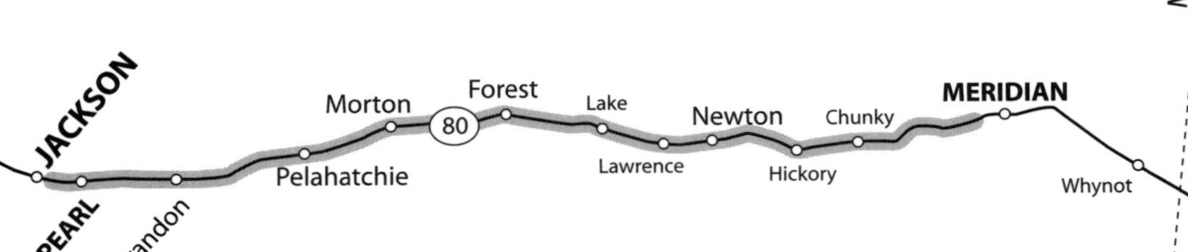

Date: Wednesday, August 15.

Distance traveled: 75 miles in Mississippi, from Jackson to west of Meridian.

Total miles completed: 2,151.

Starting temperature and time: 72 degrees at 5:45 a.m.

Finishing temperature and time: 91 at 2 p.m.

Food: breakfast—English muffin, waffle, fruit cocktail, donut; lunch—four chicken livers, one roll; dinner—cottage cheese, broccoli, pears, peaches, catfish, corn, black-eyed peas, mashed potatoes and gravy, cherry pie a la ice cream.

Additional fuel: 14 Fritos, two gallons of water, three quarts of Gatorade, one root beer.

Song stuck in my head: "Leavin' on a jet plane, don't know when I'll be back again." ("Leaving on a Jet Plane," John Denver, 1967)

Overnight: Holiday Inn Express, Meridian.

My new SAG retrieved my bike from Jules Michel and met my plane at the Jackson airport last night. Jim Shoemaker, a track-coach-turned-pharmaceutical-salesman and pillar of our church in Kansas City, sacrificed his vacation to spend eight days chasing me across the South. It was another act of unselfishness that humbled Nicki and me and reconfirmed why it's called human*kind.*

I tapped the snooze button several times this morning. The most difficult aspect of the bike ride was getting up in the morning; it was an uncomfortable reminder of the first weeks after the crash, when simply rolling out of bed took all the energy that I could muster. Today was bad because every day during the break I had slept until the slothful hour of 7 a.m., and my body had grown accustomed to the luxury.

I finally headed out into a morning so foggy that I could barely see the handlebars. Mist rose off of ponds as in a Sherlock Holmes flick. Like tragedy, the dark gray vapor was a great equalizer—black men and white men became indistinguishable from each other. Similarly, in the mists of grief, tragedy makes equals of rich and poor, of the famous and the unknown.

My mind was foggy, too. I was glad to get out of the coat and tie that I had worn during the break, but my brain took a while to return to a bicyclist's focus. My thoughts wandered back to the airplane crash and the many prominent people—such as coaches Roy Williams, Kelvin Sampson, Mike Krzyzewski, Mike Montgomery, Mack Brown, and Barry Switzer as well as television announcers Jim Nantz, Dick Vitale, Digger Phelps, Ron Franklin, and Vern Lundquist—who wrapped my family in warmth. Now I felt guilty because I had not thanked them adequately—and also Kristin's graduation gifts reminded me that I had not written thank-you notes to the thousand people who sent condolence cards. The guilt brought out the blue moth, which luckily had missed the flight to Connecticut with me, allowing me a few days of solace.

My mental meandering and the moth's visit were interrupted by the sight of two large, menacing dogs standing in the fog near the road. I went into canine-combat mode: (1) I removed my helmet to show that I was human and not monster; (2) I rode to the opposite shoulder so that they'd have to cross traffic to reach me (there was no shoulder or traffic, but that's beside the point); (3) I puffed my chest to appear large and threatening; (4) I armed myself with the pepper spray; (5) I spoke gently to the dogs, who didn't move; and (6) I was basically scared brainless.

The effort was not necessary. They were only statues of dogs. I laughed out loud at my own paranoia. I should have known; after all, the South was an exquisite yard-art gallery. Plastic pink flamingos, ceramic ducks, wooden paintings of hefty human behinds—and, last week, red cement Arkansas Razorback hogs—guarded driveways that led to rusty trailers and stately mansions alike.

A trash truck followed me through Brandon, Mississippi. Each time the truck stopped to pick up garbage, I fled past. Then the truck passed me, only to stop again. The odorous vehicle and I continued the minuet for several blocks, then the driver waved a smiling farewell when he finally turned off the main road and headed for the dump. Would the blue moth ever leave me for another dance partner? Or was I headed for the dump, too?

On the highway, my most common companions were armadillos, now the most frequent road kill. I still hadn't seen a live one. Nor had I spotted a snake. The South's national forests weren't any help in the wildlife search. They seemed to be log farms, quite unlike the idyllic playgrounds of the West. A road sign stated, "Trucks Turning. Watch For Long Logs." It was appropriate, because logs protruded far behind the trucks, with red bandanas tied on as warnings for trailing motorists—and bicyclists.

Just beyond Chunky Creek, in a lovely rolling landscape, I began to white-line. That's a biker's phenomenon—when we put our heads down and pedal for miles and miles, looking only at the white line that marks the road's shoulder and outlines the course from here to infinity. It's a lousy way to move through life, because we might miss a chance to let our imaginations invent friendly creatures in the clouds. But that doesn't stop us from going around with blinders on; we think it's necessary because a destination awaits, or a schedule must be kept. Then, suddenly, we come to our senses, slow down, and, in the words of the song, make the morning last.

Andie, sometimes you must white-line, such as when you're studying for an important science test, practicing your piano scales, or writing letters to your granddad. And that's okay. But remember to occasionally lift your head and watch the clouds slow-dancing across the sky. You may see a ballerina on her toes. You may see her loosen her hair and let it cascade earthward in the form of rain—to comfort dry cotton fields like tears comfort parched hearts.

More Questions from the E-Mail Crew

The e-mail support group had spread like kudzu. I was now spending an hour each day preparing the journal and responding to messages of encouragement.

How's the laundry situation? I have five shirts, five pairs of socks, and two pairs of bike shorts, so I do laundry every four days. In the West, at the end of the day the clothes were so crusted with salt that they would stand up in the corner on their own. Here in the South, they're soaking wet and I wring them out before hanging them to dry. Sometimes they're dry by morning, sometimes not.

Is it difficult being out in the sun all day? Not really. I use a half-pint of sunscreen every day.

Those long-sleeved shirts sound hot and miserable. Are they worthwhile? Yes, because they provide some protection from the sun. Strangely, my back is sunburned, even through the cotton fabric.

You finish riding pretty early each day. What do you do then? Eat, do laundry, talk to people, eat, read the local paper, see the sights, eat. Occasionally, I take a nap. Then I prepare for the next day: air the bike tires, clean the frame, fill my water bottles, set out my gloves and helmet. I want to be able to jump on the bike and get started early.

The trip sounds so great; do you think there will be a "do-over"? If I have a vote, there will.

How do you know so much about the places you visit? Nicki and I studied before we left. On the road, we listen to the locals, read every historical marker and try not to bypass any museums.

Are you bored yet? Nope. I knew you'd ask again, and you'll be interested in this: over the last couple of days, at mid-morning, I have become sleepy when riding. I don't suppose I would actually fall asleep on the bike, but I do stop to walk around, just in case.

What kind of dog are you getting after the trip? Very funny. If you must know, a biker-spaniel.

Are you sleeping well? Yes—but not long. I haven't slept more than three hours at once.

Almost every day, you write that riding on so-and-so highway in the middle of nowhere is a great privilege. Com'on, Pollyanna, it can't be that good. It's better than good; it's awesome. Once, in the New York City Marathon, I turned to another runner as we entered Harlem and said, “What a privilege it is to be here, and especially on foot. How many people get this opportunity?” Right on the spot, he vomited.

What should a cross-country biker not eat? My diet has been, ahem, questioned. Seriously, I suggest avoiding three things: dairy products, fried foods, and sugar.

Why no Vienna sausages lately? People gave me such a hard time that I quit cold turkey. Actually, because of the heat, I've mostly quit eating lunch. I think the Viennas will be back soon.

You never mention rain. Why? Because it hasn't rained while I've been on the bike. Not a drop.

And this, which caused a chuckle but needed no response: *Your colleagues at the NCAA have concluded that the bike ride is a hoax, that Nicki and you actually are lollygagging on a romantic South Seas island. You're making up all those reports and are generating fake photos on the computer, like the "moon landing" back in 1969.*

DAY 29

You Go, Boy

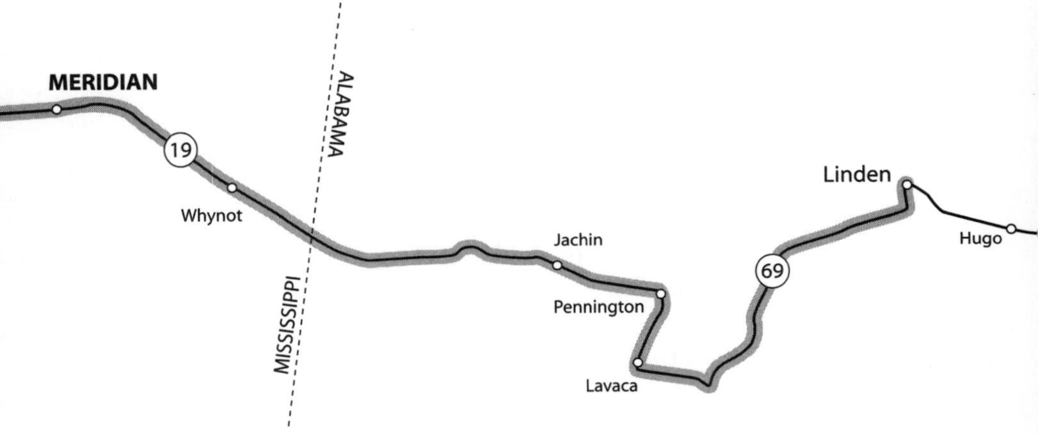

Date: Thursday, August 16.
Distance traveled: 85 miles, from west of Meridian, Mississippi, to Linden, Alabama.
Total miles completed: 2,236.
Starting temperature and time: 72 degrees at 4:50 a.m.
Finishing temperature and time: 94 at 1 p.m.
Food: breakfast—cheese crackers; lunch—Vienna sausages (they're baaacck) and apple sauce; dinner—chicken tenders, green beans, salad, broccoli, peaches, carrots.
Additional fuel: 30 Cheez-Its, 32 Fritos, two gallons of water, three quarts of Gatorade, one root beer.
Song stuck in my head: "The Entertainer," Scott Joplin, 1902.
Overnight: Depot Motel, Linden.

Fog engulfed a cemetery on spooky old U.S. 80 west of Meridian before daylight, and its headstones were silhouetted against a sky that glowed pink from the city lights. I was happy to reach the well-lit downtown, although the only other creature stirring was one police officer who looked at me as if to say, "Don't worry, I'll take care of you." Even the I-20 frontage road was deserted. Soon, I was back in open country.

The dirt southeast of Meridian was day-glo, as if someone had cooked a scrumptious bisque of Texas Longhorn orange, honeysuckle blossoms, and a Hawaiian sunset. If I'd rolled in it for a while, I could have gone trick-or-treating as a carrot. Amid the orange soil, three dogs dashed out of a junkyard and flung themselves toward me. The road was uphill, so I couldn't sprint, and there was only one thing to do—I stopped, took off my biking helmet and talked to them as if I were Mister Rogers and they had ventured into my neighborhood.

"Good morning, guys," I said as they snarled around my knees. "How you doing? How are your moms and dads? Did you watch the Westminster Kennel Club Dog Show on ESPN last winter? Wasn't that Tibetan Terrier gorgeous?"

The snarls turned to sniffs, and the monsters backed off. It was as if I had thrown water on the Wicked Witch. Maybe it was merely luck. But maybe I truly had learned to be the Dog Whisperer.

After the dog adventure I got the "biker blues," a deplorable mental condition that also strikes solo mountain climbers, trekkers, and long-distance swimmers. Some hallucinate. Some cry. Some panic. Several elements combined to lower me into the pit of depression. A spiteful voice mail from an NCAA colleague caused me to wonder why anyone ever worked in any office, period. Trucks suddenly couldn't bother to swing into the other lane when they barreled past me. And I missed Nicki—a lot. You-know-who stopped by for an unannounced visit.

The setting was hardly inspiring as well. The warm haze and fog were suffocating. The road was cracked, rutted, and rough. And large logged-out tracts reminded me of downtown Gary, Indiana, which made me recall that Will had once played trombone in the pit orchestra for *The Music Man* and we walked around the house singing the repetitive chorus to the young boy's solo from that show: "Gary, Indiana, Gary Indiana, Gary, Indiana." Now Will would never haul his horn out of the attic and play it for Andie, as I had played my Selmer clarinet when young Will and Nate would sit at my feet and listen for as long as my embouchure and right thumb held out.

Then guilt slammed me. I became obsessed with the morning that I didn't have time to play ping-pong with Will when he was 11 years old. He asked twice, but I didn't want to be late for work. Now, in my mind's eye, I could plainly see the disappointment in his trusting face, and it haunted me for miles. The blue moth clung to my heart like a mantis on the screen door.

The final blow was a pickup which sped toward me, straddling the center line. I thought it was only momentarily out of control and—as had happened almost every day—that the driver was merely distracted by reaching for something in the passenger seat. But this grape-colored truck, with two spotlights on top and mud flaps for wings, veered across the lane toward me—a wide-wheeled blue moth on the attack. Then a young man poked his head out the window and screamed like he was on Pickett's charge. I'll never forget his greasy blond trusses blowing in the wind.

"Euuuuuuasssss hoooool e."

"Hit me, dang it," I yelled back, incensed. "Get me out of this stinking life."

We are all insecure, but we handle our insecurities differently. The pickup driver whooshed past, no doubt pleased to have terrorized a defenseless stranger. For me, the general malaise deepened. I envisioned a brief candle blowing out. One Edgar Allan Poe-esque word crept into my brain.

"Nevermore."

My soul grieved for my Will—and for all the lost Lenores of the world. My concentration was lost. Just keeping the bike upright became a chore.

Then, several stars aligned to drive away the raven, the moth, and the biker blues. The first star was my entry into Alabama, where the road immediately improved. The bumps disappeared and the shoulder expanded from two inches to ten. If I were in charge at the statehouse, I would build fabulous highways near the state line, simply for the pleasure of embarrassing the adjoining state. It would be almost as good for the taxpayers' egos as a victory over the neighboring university's football team.

Second was Choctaw County Road 32, a serene rural pathway that rolled peacefully past clusters of tiny but well-kept frame houses and mobile homes, many with a circle of chairs under a large oak or pine tree in the front yard. Families and friends surely gathered there in the mellow evenings. Relaxing in those chairs must be healthier than a dozen therapy sessions and several doses of Prozac. A frail, raven-skinned woman emerged from one rusty house trailer as I approached.

"Need help, young man?" she asked.

"No, m'am, I'm okay. You sure do live in a beautiful spot."

"It's what we got," she replied. "Don't know no place else."

Third was a hand-written sign pointing the way to "Little Hope Baptist Church." If these poor people could find hope—even a little—then perhaps I could, too. It was the third "Hope" that I had visited on the ride, after the towns in Arizona and Arkansas. The message was obvious, as if it had been painted in the Alabama heavens by a skywriter. Hope is waiting on the road ahead.

Fourth was a trio of women in a little store in the community of Jachin. When I pulled under the rickety portico, one of the women waddled out into the hot afternoon to greet me. "Welcome to Alabama!" she said, smiling as if I were a prodigal son.

I followed her into the sparse establishment, where she announced, "This gentleman is riding his bicycle across the country. What do you think about that!?"

"I declare!" said one woman, almost shouting.

"Well, I'll swan," the third answered. "You go, boy!" They talked in exclamation points.

I asked about the people who inhabited the meek homes on County Road 32.

"They country folks. They churches is they circle of life. One woman who stay back there, her husband was killed in a fire. Her daughter was all burnt up, too. But she's makin' it. She love the Lord."

I realized that my own misery was only about five on a ten-point scale. Others on my side of the fence faced greater loss, and more insurmountable odds. In a strange way, it lifted my spirit. I purchased a bag of Fritos and left the Jachin Store with the biker blues exorcised and the ladies rooting me on like cheerleaders at a high school pep rally.

So far gone were those blues that I merely whispered, "Oh, golly," when I saw a sign I had been dreading since Huntington Beach: "Road Closed Ahead, Bridge Out." The alternate route would add 15 miles to the ride. Later I learned that I might have been able to walk the bike across an adjacent railroad trestle to avoid the damaged bridge. I used to walk the tracks as a kid, but now I doubted my sober adult self would have attempted such risk.

The detour became a rewarding journey through fragrant pine country and along a quiet lane dotted with tidy farmhouses. The weather was not so lovely. It was 90 degrees, and deep purple clouds assembled like evil hunters circling their prey. A hot wind swirled. Then the clouds spit out a few sprinkles, and I hauled the poncho out of my seat bag. My clothing and body were soaked with perspiration, so I actually looked forward to a cooling rain shower. But no rain fell—the clouds slid away, the sun came out, and the temperature climbed to 94.

Steam rose from the pavement as if Satan were boiling tar. The humidity was at least 176; fish could have had sex on land. My sunglasses fogged and sweat puddled in my shoes. I could feel unsightly flab draining away as if I were performing liposuction on myself. I don't think I had ever *seen* weather like this, much less ridden a bike in it. But the countryside was so peaceful, and the blue moth so distant, that I couldn't complain.

In Linden, population 2,400, I rode past the Marengo County Academy, a private high school. Laughing teenagers piloted flashy vehicles out of the parking lot. A couple of miles north was the Linden public high school. Integration had caused private schools to spring from the ground like rain brings mushrooms. In the last six days, a dozen white people had told me to avoid blacks. No black person ever turned the tables. As I struggled to find the meaning, I happened to look down at my bicycle wheel. The wheel is supported by flimsy spokes and gets its muscle from the spokes as they pull toward the center. That force, from pulling together, gives the bike wheel its strength. Somehow, many people had managed to overlook that simple technique in life: pulling together creates strength far greater than what each of us could muster individually.

The only lodging in Linden was the immaculate Depot Motel. We were the only guests, so SAG Shoemaker and I got the honeymoon suite. There was no pool, but soaking for 30 minutes in cold bath water returned my body temperature to just under "broil." I ate Fritos and drank root beer in the tub, feeling like Jabba the Hutt in a wading pool, until I spilled the root beer, which turned the bath water brown.

Shoe and I walked across the street to the snug Depot Restaurant, where we joined locals who mulled over the day's events. We made several raids on the heaping salad bar and enjoyed watching the dance of small-town life. The conversation hushed when a stunning 45-ish woman entered with her wholesome-looking college-age son and her husband. The husband bore the weary, wary look of the spouse of the prettiest woman in town. For her part, the beautiful woman held her arms in front of her body like folded angel's wings, as if she wanted to make herself invisible. I decided she should spend an hour some evening sitting under a tree on County Road 32. Maybe it would relax her—and maybe not.

After dinner, Shoe and I went for ice cream as the mellow evening fell around us like snow. Savoring our soft-serve, we asked what we should see in Linden.

"See somethin' here?" exclaimed a fuzzy-cheeked teenager behind the counter. "You gotta be kiddin' me. There ain't nothin' important in this here town."

And then his boss spoke up, "Well, fellers, you are standing in the oldest Dairy Queen in the state of Alabama."

"Mr. Johnson, I didn't know that! That's cool. We're famous!"

Andie, this was a multi-lesson day. When you get the blues, hang in there and they'll go away. As Dr. Ralph Phelan in Hobart often said, "The best medicine is Tincture of Time." As I discovered on Choctaw County Road 32, hope is the most precious commodity.

8

Doubt in the Deep South

DAY 30

THE WHEELS COME OFF

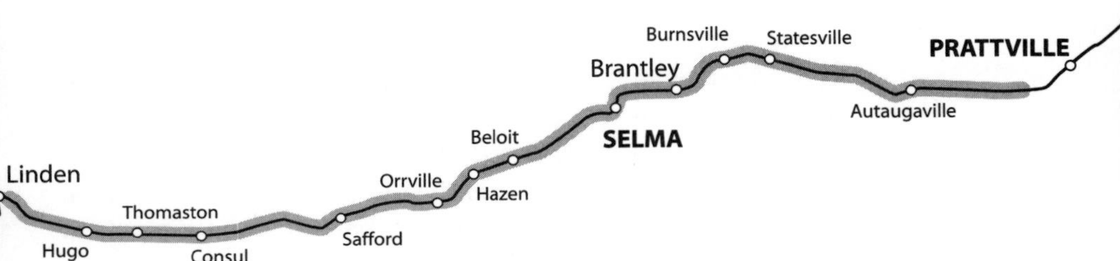

Date: Friday, August 17.

Distance traveled: 82 miles in Alabama, from Linden to a few miles west of Prattville.

Total miles completed: 2,318.

Miles to go: all of a sudden, not too many.

Starting temperature and time: 71 degrees at 5 a.m.

Finishing temperature and time: 89 at 2 p.m.

Food: breakfast—apple, sausage biscuit; lunch—cheese crackers; dinner—spaghetti, salad.

Additional fuel: 18 Fritos, two gallons of water, three quarts of Gatorade, one root beer.

Health: In the heat of the day, the nausea returned.

Song stuck in my head: the Woody Woodpecker theme, written by George Tibbles and Ramey Idriss, 1947.

Overnight: Hampton Inn, Prattville.

America had yet to reach its capacity to surprise me. As the newspaper reported, "The meeting of the Clairvoyance Society was cancelled because of unforeseen circumstances." In rubber-chicken banquet speeches, old coaches say there's no defense for the unexpected, but there is preparation. Dealing with the unpredicted is an art, and on this trip I had plenty of practice. Usually I was prepared, but not today.

I enjoy the elements. The hotter, windier, foggier, colder: the better. I enjoy jogging at noon when the temperature is 106. Conversely, I invented a scoring system for running farther than the temperature; my record is 14—six miles with the thermometer at eight below. No matter who is playing, football on television is best when the game is played in rain, snow, sleet, or hail. And so I eagerly anticipated uncomfortable weather on the bike ride, just for the experience. Yesterday's humidity had been pleasantly wicked.

But today was too much. First fog, then overpowering heat, like standing beside a kiln, made me wish that I had taken a more northerly route across the continent—say from Alaska to Greenland with a stop for lunch at the North Pole.

DAY 30

I rode for nearly four hours in the fog—not merely the ground clutter that I had been enjoying for a week, but dungeon mush that limited my vision to one bike-length. When moisture collected on my helmet and trickled down to the visor, I entertained myself by catching the drops with my tongue. My clothes and shoes were soaked; I squished when I walked and I left wet footprints in stores. A lean banker-type man squinted over his glasses in the limited visibility and said, "Boy, somebody's gonna run you over." I hoped not on purpose.

The fog had diluted somewhat by the time I wheeled into the village of Orrville, home of 230 people and just about as poor as a town could be. But a hand-painted sign on the side of a garage proclaimed, "Orrville, Where the Livin' Is Easy." A dozen people sat idly on long benches under porches in the one-block downtown.

Two men smiled and waved from their perch on a car hood, so I swung by for a chat. One of them, whose scraggly beard resembled four long-legged black spiders lying on their backs, said, "We got a nice life here. Do you like football? We love college football; it gives us something to foller. I'm for Auburn when they playin', Alabama when they playin', and I stay out of the way when they play one another. They's some crazy people."

The small-town tempo—much more *Canon in D* than *Flight of the Bumblebee*—was ironically energizing. Perhaps all the people in a hurry have moved to the city. In the same sense, I enjoy the first round of the NCAA tournament more than the Final Four because there are fewer high-octane celebrities; the humble Northern Arizonas, Butlers, and Alcorn States cherish their moments in the sun.

The real sun emerged after Orrville, when the road abandoned the woods and settled into flat cotton land. Crushing heat rolled like a baseball-stadium tarp over the countryside. I wondered how people survived here before air-conditioning. Some of them, it turned out, endured through creativity. The people of Enterprise, Alabama, cleverly honored the boll weevil by constructing what was probably the world's only monument to a pest.

Before the boll weevils invaded in 1915, farmers around Enterprise grew cotton almost exclusively. After the weevils destroyed most of the cotton crop that year, many farmers turned to peanuts. The nuts were well-suited to the climate, and the diversification solidified the area's agricultural future. Peanuts had Wally Pipped cotton. Enterprise businessman Bon Fleming dreamed up the monument to honor the boll weevil for forcing farmers to put their eggs in more than one basket, as savvy financial planners advise investors to do today. The popular statue of a woman dressed in white and holding a giant black boll weevil, a sight you just have to see for yourself, has helped Enterprise expand its economy into yet another area—tourism.

There were no tourists on the road to Selma, but oncoming vehicles were swinging over the center line into my lane. As I drew nearer, I saw that the cars swerved to avoid a person who was hobbling like a sleepwalker in the traffic. As if in a daze, the overweight black woman kept her eyes straight ahead. Vehicles whizzed past the zombie-woman, billowing her white skirt. Some drivers gestured angrily and gave the same "you idiot" honk that I had received on occasion.

She shuffled down the road the same way that I had moved through life since the crash. Her halting steps symbolized absolute despair. Obviously, something was terribly wrong. When I rode past, I could have reached out and touched her. I could have stopped. I could have suggested that she walk in the grass. I could have called 911. But I chose to continue on my way—a regular Levite when a Samaritan clearly was needed—leaving her to fend for herself in the highway. Perhaps I ignored the woman because I didn't want to get involved, or because I was not trained in *how* to help her, or simply because she was different from me. Whatever the reason, I had been given the chance to help someone, and I had taken the easy way out. I had taken a horrifying step backward, forsaking all that I had learned since the crash. The blue moth fluttered around my ears as I pondered Will's disapproval.

I stopped at an aromatic restaurant for a glass of cold water and tried to think about anything but the woman in the road. The sign told me that I was at Hancock's barbeque place, so I wondered what had led the Alabama Hancocks (no relation) to produce warm, spicy food while the Oklahoma-Kansas Hancocks had produced such a cold lack of concern for others. I dallied in the air-conditioned restaurant as long as I dared, hoping the cool air would dispel the image of the woman—and the blue moth.

I was not to escape. Almost immediately after I left the restaurant, I saw the woman again, slumped on the side of the road. She was surrounded by a half-dozen citizens and a police officer.

"Don't give up hope, honey, the Lord is always there," a woman said as she placed a wet towel on the stranger's forehead. A bystander told me that the woman had been walking in the road as a suicide attempt. How awful would I have felt if she had been successful, after I made no effort to help her? Crushing guilt overwhelmed me and the blue moth returned with a vengeance, trying to drill a silo into my brain.

I had hit rock bottom, emotionally, and Nicki was not here to console me. As I stood in the hot sun and watched others care for the woman, I remembered talking to young Will about a blind man whom we saw on the University of Oklahoma campus. "He can't see," I explained, when Will asked why the man was tapping the sidewalk with his cane. "He takes pretty good care of himself, but it's our job to help him when we can."

Like most parents who give advice to children, I had no idea whether Will understood. But now I knew that I had neglected my own message. I felt a strong urge to ride hard to Selma as if the moth were sarcastically egging me on—challenging me to learn more about myself. And so I headed east, past Selma's quiet cemetery shrouded in Spanish moss, to the Edmund Pettus Bridge downtown.

A dignified-looking elderly gentleman in white trousers and a pressed white shirt made a statement that sent a shock wave through me. He said, like a tour guide from Hell, "That bridge was designed by one of our Alabama niggers." The word stung. It was a uniquely ugly moment for me, the offspring of open-minded parents who, despite their Southern origins, taught me to respect others and to avoid painful labels. Then, in the NCAA national office, I worked in a colorblind bubble, hermetically sealed to keep prejudice out and diversity in. So I had scant experience with racism.

Naively, I had not expected to hear the "n" word in Selma. The town's very name stood for a landmark event in civil rights history. In 1965, crowds of protesters gathered in Selma where the Brown Chapel African Methodist Episcopal Church was hosting the Southern Christian Leadership Conference. Another church was headquarters for the organizers of the Selma Campaign—the Student Nonviolent Coordinating Committee—seeking voting rights for Alabama's disenfranchised. Governor George Wallace had banned protest marches, but on Sunday morning, March 7 (a date that would become known as "Bloody Sunday"), about 600 blacks gathered outside Brown Chapel to march from Selma to the state capital in Montgomery.

At the Pettus Bridge over the Alabama River, mounted troopers confronted the throngs of marchers and ordered them to disperse. The marchers stood their ground, and the troopers brandished billy clubs. Several protestors fell, screaming, as white onlookers cheered. Then Sheriff Jim Clark's deputized posse charged, firing tear gas and swinging bullwhips and rubber tubing wrapped in barbed wire. Fifty-seven people were injured in the chaos that ensued.

That night, ABC interrupted its showing of the movie *Judgment at Nuremberg* to air footage of "Bloody Sunday." By morning, news of the event had spread across the country. Thousands of supporters flocked to Selma. Federal Judge Frank M. Johnson overturned Governor Wallace's ban on protest marches. On March 21, the National Guard, acting as SAG for the marchers, opened the way, and some 25,000 people completed the five-day walk to Montgomery. The events in Selma got the country's attention. Less than five months later President Johnson signed the Voting Rights Act.

As I leaned my bike against the stately Pettus Bridge and sipped water, I thought about the good that evolved from the crisis that occurred on this very spot. But, could any good come from the Oklahoma State airplane crash? The price paid by our family was too steep—but I couldn't stop thinking about it until two meter maids approached to break my concentration. "I wouldn't have started talking to you, except you were smiling," said one. I had not known that I was smiling. Was something worthwhile germinating inside me, and was its light shining out of my eyes?

The light didn't shine for long. I changed clothes in Selma and, out of morbid curiosity, I weighed the heap of steaming cotton and nylon. Just by undressing, I had shed ten pounds; but I could not easily shed the heaviness of my failure to help the woman in the road. And I couldn't change bodies. My eyes wouldn't focus, and the nausea returned like I imagine morning sickness does. It was hair-dryer hot—heat was heaped upon heat. I began to dream of wading into the Atlantic Ocean, where I would eat one last can of Vienna sausages while standing in the cool waves. Could the end really be only five days away?

Like Heartbreak Hill in the Boston Marathon, when at the 16-mile point legs begin to turn to burlap and willpower evaporates, the rolling terrain east of Selma came at the worst of times—noon on the steamiest day of the ride. I decided that bicyclist Jimmy Casper had been wise in the Tour de France one year when he grabbed the rearview mirror of a moving car to keep up with the pack. Oh, I was tempted when Shoe rolled slowly past in the minivan.

Reaching into my bike bag for the last bottle of water, I noticed that the bag itself, which had been night-on-the-town black when I left the Pacific Ocean, had been bleached the color of brooding purple by four weeks in the sun. The demoralizing sun was taking its toll on me as well. I couldn't urinate, despite having consumed nearly three gallons of fluid. At one rest stop, Shoe scowled. "You okay?" he said. Later, he told me, "When you said, 'Schure, I'm jusht fine.' I knew you were in trouble."

Ten miles later, and eight miles short of my goal of Prattville, Shoe stood on the edge of the pavement, hands on hips and glaring at me.

"You're done," he said. "Remember, the goal is Tybee Island next week, not Prattville today. We're packin' it in for the day."

Like race director Jock Semple—who darn near tackled Katherine Switzer in 1967 to prevent her from becoming the first woman to run the Boston Marathon—Shoe pulled me off the course. I could hardly disagree. I slid my soaking pink body into the van. For the first time since the desert, I had stopped short. More importantly, a cloud of doubt entered my mind: could I complete the journey? The specter of failure was ugly; how could I live with myself after riding only part way across the country? All that I knew for certain was that I wanted to go to bed and stay there, rotating the pillow to keep the cool side up.

A half-hour of sipping root beer and eating Fritos in Prattville's Hampton Inn pool helped my disposition slightly. I phoned Nicki back in Kansas; she cheered me up with reports of her new batch of eager senior English students. The ups and downs of the entire trip—of our entire lives since the crash—were symbolized in this one humid Alabama day. We would worry about the weather tomorrow, Rhett.

Andie, I felt plenty of hate today, and I hated myself for a while. Don't hate another human being. Hate that your dad died. Hate beets. Hate ants. But hating a person—even yourself—will give you a stomach ache. And a heartache.

DAY 31

TRY A FAITH LIFT

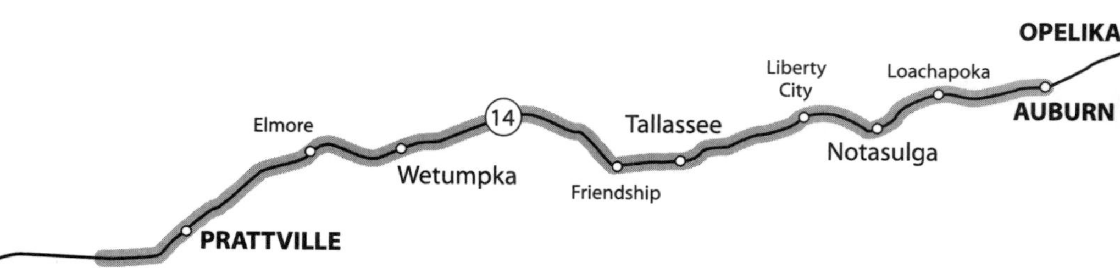

Date: Saturday, August 18.

Distance traveled: 76 miles in Alabama, from a few miles west of Prattville to Auburn.

Total miles completed: 2,394.

Miles to go: fewer than 400.

Starting temperature and time: 73 degrees at 4:45 a.m.

Finishing temperature and time: 88 at 12:30 p.m.

Food: breakfast—crackers, banana, sausage biscuit; lunch—spaghetti; dinner—four corn fritters, three fried-cheese sticks, three quesadillas, hamburger.

Additional fuel: Pretzels, two gallons of water, four quarts of Gatorade, one root beer.

Song stuck in my head: "For the darkness shall turn to dawning, and the dawning to noon-day bright. For Christ's great kingdom shall come on earth, the kingdom of love and light." ("We've a Story to Tell to the Nations," written by Henry Ernest Nichol in 1896.)

Overnight: David and Susan Housel's home, Auburn.

It was a miracle. Period.

As I hauled the bike out of the van near a cotton field west of Prattville, stars glittered in the sky. There was no fog. An overnight weather front, a summer version of the blue northers of my Oklahoma childhood, had swept the humidity out to sea. I danced a little jig in the dust. Could a similar miracle—a permanent one, not like the illusions we had experienced—intervene in the battle that I waged against the blue moth? The moth had ridden with me for 30 days across the desert, over the Rockies, and into the South. After all that, I decided it would never leave. But could my relationship with the moth be different, somehow less hostile?

I pondered the question while relaxing in Wetumpka, a storybook town of beautiful churches and fine homes, curled up against the Coosa River. An elegant bridge spanned the river. Three people perched on a logjam in mid-river 50 yards upstream, their boat tied up and bobbing in the slow current. In this era of the phony outdoor adventure—it is the age of aquarium—they were seeking real fish in a real muddy river. I was jealous of their carefree world; then I laughed at my own silliness. On the bike, I was as near nirvana as a person could be, yet I wanted more. I wished that Nicki were here to watch the fishermen; I wished that Will were here to skip rocks across the Coosa.

Huntin' and fishin' are important in the South. But maybe not bigger than church-goin'. And maybe not bigger than auto racin'. And maybe not bigger than college football. The South has many religions, some of which actually have something to do with church.

As I rode up, elderly Bill Lumpkin was changing the sign outside a Methodist church near the tiny community of Friendship. Upon learning that I was riding across the continent, he said, "Sure 'nuff? That's a right far piece. For me, this life here in Friendship is good enough." Mr. Lumpkin organized unwieldy plastic red letters, like a child with slick flash cards, to post another in a series of occasionally witty signs that I had seen posted in front of churches since Oklahoma:

- *Make your eternal reservations now: 'smoking' or 'non-smoking'?*
- *Life is fragile, handle with prayer.*
- *A lot of kneeling will keep you in good standing.*
- *Don't wait for the hearse to take you to church.*
- *No Jesus, no peace; Know Jesus, know peace.*

•*This church is prayer-conditioned.*
•*Don't have anything to be thankful for? Check your pulse!*
•*Need a new look? Try a faith lift.*

* * *

A sign of a different sort hung on the majestic Coosa River bridge in Tallassee: "Walk Your Bike Across Bridge," it read. I figured that I could cheat because there wasn't much traffic. But a motorist leaned out the window and said, quite pleasantly, "Sir, you're 'posed to walk your bike." It was another warning, like I had received before Yarnell Hill back in Arizona. Pay attention, I told myself, because most of the signals are important.

The only Confederate armory not destroyed in the Civil War was the one in Tallassee. It survived primarily because Yankee general James Harrison Wilson had a bad map and couldn't find Tallassee. I recalled my faulty view of the Arizona map and decided that nothing really changes.

Like a schoolboy on a summer afternoon, I rode on and soaked in the sights, fenced in by Bermuda grass on the highway shoulder that grew as high as British Open rough. Women mowed lawns. A man strung laundry to dry on a line. Black children sold "hot fish" sandwiches in the shadow of their church. Firemen in the community of Notasulga were conducting a fund-raising car wash and offered to clean my bike for free. There was no hint of tragedy—past or future—in the air. I hoped every person that I passed cherished every moment of ordinary life. After yesterday, today's ride was a faith lift, indeed.

* * *

The campus of Auburn University bristled with back-to-school energy. "Aubie," the Tiger mascot, rode down the street in a convertible, and Auburn-legacy parents pointed out ancient haunts to their freshly scrubbed student-children. New life was blossoming on campus as the fall semester beckoned. It rang a bell for me, too, answering the question that I had pondered earlier in the day. Maybe there could be a new life for Nicki and me. It would take wide-open eyes and a commitment to trust life once again.

I remembered sending Will off to his first year of college—and Nate, too. They were both apprehensive.

"You'll love it," I told Will.

"But I won't be home with you and Mom and Nate," he said.

"Yes, but there's a new life ahead. Go for it!"

I identified with those Auburn parents more than with the students—more with the people giving comfort than with those receiving it. That, I thought, was a good sign.

* * *

SAG Shoe and I toured the campus with Auburn athletic director David Housel, and his charming wife, Susan. Because he is also Auburn's resident historian, raconteur, and keeper of the faith, David could walk no more than a few steps without greeting an Auburn admirer. Yet he was the same humble, quietly brilliant person that I had known for 20 years. It was a privilege to watch such a gentle man enjoy doing what he loved. To stand with him at legendary Toomer's corner—the intersection near campus where Auburn stalwarts have gathered for years—was like visiting Frontierland with Walt Disney. David pointed out the railroad tracks where Auburn students greased the rails in 1896, causing the Georgia Tech football team's train to slide a half-mile beyond the station. Then I rode two "victory" laps inside Jordan-Hare stadium—where the Tigers play football—laughing all the way.

Later we had a fascinating face-to-beak meeting with War Eagle V, the magnificent eagle that swoops from the sky to a perch at the stadium before each home game. The bird is cared for by the Southeast Raptor Rehabilitation Center at Auburn's veterinary medicine school. The center is SAG to the eagles in much the same way that David and Susan Housel were rehabilitating me today.

War Eagle is also one of the most famous of college battle cries, like Texas A&M's "Hulla-Baloo Ka-Nick Ka-Nick" and Alabama's "Roll Tide" and Texas's "Hook 'em Horns" and Oklahoma's "Boomer Sooner."

According to legend, the "War Eagle" tradition originated during an 1892 football game between Auburn and Georgia at Atlanta's Piedmont Park. A veteran sat in the stands with an eagle that the old soldier had found on a Civil War battlefield. The eagle is said to have escaped from its master and circled over the playing field as Auburn drove toward the Georgia end zone. Auburn students and fans yelled, "War Eagle" to cheer on the team.

The eagle took a sudden dive, crashed to the ground and died as the game ended. And "War Eagle" lives today. There was that metaphor again: the end is not what it seems.

Andie, you're lucky to live in Stillwater, a college town where tradition is cherished and where new life begins every autumn. Enjoy your part of America—the Homecoming decorations, the student recitals, the coins in Theta Pond, the excitement of thousands of young people starting down the road ahead.

DAY 32

WRONG TURNS AND FDR

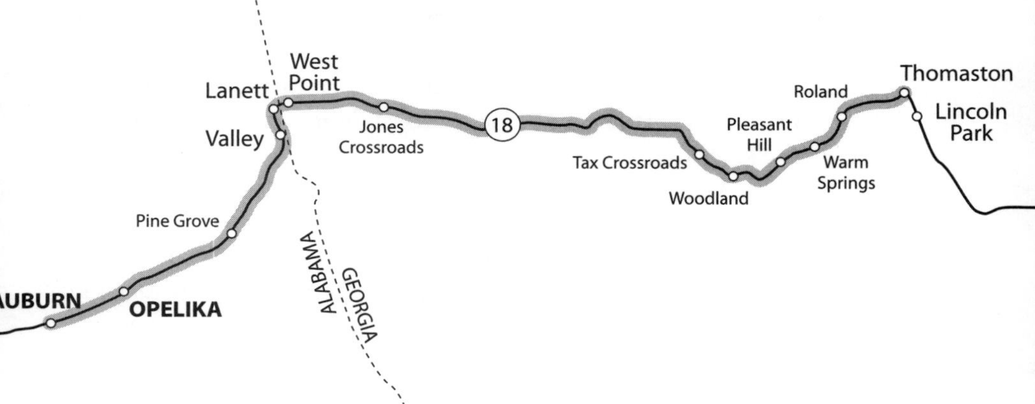

Date: Sunday, August 19.

Distance traveled: 99 miles, from Auburn, Alabama, to Thomaston, Georgia.

Total miles completed: 2,493.

Starting temperature and time: 72 degrees at 4:45 a.m. Central time.

Finishing temperature and time: 91 at 4:45 p.m. Eastern time.

Food: breakfast—toast, two bananas; lunch—sausage biscuit and Vienna sausages; dinner—Pringles, supreme pizza, and ice cream.

Additional fuel: two gallons of water, one gallon of Gatorade, one root beer.

Song stuck in my head: "Solo for the President … When I'm faced with a day that's gray and lonely, I just stick out my chin and grin and say, oh, the sun'll come out tomorrow." ("Tomorrow," from the musical Annie by Charles Strouse and Martin Charnin, 1977.)

Overnight: Jameson Inn, Thomaston.

As I pedaled through the Auburn campus long before dawn, a few hardy students were headed home after opening day of the Saturday-night party season. The Waffle House was packed. A young man wearing a tie and white shirt drove cautiously down Highway 29; his date somehow managed to look both sleepy and perky at once. Another student sat alone on a porch listening to Eminem as if waiting for the party to resume—which it would in a few hours, no doubt.

Then I got lost in Opelika, long before daylight. If a man had to get lost, Opelika was a comfy place to do it. "Nah, Highway 29 doesn't go thataway," said a friendly Fritos-delivery man. "It goes *thataway* and keep going until you get to a school, then bear right." So I headed *thataway*, but saw no signs for 29, nor any school.

I'm a typical male—asking directions is not in my nature. But I was lost and ready to admit it. "Onliest way to Lanett is the interstate," answered a bleary-eyed gas-station clerk, who seemed relieved that I wasn't a robber. A young man drove up, piloting a pulsating jam box with a Chevrolet built around it. He couldn't hear me ask directions because of the thundering music that created a hurricane in my water bottle. A chalky-cheeked woman at a truck stop was a bit more helpful: "You might be able to get to 29 by taking this here road about two miles and then going left a quarter-mile past the pond. But maybe not."

I pedaled around Opelika like a rat in a maze. Oddly enough, considering that I had often felt disoriented on this trip as I battled the moth, the sun, and dogs, I hadn't been truly "golly-where-am-I?" lost until now. This was new territory for me, and quite frustrating. Just as I was about to go into a true panic, Shoe the SAG arrived in the van and hauled me eight miles back to the spot where I had let my intuition override the advice from the Fritos man which, of course, had been correct. I simply hadn't gone far enough. There was the school, right where it was supposed to be. There was the promised right turn. Before long, I was on shady route 29 enjoying another cool morning in the country.

Maybe, I thought, this trip is a like an entertaining television sitcom—a break from the real world. Soon I must get on with my real life, but I will be better for having swallowed bugs and searched for live armadillos. I was beginning to dread the end, when I would no longer be branded a "sweaty biker," but would return to life as a grieving dad or a workaholic NCAA guy.

The eastern counties of Alabama were more heavily populated than I had expected, and there were more dogs than I wanted to meet. All of the latter seemed to be on my trail. I watched a pit bull that was connected by a long chain to a stake in the ground. The dog raced toward me; then, much to my relief, it recoiled like a ball-cord-and-paddle toy when it hit the end of the chain a few yards from me. Tied-up dogs—now there's a concept—provided me with some subtle relief. Despite my bravado about being the Dog Whisperer, the best protections still were dog chain and—even better—dog fence.

Outside Lanett, another biker silently sprinted past me. I said, "Good morning" pleasantly. The other biker said nothing. "Hel-LOW-oh!" I yelled. No response. It was highway snobbery: an affront to the brotherhood of bikers. Surely he saw me; otherwise he'd have gored my rear wheel. I decided to catch him. I slapped my bike into high gear, took one mighty pedal stroke—and my chain came off, leaving me inert and frustrated. It was a perfect metaphor for my competitive athletic career—intense intimidation followed by abject failure. I watched the rider's multicolored bicycling clothes gradually fade into the distance as I pulled over to replace my chain. Myself, I didn't wear fancy biking outfits because I didn't want to be branded as a serious biker. I preferred to be a jovial biker instead.

Near the Alabama town of Valley, a teenager asked, "Where you headed?" I responded, "Georgia!" which for 31 days had drawn appreciative gasps from bystanders. This young woman was not impressed; I was only eight miles from the Georgia state line.

Like a good newspaper column, Alabama ended before I was ready. But happy tears flowed as I crossed the Chattahoochee River into the land of Jimmy Carter, Margaret Mitchell, and Ty Cobb. Historians quote World War II soldiers in February, 1945, as saying to themselves, "Hey, I might just make it!" That's how I felt: I might actually ride to the Atlantic Ocean; I might return from the war of grief we had waged since the crash.

The war abated when my friend and fellow cyclist Khalil Johnson, who runs Atlanta's magnificent Georgia Dome stadium, met me west of Roosevelt State Park. Khalil was a member of the e-mail support crew. He has a linebacker's body, a professor's mind, and a poet's soul. Modestly, he claims a professor's body, an offensive guard's mind, and a poet's self-discipline. A companion—linebacker or poet, it didn't matter—was most welcome. My new partner was like a shield of invincibility: the blue moth never approached while Khalil rode alongside. Shoe kept us supplied with water and Gatorade.

Khalil brought along a gift—a t-shirt that draws sweat away from the body and releases it into the air. I immediately removed my soggy white cotton shirt, tossed it into the van with Shoe, and put on the new one. It kept me dry the rest of the day. Perhaps a scientist one day will prove that such miracle fabrics cause asthma in armadillos or heart murmurs in mice. But for now I was happy. My long-sleeved cotton shirts were appropriate in the dry West, but not in the South's humidityville horror. I would wear Khalil's contribution each of the last four days, tromping it semi-clean each evening in the shower, like stomping grapes.

Tools are available to help us through difficult times—from mundane ones like magic shirts to serious ones like dear friends—if we will only reach out and grab them. That was a lesson worth learning for me. After I returned to work following Will's death, I had spent my evenings holed up in my Indianapolis apartment, left to deal with my despair as a one-man wrecking crew, instead of leaning upon my friends and colleagues for support.

Khalil and I played like tourists, rocketing down a massive hill to Franklin Roosevelt's Little White House in the woods outside the quaint community of Warm Springs. The president had come to this area in response to a tip that the Georgia springs would relieve the pain caused by his polio. Apparently he did find some comfort, but not the miracle cure that he sought. Still, he loved the place although he was able to visit only 16 times. Republicans will complain that I visited both Bill Clinton's birthplace and the house where Franklin Roosevelt died. In fairness, we did attempt to begin the journey near the Nixon home in San Clemente, but couldn't find a suitable route from there over the mountains. And I did ride through Texas and Oklahoma, where true Democrats are as rare as living armadillos.

Speaking of politics, Khalil pointed out a snake, the first of my trip. It was merely a little green one wiggling across the road, but a snake was a snake. Now I needed only to find the elusive live armadillo.

In the stately burg of Woodland, we met a delightful 10-year-old child riding a bike and a sweet 90-ish woman leaning on a cane—alpha and omega. The child was wearing a D.A.R.E. t-shirt (Drug Abuse Resistance Education). Khalil asked the boy what was the first thing that D.A.R.E. teaches. "Avoid peer pressure," the boy said, flashing a smile so alive that it sprung from his face. Then it was the youngster's turn to ask a question. After we told him that we were biking to Thomaston, 18 miles away, he replied, "What?" in the stunned, disbelieving, staccato tone of a Jewish comedian. In his fresh young world, bicycling to Thomaston was as incomprehensible as riding a pogo stick along the Oregon Trail from Missouri to California.

The woman hobbled across the road on legs that seemed to be held together by duct tape. She smiled and said, "Don't run over me, young men. I'm not ready to go yet." Before the crash, our own family's lives had been as sheltered and optimistic as the boy's; now we possessed the old woman's wisdom.

Khalil and I sped down the highway like superstars, buoyed by a refreshing tailwind. Puffy white cotton clouds danced against a deep blue backdrop overhead; it was a lovely and temperate summer's day. Birds whistled arias. Khalil's presence and the stimulating conversation pulled me down the road; I could have ridden 200 miles without stopping. We drafted for each other; we called "car back" when a vehicle approached; we were a team. Too soon, Khalil bade farewell to Shoe and me and headed back toward his car, facing a 40-mile ride into the headwind. I was left alone for the last 14 miles to Thomaston, sad to lose him but grateful for the moments.

I rode 99.2 miles today. At one time in my life, I would have ridden six laps around the stately Thomaston courthouse, just so I could say that I'd broken 100 miles. Now, 99.2 was plenty.

In a shady yard near downtown Thomaston a boy was throwing a skateboard at the lower limbs of an oak tree, trying to dislodge a basketball.

"Think you can get it?" I asked.

"Maybe," he replied. "Havin' fun, anyway—wanta help?"

On his next throw, the skateboard struck paydirt and popped the ball free. But the board stayed in the tree, hanging by its wheels between two other branches. The boy looked at me, shrugged his shoulders, and grinned.

He was the kid that I used to be, concerned only with stretching out a fine summer afternoon as long as possible, until it reached a satisfying evening that probably included a cook-out with root beer floats for dessert. His life was as simple as it was full. Neither a fancy job at the NCAA nor the top of the career ladder was in his viewfinder. For him, the future was only tomorrow.

I arrived in Thomaston too late for the free band concert, but a 58-year-old motel clerk entertained me with tales about local guests, including the preacher who overnighted with a parishioner, and the banker who didn't pay his bills. There are no secrets in a small town.

Andie, Mr. Roosevelt had the most important job in the world, but it's sad that he couldn't enjoy his paradise in the Georgia woods more often. When you find your own special place, make good use of it.

DAY 33

LEAVE NOTHIN' SHORT

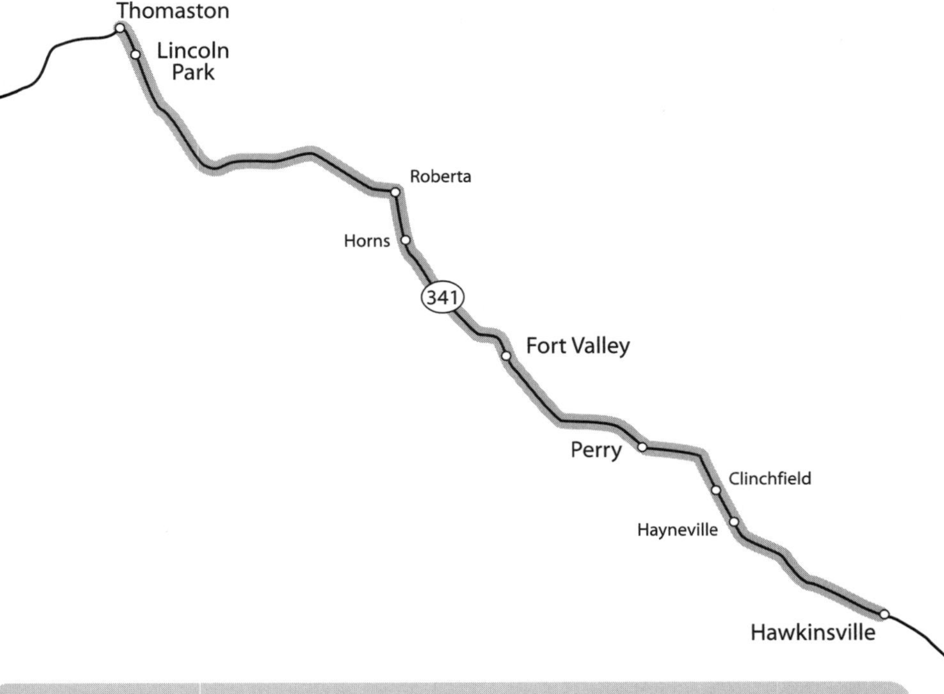

Date: Monday, August 20.

Distance traveled: 75 miles in Georgia, from Thomaston to Hawkinsville.

Total miles completed: too many—2,568.

Miles to go: too few.

Starting temperature and time: 71 degrees at 6 a.m.

Finishing temperature and time: 84 at 12:45 p.m.

Food: breakfast—bagel, banana; lunch—sausage biscuit; dinner—chicken livers, salad, baked potato, ice cream.

Additional fuel: 19 Cheez-Its, six small chocolate chip cookies, two gallons of water, one gallon of Gatorade, one root beer.

Song stuck in my head: "I got a girl and you got none, Li'l Liza Jane." ("Li'l Liza Jane," traditional from the early 20th century performed by Nina Simone, among others.)

Overnight: Best Western, Hawkinsville.

As I stood in the soft, golden summer morning watching three people paint a water tower in the little town of Roberta, a tiny man in a fragile pickup told me that he was a golfer. Had he watched yesterday's electrifying PGA tournament final round?

"I'd ruther play than watch," he said. "But the toonamint was still on television when I got home from the course. I saw that Pheal Mickasin (Phil Mickelson) and another guy were on the last hole; Mickasin had to make a birdie to win and he left it short. Don't leave nothin' short."

Bad grammar, but good advice, especially for a cyclist with only a couple hundred miles separating himself from the finish line. It became clear that the stifling humid days last week were a blessing; after that gloom, the rest of life seemed easier. Easier, that is, except for the ants. They were everywhere that I sat today. And yesterday. And the yesterdays before that. Big black ants that tickled when they crawled up my thighs, small ones that bit, flying ants, listless ants, ants in bunches, single ants. I decided the ants were attacking because I killed their red cousin back in the California desert, and that word had traveled quickly via the antformation highway.

DAY 33

Near Fort Valley, my thoughts turned from insects to flora when I saw my first Georgia peach orchard. I had vowed to sample at least one fresh peach, but the trees were decidedly bare. I continued through dark green pecan groves, at one time waiting in a cool pecan-tree tunnel for a road crew to finish laying new asphalt. A million pecans surrounded me, their shells protecting the fruit inside from insects much like the armor I wanted to shield me from the blue moth. I wondered where the critter had spent the weekend because it hadn't pestered me in two days. Maybe it needed a rest after hurling those bombs at me in Selma. Perhaps it wasn't easy being a blue moth.

My route took me past the Blue Bird bus factory in Fort Valley, where a school bus is born every 20 minutes. Then I almost achieved a rare sighting of a live armadillo. A shell was still intact in the road, which meant that no car had ridden over the poor fella since the one that took its life, so I surmised that the animal had been dead only a half-hour or so. Not quite scientific, but not too shabby for a drive-by autopsy.

A yellow baritone dog walked beside the highway near Perry, and I prepared for combat. The canine stopped, looked at me, and strolled on down the road. If I lived here and that yellow dog ran for dogcatcher, I would vote for it.

When I wasn't dog-whispering, I was conversing with common folks all across the country. I had talked to farmers, editors, storekeepers, and preachers, but until today, I had not met any lawyers. I identified the man in downtown Perry as an attorney because he walked quickly, carried a legal-sized file folder, bore a harried scowl, and perspired heavily in a green sport coat.

"Good mornin', sir," I said. "What things should I see while I'm in Perry?"

He scratched his bowling-ball belly with the accordion folder.

"Uh, well, uh, I dunno," he said. "If you're still here when I come back, maybe I can help you." Then he hurried away. To return phone calls, I hoped.

On its courthouse square, the town of Perry did feature the obligatory Confederate soldier monument. It was surrounded by red and white crape myrtle bushes that resembled giant Homecoming mums. In sharp contrast to the delightful Southern ambience was a stand of prickly pear cactus in the front yard of a beautiful home outside town. All across the country, I had encountered things that were out of place.

For example, Palm Springs residents planted tamarisk trees in the 1940s because they grew quickly, made good windbreaks, and provided shade. Unfortunately, the trees produced millions of tiny seeds that have blown to remote locations and taken root miles away, siphoning water that for centuries has helped other plants grow.

Mesquite seeds were carried to Oklahoma in the stomachs of cattle being driven from Texas to the Kansas railheads in the 1870s. They spread through excrement. Mesquite trees are a nuisance to ranchers; their roots are the strongest underground network since the New York subway system.

Imports were everywhere: On the White Sands Missile Range in New Mexico, I saw a herd of oryx, antelope brought from Africa in 1969 by the New Mexico Game and Fish Department. Wheat and cotton are not native to Texas and Oklahoma, nor rice to Arkansas, nor peanuts to Georgia. There was much more. Coyotes in Mississippi. Boll weevils. Siberian elm trees. Kudzu.

Franklin Roosevelt, the New Yorker, semi-relocated to Georgia. Snowbirds from Big Ten country overrun Southwest Arizona each winter. In fact, all the people—dating back to Clovis Man—are invaders on this continent. What belongs? What doesn't? Should a man ride a bicycle in the desert, or in the Rocky Mountains, or in the Georgia woods?

It isn't normal for a child to die before his parents. But what is normal? Is "normal" sameness or change? Who makes the rules? I had become a regular bicycle philosopher.

My head was nearly overloaded by the time I saw the rules that were displayed on the front door of Brown's Auction in Hawkinsville. They were written far too succinctly to have come from the pen of that Perry attorney: "No drinking. No cussing. No fussing. Welcome, as long as you do right, or we will call the law. We love y'all." Did Martin Luther state the rules any more profoundly when he nailed the "Ninety-Five Theses" to that door in Wittenberg?

Andie, remember that small-town golfer who said, "Don't leave nothin' short." Those are words to live by. Whatever you do, give it your best. Don't do anything halfway.

A Precious Thing

DAY 33

The e-mail crew had grown beyond my wildest imagination. I was now enjoying 90 minutes each day communicating with the friends and strangers whose enthusiasm and support pushed me toward Tybee Island as surely as Will had pushed me up to the Mogollon Rim back in Arizona.

What's been your favorite state? That's like asking a parent to select the one day when he loved his children the most. Every state has been wonderful. And unique. Sampling the states has been like hearing a terrific concert where the program ranges from Beethoven to The Beatles.

I won't accept that. I'm holding pepper spray to your head: which state was best? Okay, okay: New Mexico.

What were you going to do with that fancy biker if you had caught him? Force him off the road and sit on him until he said "hello" and told me what he had for breakfast. Or, maybe just help him realize that he is not alone on the planet.

Then this, from a 72-year-old Oklahoma farm girl who has known the blue moth herself and was awaiting the finish of my journey: *A precious thing is within your grasp. Hold it like a butterfly. Lightly. Control the excitement and the euphoria. Listen to your SAG advisors; take deep breaths, be calm. If I sound like a labor coach or a schoolmarm, I was those things. I am so excited myself, I feel breathless.*

9
To Sea Again

DAY 34

Stars Through the Fog

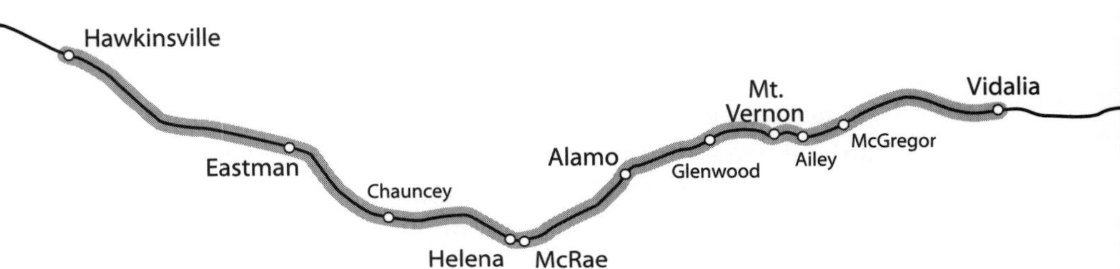

Date: Tuesday, August 21.

Distance traveled: 77 miles in Georgia, from Hawkinsville to Vidalia.

Total miles completed: 2,645.

Miles to go: I can see the light at the end of the tunnel.

Starting temperature and time: 68 degrees at 5 a.m.

Finishing temperature and time: 89 at 12:45 p.m.

Food: breakfast—banana, sausage biscuit; lunch—sausage biscuit, 17 Cheez-Its; dinner—tamales, rice, beans, ice cream.

Additional fuel: one root beer, one gallon of water, one gallon of Gatorade, 16 boiled peanuts, one awesome fresh peach.

Song stuck in my head: There were lots of obvious possibilities, such as "Georgia," "Georgia on My Mind," "Rainy Night in Georgia," "Sweet Georgia Brown," "Dixie," "Battle Hymn of the Republic," Stephen Foster's entire repertoire, etc. Instead, the following swam through my head... "Slow down, you move too fast. You got to make the morning last. Just kickin' down the cobblestones, lookin' for fun and feelin' groovy." I even heard the instrumental break; is this the only rock tune featuring a bassoon? ("59th Street Bridge Song," Simon and Garfunkel, 1967.)

Overnight: Comfort Inn, Vidalia.

DAY 34

As I rode into a patch of ground fog this morning, I could still see bright stars overhead. Stars through the fog: it had a nice ring to it.

There was energy in the remarkably cool air, like the morning before Christmas. For the third consecutive day, a tailwind shoved me down the road like skipper Dennis Conner on his boat, *America II.*

A sign on a nifty little store advertised breakfast sandwiches, so I skidded to a stop and found two elderly female owners. "Sorry, we're sold out of sandwiches," one said, in a tone as contrite as if she had driven her car into my tulips. "I'll make one for you from scratch." I begged off but marked her down as a treasure.

This morning I decided that I didn't want to make it to the city of Savannah, the gateway to the Atlantic Ocean and Tybee Island. Oh, sure, I wanted to reach the ocean, but conversely I didn't want the journey to end. Moreover, although I found myself daydreaming more each day about my NCAA career, returning to life inside an office had as much appeal as a week's vacation in a bank vault. As John le Carre wrote, "A desk is a dangerous place from which to watch the world." I preferred to turn left and pedal north to Millinocket, Maine, where I'd trade the bike for a good backpack and climb to the top of Mount Katahdin to look down upon the ponds that Thoreau likened to broken glass glistening in the morning sun. Then I'd hike the 2,100-mile Appalachian Trail, and arrive back in Georgia just in time for the Final Four.

The daydream ended when road construction marred my trail for 24 miles southeast of Hawkinsville, where there was no shoulder, and traffic was as jammed as on a football Saturday in Auburn. The department of transportation had commandeered a house and yard for an office compound, like the bomb-makers took over the MacDonald ranch in New Mexico, and like the blue moth was trying to take over my character. Near that house-office, I heard the rooster for the 33rd day of 34. Today I also heard a quail's call so clearly that I thought he was perched on my helmet, and I abandoned all hope of seeing a live armadillo. It had been a noble quest, but quixotic in its failure.

Shoe's wife, Cheryl, flew in from Kansas City to join us. Nicki would arrive tomorrow, and I was ready. We had talked every day since she went home, but you can't *smell* someone on the telephone.

I was surprised when Savannah Hyatt Regency general manager Shelly Fox and WTOC-TV news anchor Sonny Dixon both called my cell phone today. Tim Lindgren, the Hyatt vice-president, had been forwarding my daily journals to them. Shelly offered us a room in his hotel. Sonny dispatched reporter Dal Cannady to find us on the road and produce a news story. While SAG Shoe drove, Dal balanced himself in the back of the minivan with the hatch open, conducting an interview while I rode.

The blue moth was nowhere in sight.

Andie, I will never forget the roosters who sang those wake-up calls like clockwork every morning. The simple wonders of the world are the best.

The Peach Angel

DAY 34

I met the Peach Angel east of McRae, Georgia. His real name was Steve, and he was assembling a stand to sell peaches by the side of the road. As I approached, he was unloading supplies from the back of his old pickup truck. The truck—ironically, it was peach-colored—had a faded "For Sale By Owner" sign in the back window. When I asked to purchase a peach, Steve said, "For a gentleman on a bicycle, no charge." Then his eyes lingered as if he knew me, although the closest I'd ever been to this spot on Highway 280 was Hartsfield International Airport, 160 miles away in Atlanta. Unlike other strangers that I had met, he was unfazed by a biker in rural America. I rinsed the fuzzy peach with a splash of Gatorade and bit eagerly, spewing juice down my chin. The sweet flavor filled every molecule of my body.

Steve placed boards on sawhorses to form a crude but effective sales table in the unkempt Bermuda grass. A fountain of perspiration, he weighed perhaps 300 pounds, and his black shirt was nearly as much hole as cloth. He didn't bother to wave away the gnats that hovered around his eyes and ears.

"I'm a little late today, sir," he offered as an apology. "I wish you were here later; this place will look real nice. I got three good umbrellas: one for the peaches in the back of the truck, one for the table, and one for me."

Four hefty semi-trailer trucks pulled sections of double-wide mobile homes down the road past us while we talked. Would I be plagued by the monsters all day? My face must have reflected my apprehension, because Steve said, "Sir, it's Tuesday. That's the day they move them house trailers. But they'll turn off this road a mile down the way. Sir, you'll be okay."

If I had been riding my bicycle instead of getting wisdom from the Peach Angel, I'd have been forced off the road then and there because those massive trailers occupied a lane and a half. Instead of dodging them, I observed them in safety as I watched Steve set up his peach stand.

Steve went on, as if he had a message to deliver and he knew our time together was limited.

"Sir, I been sellin' peaches for 13 years, since I was 12 years old," he told me. "It's all I know. My daddy's daddy sold peaches and then my daddy did. My brother and sister don't like the peach business. They couldn't stay out here in this heat five minutes. The season lasts—let's see—one, two, three, four months. It'll be over real soon. Then I won't have nothin' to do 'til next year."

Steve cast a reflective look at the baskets of golden fruit in the back of his pickup. "Sir," he said, "my daddy and momma grew me up real good. I don't ever want them to die. But if they do, sir, I don't want no money. Don't want no house. Don't want no vehicles. I just want what I know—sellin' peaches."

Then there was silence. A rivulet of sweat cascaded down Steve's left cheek. His eyes did not waver from mine. It was the most awkward—the most transcendental—moment of my life. It was as if he were saying to me: "Sir, do you get it? What you have, is what you have. Treasure it."

The sparkle in his eyes hit me like a sudden blast of Bach from a pipe organ: I realized he could be an angel. He did not meet the common image of an angel, but if there was a point that was hammered home on this trip, it was that looks could be deceiving. He turned slowly and went back to work.

Wiping the peach nectar from my chin, swatting the gnats, and watching him open his umbrellas, I decided that Steve was simply another in a series of angels who had helped me cross the country. Nicki. Desert Construction Worker. Talkative Freeway Samaritan. Nicki. Arizona Bud Man. One-Eyed Pop in Pie Town. Nicki. John D. and Gracie. DeWayne Lindley. Arkansas Game Warden. Washington Cooks. Nicki. The Suicidal Woman. SAGs Jim and Shoe. Nicki. Tim Lindgren. David and Susan Housel. Khalil Johnson.

Most importantly, Nicki.

My mind raced. Was I hallucinating in the morning heat? Had the sugar from the peach scrambled my brain? Was it just another daydream?

No sir, it was all very real. God had sent a series of angels like Clarence Oddbody—who got his wings in *It's a Wonderful Life*—to protect me, and Steve the Peach Angel was here to conclude their work. Steve's mission was to seal the deal, to ensure that I learned something about myself—about life—from this journey.

I had been wrong to have discerned that *It's a Wonderful Life* had to be about Will. Instead, it was I—not Will—who was George Bailey, earning a second chance at life. The angels whom I met while biking across the country showed me how do to it. They stayed with me until I could fly on my own. Sure, as Karen said, I would have a Will-sized hole in my heart for the rest of my life. But I could live again. I could open my shell and help others. Just a regular guy, I stood in tall grass, sweating like 14 linebackers and smiling. A wonderful sense of peace settled in my soul.

* * *

After I bade farewell to the Peach Angel, I daydreamed again on the road to Vidalia, like in Palm Springs when my mind's eye saw cheerful families cavorting happily in the green grass and the rest of us—those who had experienced tragedy—wandering sadly in a rocky desert behind an ugly split-rail fence. Dark waves of crying people crossed the fence to join us.

But now I saw the two groups of people differently. We on the desert side were wiser. The harsh crossing of that splintery barrier had shown us what so many know, but so few accept—that death is a part of life. We had learned that earthly pleasures are as fragile as the first blossoms of spring and must be held dear. On the blissful side of the fence only poets and saints—and perhaps a few children shooting baskets—understood the words of warning that were crystal-clear to everyone on our side: *Life is precious. Cherish every minute.*

Few of the innocents heed that warning, like a center fielder who pays no attention to the warning track en route to smashing into the outfield wall to make a catch. They hear, "Yarnell Hill is ahead—are you ready?" without fully comprehending just what they are about to confront. From our elevated vantage point on the other side of the fence, we know to pay attention to the signs. It was all so logical. My nightmare 10 days before the crash and Nicki's premonition had both been warnings, early signs that I could not comprehend.

More importantly, they were undeniable proof that God is omnipotent and compassionate. God had spoken directly to Nicki and me through the premonitions, proving that He is in control. It was raw mathematical logic; we had undeniable proof! Through messages and messengers like the Peach Angel, He was trying to tell us the simple truth—that new life awaits here on earth and, later, in Heaven.

Now for the first time, in my daydream I looked beyond the desolate wilderness on our side of the fence and saw a pathway lined with desert creosote, sage, and lavender. The fragrant path led to a welcoming grove of Ponderosa pines—with one Australian coolabah tree standing front and center. A man rode a yellow and orange Cannondale bicycle steadily toward the cool shade, one pedal stroke after another. A second man—holding a trombone and wearing a U.S. Olympic team shirt—stood in the shade, patiently waiting for him. Somewhere, a chorus sang "Waltzing Matilda."

On a rocky hillock near the pines, the blue moth reclined with spread wings, its tendrils moving gently so that it seemed to be nodding in affirmation. It almost seemed to be smiling. I recognized the moth as a vital presence on our side of the fence—admittedly not exactly Mr. Chips or Mr. Holland, but indeed a stern but loving professor explaining the deep truths of life to all who will listen.

In a day of epiphanies, it was yet another. There was joy in the morning. I had a chance to live again: to ride, to breathe, to laugh—to be an angel myself, a mentor shepherding strangers across the barren desert. I intended to take advantage of it. For starters, I would share this realization with other generations of Hancocks, beginning with Andie. She would need to know that angels are all around her—whether she recognizes them or not. Sometimes, a peach is not just a peach. God sends angels to care for us; in our turn, He will send those our way who are in need of our care.

DAY 35
HUMAN BATON

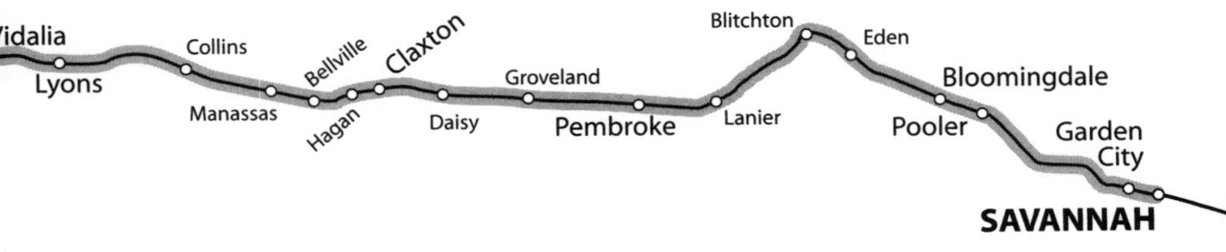

Date: Wednesday, August 22.

Distance traveled: 83 miles in Georgia, from Vidalia to Savannah.

Total miles completed: 2,728.

Miles to go: oh, my goodness—only 18!

Starting temperature and time: 66 degrees at 5 a.m.

Finishing temperature and time: 85 at noon.

Food: breakfast—banana, tortilla, oatmeal-raisin cookie; lunch—sausage biscuit, hotdog, chips; dinner—Caesar salad, New England clam chowder, tuna, rice pilaf, crème brule.

Additional fuel: 14 Fritos, eight strawberries, one root beer, two gallons of water, six quarts of Gatorade.

Song stuck in my head: "The Star-Spangled Banner" (Francis Scott Key, 1814), inspired by a tattered American flag fluttering in a headwind near Claxton. In my head the anthem played itself as a march, then a boogie, a waltz, a blues riff, a syncopated Bernstein song. It was a day for dancing.

Overnight: Hyatt Regency, Savannah.

Instead of the routine cock-a-doodle-doo, this morning the bright rooster's call said, "Awake, the dark night is over." For the first time since the crash—rather, for the first time in my life—I was truly aware. As if in celebration, lightning pyrotechnics illuminated orange mushroom clouds; then, as if tugged by a pulley, the clouds separated and the sun rolled out of a purple haze to paint the world with a golden brush. All such glorious sunrises come with clouds.

I was in the bootheel of the Low Country, the swath of land near the coast that extends from North Carolina through South Carolina and Georgia. Onion country. Unfortunately, the Onion Factory and Gift Shop in Vidalia was closed when I left town. "Darn," I thought, "I won't be able to sample those chocolate-covered onions." The famous Vidalia onions come from a 20-county area surrounding the town. They're sweet and mostly don't smell like onions because of the local soil, which has very little sulphur. Sweet onions from a sour soil, a good sign for my next-to-last day on the bike.

When I inquired about the distance to the town of Claxton, a troll of a storekeeper in Collins said, "Don't matter. Just foller yonder road and you'll get there." Put one foot in front of the other, I told myself. And I smiled. Yes, I smiled.

Then I saw a road sign: "Savannah 55." After a week of repeating to myself, "Don't peak too soon," I was starting to get a little excited. A little nutty. Coincidentally, Claxton claims to be the fruitcake capital of the world. Workers inside a fruitcake factory prepared the holiday delicacies as I rode past.

I headed east through a tunnel of oaks with Spanish moss hanging like blue-green stalactites and past other trees that, Oz-like, appeared ready to throw apples at me. Just before the town of Bloomington, a police officer pulled alongside and waved me off the road.

"Am I under arrest?" I asked naively.

"No, but are you Mr. Hancock?" he responded, and I nodded yes. "Follow me. I'm going to escort you to Pooler. By the way, I think your bicycle ride across the United States is an incredible accomplishment."

It was astounding. Tim Lindgren, Shelly Fox, and Sonny Dixon had arranged a police escort—a cadre of officers would accompany me all the way to Tybee Island. The police represented all the angels who had guided me across the country, like a bucket brigade carefully passing me from one to another. When we reached the town of Pooler, another officer was waiting. He drove in front of me for four miles, with the Bloomington officer behind me. Pooler then handed me off to Garden City, who took me on to Savannah. I was a baton in a relay. The Peach Angel had shown me that I could let the angels carry me, so I relaxed in their arms.

Now I knew how it felt to be leading the Boston Marathon. It was like the scene in *Field of Dreams* when Ray Kinsella—scarcely believing reality—said to himself, "I am pitching to Shoeless Joe Jackson!" To the bewilderment of onlookers, the policemen stopped traffic as we crossed intersections. It was my own private ticker-tape parade; I pinched myself to make sure this wasn't just another daydream.

Tucked as closely as possible behind the police car, I pedaled hard. I was certain the officers had better things to do, and the faster I sped through their towns, the sooner they could return to their regular duties. My legs ached. My lungs burned. The attention was embarrassing. I needed a restroom, but I didn't dare stop the parade.

Pain aside, I did not want the day to end. But all too soon our little convoy arrived at the shady front drive of the Savannah Hyatt, where a television crew and newspaper reporter were waiting for me. "Will you be conducting a press conference?" asked the reporter. I laughed and said that I was just a regular guy out for a little ole bike ride and suggested that he interview someone with a story to tell. Someone with a cause. Someone important. But he insisted, so we did the interview—after I found the restroom.

A crowd of conventioneers in the Hyatt lobby applauded when I walked in. A sign read "Welcome Bill. Pacific to Atlantic." It was quite embarrassing, but I did allow a small dose of ego into my now-cracked shell. A smile tugged at my lips. I had done it—almost.

Ego plays no part in the life of Shelly Fox, who ran the Savannah Hyatt. He has dueled with the blue moth himself. A former marathon runner, he underwent a foot amputation because of cancer, which also took the life of his twin brother and another brother. He was an inspiration; I knew he was an angel, like the one I wanted to be.

Shelly's Hyatt hotel sits on the spot where James Oglethorpe landed on the shore of the Savannah River in 1733 and chartered the 13th and final crown colony in the name of King George II.

Oglethorpe was intrigued by the river's tropical shoreline. I was fascinated by the lovely city squares, including the one where the celluloid Forrest Gump sat waiting for the bus and describing life as "like a box of chocolates." Nicki and I had bitten into the wormwood in the chocolate box, but we were learning to find a few candied cherries to temper the bitterness.

The Hyatt's gentle people transported Nicki from the Savannah airport to the hotel, and only Nicki's reserve and my basic shyness kept our reunion from being like something out of a movie. We kissed and hugged, but we were so impressed by the Hyatt suite provided by Shelly Fox and Tim Lindgren that we forgot to cry.

As I propped my bike against one wall of the suite—the bike had fit nicely into the hotel's elevator—the hotel's executive chef phoned to ask what I wanted from room service before tomorrow's 18-mile ride to the sea. The generous offer caught me off guard and all I could think of was an English muffin, grits, a banana, and some tea for Nicki.

"Are you sure that's all?" he asked, with disappointment in his voice. I think he hoped to deliver eggs Benedict, a soufflé, or a frittata. Truth was, I would have been more comfortable eating a sausage biscuit while sitting in the hotel driveway and talking to the bellhops about the least-traveled route to Tybee Island.

Nicki and I did enjoy a gourmet dinner in the Hyatt's beautiful restaurant with the Shoemakers, Mr. and Mrs. Dixon, and Mr. and Mrs. Fox. I ordered pan-seared Vienna sausages on a bed of Fritos glazed with root beer reduction. Everyone laughed and the gracious waiter brought fresh tuna instead. Shelly and Sonny, having deputized themselves as vice-mayors, presented me with a key to the city of Savannah.

If the bike ride were a marathon, I was at mile 26 with just "point-two" to go. The tape stretching across the finish line was in plain sight. The roar of the crowd was thrilling. And I, frankly, was a bit overwhelmed.

Andie, when I rode into that hotel driveway with a police escort, I was so happy that I wanted to sing. But please remember that you achieve little without the help of others. A chorus is more impressive than a solo.

DAY 36

Marsh Grass and Ocean Water

Date: Thursday, August 23.

Distance traveled: 18 miles in Georgia, from Savannah to Tybee Island.

Total miles completed: 2,746.

Miles to go: zero!

Starting temperature and time: 69 degrees at 6 a.m.

Finishing temperature and time: 72 at 7:45 a.m.

Food: breakfast—banana, English muffin, grits.

Music that wouldn't leave my brain: There were two tunes today. Before daylight, it was that old Australian folk song, "Waltzing Matilda." Then, just after another sunrise of Biblical proportions, Beethoven's Ninth Symphony, Fourth movement, "Ode to Joy." (Ludwig van Beethoven, 1824.)

Overnight: In the minivan, on an all-night drive back home to Kansas.

Alas, this morning there was no rooster. Instead, a seagull hovered overhead like a good omen. I felt as if Will Hancock were riding on my shoulders, as he did when he was three years old and I took him on my bike to the Sooner City day care center. It was dangerous, but both of us loved that daily commute. He would hook his legs under my chin, and sometimes his little arms would fall down around my eyes, and he would giggle, and I would scream, "Will, I can't see!" Then he would move his arms away and I could see again. I could live again. Today I knew that he was there with me.

The Bull River Bridge east of Savannah rises over a vast expanse of green salt-water marsh that resembles the pastoral Arkansas countryside. As I climbed over the bridge, I inhaled my first whiff of salt air. A huge ship in the nearby channel loomed above the trees like a rabbit in a 1950s arcade shooting gallery. I speculated about its distant ports of call. Los Angeles, perhaps? How long would the trip take? More than 36 days?

An airplane painted a white contrail in the pink sky, reminding me of the vast distance that I had covered. I could have flown in a plane from Los Angeles to Savannah, but that would have been like transplanting a full-grown tree into the back yard. I would have missed the growing-up part.

The bike and I were part of a little caravan that included two police cars, the minivan carrying Nicki and the Shoemakers, a television station car with Sonny Dixon and a camera operator inside, and the station's traffic helicopter. Traffic was thin after we passed historic Fort Pulaski, which was engineered in the 1830s by West Point graduate Robert E. Lee. It was a final rendezvous with this country's vibrant history that I had encountered on my trip. The last cattle trail, the Trinity Site, Roswell, Coronado's route across the Southwest, Vicksburg, Selma, and Warm Springs—each had left an indelible impression on me.

When I stopped on the almost-deserted highway to photograph one last magical sunrise, I almost told the police officers to go home. Then I realized that they were no longer necessarily tagging along for my sake; now they were there for themselves. I preferred to be alone, but how dare I deny them the opportunity to share in the moment? As our entourage passed, a smiling woman in a minivan shouted from her window, "What's the occasion?"

She hadn't asked, "What's the cause?" I grinned. The journey and the cause had finally become one.

I said, "I rode here from Los Angeles."

"I'd love to do that," she responded.

"You can!" I shouted. "Just put one foot in front of the other."

I meant it. Anyone can travel to an incomprehensible place, or away from one—all you need is good health, a bike, Vienna sausages, plenty of time, and an army of watchful angels.

A mile from Tybee Island, the Savannah policemen halted the procession and stepped from their squad cars to shake hands with me. "We've enjoyed being a part of this," said one. "I will never forget it." Then they handed me off to officer Renee Kaminsky of the Tybee Island police department.

Officer Renee was my trip's final angel. She could see that I no longer needed an escort and said, "Okay, so what do you want me to do?"

"Would you mind driving to the beach and waiting for me there? If you see anything dangerous before then, such as pirates, please stop and help me deal with it. Otherwise, I'll see all of you at the ocean."

And so I rode the last four miles alone, but with 100 heavenly musicians performing Beethoven in my head, and the blue moth now flying escort. Most of the real angels who had helped me cross America didn't know that I was about to achieve the goal. What I sincerely wanted to do was to turn around and ride back to thank all of them. But angels don't need thanking. They are repaid when we pass the kindness along to others.

I realized that the blue moth had been a leading angel, one with a less-defined but still necessary purpose. For the better part of nine states I had tried to lose the moth once and for all around a street corner, or hoped to see it squashed on the windshield of one of the trucks that barreled past me on the highway. I had thought of the moth as a burden, a continual reminder of Will's passing. Now, finally, I realized that the moth had forced me to grow in strength, understanding, and compassion—growth that I had been unable to measure as I pedaled blindly across the heart of America. Its presence caused me to reconsider how I thought about life—from the important things like my wife and family to the mundane things such as exercise and work. The blue-moth angel would be my welcome navigator on the rest of my trip through life. It could ride shotgun.

I pedaled slowly and deliberately to preserve the memory of every nanosecond of this final leg of the trip. I stopped at a convenience store on Tybee Island for one final bottle of Gatorade—it cost $1.09, same as in Parker, Arizona. Then I rode down to the ocean. The morning was soft and warm and sunny; two dozen towering white clouds gathered themselves on the horizon, ringside spectators to the finish.

The beach and pier on Tybee Island were mostly deserted. The pier was eerily similar to the one at Huntington Beach that I had left 46 days before. The salty Atlantic air smelled the same as the Pacific air; gulls sang similar tunes; waves lapped the sand just as they had some 2,700 miles away. But I was different—mellow and at peace because now I knew that the angels were there to protect me.

A friend had suggested by e-mail that I ride the Cannondale off the pier into the ocean, mimicking the women in *Thelma and Louise*. Another, more poetically, wrote, "Remember, Tybee Island is not the end."

Nicki and I walked the bike across the sand to the water, holding hands like we did on dates back in 1967. My eyes filled with tears until they spilled down my cheeks, mingling with sweat and cascading into the warm, gray ocean water. I repeated the biker's tradition and dipped my front wheel into the ocean. The ride was over.

Policewoman Renee kindly looked the other way as Nicki, dabbing at her own tears, served sparkling champagne to Tybee Island Mayor Walter Parker, Sonny Dixon, the cameraman, the Shoemakers, and me. I walked back into the ocean munching on a Vienna sausage and sipping one final root beer. There was whooping and hollering behind me and—I'm certain—above me, too, by Will in heaven.

I stooped to fill a little bottle with Atlantic Ocean water, matching the Pacific bottle which I had carried in the bike bag from Huntington Beach. I held the two of them up to the bright morning sun as tiny gray particles settled to the bottom of each, leaving clear water at the top. I hoped that Andie would someday teach her grandchildren the lessons represented by those little bottles. Lessons from the bike. Lessons for Andie. And for me.

Epilogue

I did not have long to adjust to life after the bike ride. After dipping my front tire into the Atlantic, I took a hasty shower at the home of Officer Renee Kaminsky on Tybee Island. Then the Shoemakers, Nicki, and I loaded my bicycle into the back of the minivan and made a 20-hour drive non-stop to Kansas City, arriving Friday morning in time to hop on a flight to Colorado. The next day we took part in Oklahoma State University's dedication of a granite memorial at the crash site.

The transition from the pastoral bike ride to the midst of all 10 grieving families was a shock. We gathered in tears in that hardscrabble field where Will's life ended. But the other families, the leaders at Oklahoma State, and the people of Adams County, Colorado, who had cared so much for all of us, truly comforted Nicki and me.

Over four years after Will's death, we have gradually come into a life that imitates normality.

Nicki returned to Olathe East High School, where she continues to draw consolation from her senior English students. Their curiosity and youthful energy give her an affirmative boost—it is a case of the students teaching the teacher. She has received additional help from the members of Compassionate Friends, a support group for parents who have lost children.

I was doubly proud when Nicki was chosen as Kansas "Master Teacher of the Year" in 2004—proud because she was named and proud because she allowed herself to enjoy it. Since our bike adventure, Nicki has slowly and steadily improved. Still, the sunshine often makes her cry, and on some days it is hard for her to be alone with her thoughts. The girl of my dreams is waging the most difficult battle of her life, and I am trying to help.

Karen has also earned her share of honors. She is in her 10th year as head coach of the Oklahoma State women's soccer team. The 2001 season was difficult—as was everything about 2001 for our family and for the thousands of families who crossed over to our side of the fence on September 11. But in 2002 she was named Big 12 Conference co-coach of the year. And Karen's 2003 Cowgirls team won the conference championship.

Karen, like all of us, continues to miss Will tremendously. "He was the love of my life. He was my soulmate and more," she says. To say that she has moved on would imply, incorrectly, that she has simply stepped over the loss of Will and strolls on, unaffected, through life. Instead, she carries the tragedy as gracefully as if she were toting that portion of her life in a backpack that never leaves her shoulders. She smiles, laughs, coaches her team, travels, and nurtures Andie. But that extra load is always there.

She seems to be determined to be the best darn single parent in Oklahoma. She dotes on Andie without being possessive, all the while showering our granddaughter with love. "The best thing you can do for your child is to be happy," she says. Karen has plenty of help from friends in Stillwater and from her parents and her warm, supportive extended family.

Nate is also making good progress. He is our leader, our rock, and has accepted his new role as Son No. 1—but some things will never be the same for him. His major in college was vocal music, and Nicki and I dreamed of him performing at the Met some day; but he no longer sings what his dad innocently calls "good music." He has found solace by singing and playing keyboard in a rock band. Perhaps the unbridled freedom of rock music is more cathartic than the sophistication of opera. Or perhaps rock is a good way to vent—just like it was for my generation in the sixties. Or perhaps opera simply conjures too much emotion. After all, it's difficult to sing with a lump in your throat. (I should know; after the bike ride, I re-joined the church choir. Frequently the great hymns—and even the Doxology—bring back the tears.)

We've decided that Andie is yet another of those angels sent from heaven to help us deal with life on the rocky side of the fence. Her smile exudes pure joy, and her intellect matches her dad's. She doesn't look like Will but has his curls. Andie is as curious as little Will was, and as engaging. She is a statuesque four-year-old—the doctor says she may grow up to be more than six feet tall—but she is more interested in ballet and frilly dresses than in sports. Of course, she has learned the familiar OSU refrain of "Ride 'em Cowboys," so sports may yet become a part of her life.

Andie knows that she lives alone with her mom because her dad died in an airplane crash, and I believe she understands what that means as well as any of us can understand. She doesn't call him Daddy; he's "Will" to her, and she seems to feel his love, as we all do.

I returned to the tournament-director's job that I treasured at the NCAA, working during the week in Indianapolis and flying home to Kansas City on the weekends. But I could hardly bear to be away from Nicki; I could no longer settle for those slumber-party weekends. Also, I desperately missed the freedom of the bike ride, the feel of the breeze in my face, the smell of new-mown hay, the opportunity to daydream, the liberty to stop and get off whenever I desired. I had ridden the bike to a place where I could see the world differently, and the backside of a desk was no longer the vantage point that I desired.

On the other hand, I needed the camaraderie of the people in basketball—the coaches, referees, writers, broadcasters, athletic directors, publicists, and arena managers. I was afraid of a life without the support of our tournament family. I couldn't stay with the NCAA, and I couldn't leave it. What to do?

The answer came after Greg Shaheen—coincidentally one of Will's good friends—was named vice-president for NCAA Division I Basketball. Greg and my boss, Tom Jernstedt, graciously conceived a plan that let me stay with the basketball family as an NCAA contractor. I have returned to my roots—and to Will's—by handling media services for March Madness. I travel to my cubicle in the NCAA office one week each month. The rest of the month I work at home, with Nicki and my family.

My time is now mostly my own. And Nicki's. And we cherish every minute together. We've hiked the Grand Canyon. We've giggled and bought a goofy hat at the Kentucky Derby. From a magical perch high in the wondrous Alps, we've watched biker Lance Armstrong win the Tour de France. Even though Nicki and I are dealing with the loss of Will differently, that cord of trust and love still connects us. She knows when I need to sit quietly with a book or a box score, I realize that there are times when she must cry. We are closer than ever—almost as if our loss has welded us into one.

As for me, my identity has changed. Whereas before I was known as the NCAA tournament guy, now I am labeled as the father of one of those young OSU men who were killed. I do not like the tag, but I cannot shake it any more than I can shake the blue moth. Of course, I now know that the moth is a helper.

People sometimes compliment me on my resilience, but I feel as fragile as a cricket under a biker's wheel. People don't know about the crushing, lonely nights. They don't see the tears that flow—almost always behind closed doors. But I am different. No one has mentioned it, but I know that it is true. I am more appreciative of life, yet more comfortable with the reality of death. More patient. Less judgmental. More interested in other people.

After the bike ride, people often asked me if I could do it all over again, would I? My answer was always the same, "In a heartbeat." In fact, Nicki and I took Roci and the Cannondale on another cross-country bicycle ride in 2003—a 17-day, 1,700-mile jaunt from the banks of the Rio Grande River near Comstock, Texas, through the fragrant Great Plains to the International Peace Garden at the U.S.-Canadian border in North Dakota. In many ways, the second ride was like stepping into a time machine and reliving that awesome first trip. There were morning roosters again, more root beer and Vienna sausage, wonderful people, hills, and, yes, visits from the blue moth. Even the Dog Whisperer was happy to resurface when needed. One friend surveyed my south-to-north route on the map and joked that the ride must have been tough because I rode uphill all the way.

When planning the second bike ride, I pondered the Cannondale's front tire and tube that had carried me across the continent without a flat. I considered changing them before heading north from Mexico, but decided that my loyal rubber companions deserved to be a part of the new adventure. Miraculously, the tire and tube held up all the way to Canada. They survived two cross-country rides for a total of 4,400 miles, plus a thousand more miles of training. Dave Clements at my Kansas City bike shop was amazed. "This tire has dry rot," he said. "And the tube is almost brittle. I don't know how they lasted." I'd like to be as tough as that old tire, which now rests in a place of honor in my office alongside my treasured little bottles of water from the Pacific and Atlantic Oceans.

The blue moth is still with us, swooping in with a load of sadness when we least expect it. The moth remained by my side for a long time when my sister died of complications from diabetes just six months after the first bike ride ended. "What else could happen?" I wondered.

Yes, there is fear. Nicki, Karen, and I have talked about how we might respond if unthinkable tragedy were to strike again in our lives. Frankly, I cannot predict. We all worry about it.

Still, there are many hints that my relationship with the blue moth has matured. The moth and I watched *It's a Wonderful Life* one November evening; then we finally sat together for *Field of Dreams* in an Indianapolis hotel room. The moth cried along with me when Ray

Kinsella shook hands with his father. I know the moth will come and go as it pleases, and not as I dictate. Now I do not try to escape when it arrives. I simply listen to what it has to say, and wait quietly for it to fly away. And it has always done so.

I continue to find new meaning in the bike ride. For years, my prayer each evening had been "Lord, make me an instrument of your peace." But I didn't know how to be one. Then I realized that others are similarly untrained and naïve but serve as agents of peace anyway. For example, Steve, in McRae, Georgia, didn't know he was my Peach Angel. He was just a regular guy doing his job—an unintentional angel.

A friend suggested that I turn the bike-ride e-mail journals into a book, so that I could possibly serve others desperately searching for resolution in their lives—and maybe find a bit more in my own. I took a stab at it, creating a memoir about the 36 days of bike riding and nothing more. A friend sent the manuscript to a New York editor who said, "This story is incomplete without the pain." But to write about January 27, 2001, and those following few weeks would be difficult—not to mention seeming exploitative and maudlin. And it would ask too much of Nicki, I thought. So I shelved the book project.

I kept putting one foot in front of the other, like a toddler learning to walk. Slowly, very slowly, the music of the bike played again in my head. Now the song was my prayer set to music. "Lord, make me an instrument."

Be careful what you pray for. Will—the elegant word player with a puckish wit—must have whispered into God's ear. The Lord has made me an instrument in the form of this book. It would be my clarinet, my sax, and my piano. Its theme, I hoped, would help others deal with the blue moths in their own lives. It certainly helped me deal with mine.

To conduct additional research for the book in the spring of 2005, Nicki and I visited the town of Congress and Arizona's Yarnell Hill, that beast that had nearly been my undoing on Day 5. In what I will always consider divine intervention, we met a solo bicyclist who—without knowing anything about my journey—had followed my route across the desert from Twentynine Palms. He was preparing to ride his bike up the fabled hill.

"I thought I was the only one nutty enough to try this," said the 41-year-old rider, Jud Davis of Louisville, after we told him our story. "No one can understand except someone else who has done it."

I was struck by the similarity between bike-riding and living with the blue moth.

"I'm gonna find a camping spot halfway up Yarnell Hill," he continued.

"Golly, I'm afraid that won't be possible," I replied. "There's nothing outside the road but guard rails and cliffs."

I was surprised to hear myself explaining what was ahead of the biker—just as I wanted to tell new folks on our side of the fence about the blue moth. He frowned at the prospect of being unable to find an overnight resting spot on the hill, and I diverted his attention with a question.

"Jud," I said, "When you are riding your bike all day, what do you think about?"

"That's easy," he responded. "I write music in my head."

I smiled, glad to be a kindred tune pedaler. As we bade farewell, Jud had one more comment for me.

"I met a real grumpy store owner back down the road a few miles," he said, and I remembered my encounter with the nasty man back at the same place four years earlier. "But most people have been friendly and helpful."

* * *

People remember Will in several wonderful ways. At last count, seven infants have been named for him, as their parents proudly informed us. There are scholarships endowed in his honor at Oklahoma State University and the University of Kansas, and each year a bright young person serves as the "Will Hancock intern" in the Big 12 Conference.

Others will come to know him from this book. I believe Will knows about the book. After all, he was with me for the entire trip, and his presence comforted me when tears came while I was writing. But it's not the same as if he could sit across the desk and suggest edits. I will miss my son every day for the rest of my life.

A year after my first bike ride, Nate and Kristin delighted us all by moving from Connecticut back home to Kansas City, and soon we became grandparents a second time when Kristin gave birth to William Patrick Hancock.

Andie and I have already begun to teach little Will his lessons.